THE
WARRIOR
WORKER

THE
WARRIOR
WORKER

The Challenge of the Korean Way of Working

ROBERT P. KEARNEY

HENRY HOLT AND COMPANY
NEW YORK

Library of Congress Cataloging-in-Pubication Data
Kearney, Robert P.
The warrior worker : the challenge of the Korean way of working /
Robert P. Kearney.—1st ed.
p.   cm.
Includes bibliographical references and index.
ISBN 0-8050-0978-7
1. Work ethic—Korea (South)   2. Korea—Economic conditions.
3. Korea—History.   I. Title.
HD8730.5.K43   1991
306.3′613′095195—dc20   90-42096
CIP

Henry Holt books are available at special discounts
for bulk purchases for sales promotions, premiums,
fund-raising, or educational use. Special editions
or book excerpts can also be created to specification.

For details contact:
Special Sales Director,
Henry Holt and Company, Inc.
115 West 18th Street
New York, New York 10011.

First Edition

Designed by Katy Riegel

Printed in the United States of America
Recognizing the importance of preserving
the written word, Henry Holt and Company, Inc.,
by policy, prints all of its first editions
on acid-free paper. ∞

1   3   5   7   9   10   8   6   4   2

Portions of this book originally appeared in PLAYBOY Magazine.

Contents

Contents

Acknowledgments

My research for this book was directed and made easy by the many scholars and journalists who have labored arduously to make the Korean culture and economy understandable to Western eyes; they are, unfortunately, too numerous to mention. I also relied heavily on interviews (and inspiration) from the following individuals: Kim Kyong-Dong, Park Young-Ki, Park Fun-Koo, Choi Song-Hyun, Kim Seung-Don, Oh Hong Keun, Han Sung-Taik, Dong Seob Sim, Chang Seung-Woo, Lee Hong Kyu, Park Hyun-Soon, Lee Sang-Joon, Harry G. Kamberis, Phee Jung-Sun, Jang Song-Hyon, Peter Bartholomew, Peter Underwood, Gary Sullivan, Mario (Mike) Bognanno, Ilse B. Dorman, Kim Myung Chul, Lee Dong Kon, Kim Nam Suk, Theodore M. Moscheau, Jeffrey L. Goldstein, Fr. Dale Tupper, Fr. Russ Feldmeier, Kelly Im, Kyung Suk Soh, Shim Sang Wan, and Pharis J. Harvey. Mickey Oh was a good friend and interpreter of events as well as words, during our time in Korea and after. Thanks also to Steve Randall for editorial assistance when I first began to explore the subject of Korean labor, and to the late Don Hutter, for his enthusiastic support and guidance.

After much thought, I have decided not to acknowledge the many individuals within Korea's conglomerates who answered my inquiries and directed me to other sources of information. I regret not being able to thank them formally, but I am reluctant to implicate them in this book's findings and conclusions, which are at times unflattering to their employers. Suffice it to say that without their open and often repeated contributions, this work would have been impossible.

I owe a particular debt to my wife, Virginia, for her insights and observations of Korean life and for her patience. Her embrace of this project, despite its occasionally extreme demands, has made a rigorous task joyful.

This book is dedicated to my father, Robert J. Kearney, and my mother, the late Ellen L. Kearney, for all their labors.

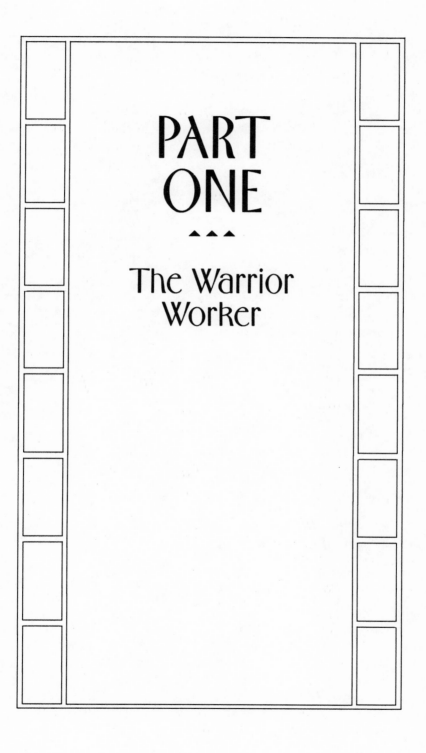

PART ONE

▲▲▲

The Warrior Worker

I
▲ ▲ ▲

Sacrifice and Glory

Every month, the fifth-largest city on the planet shudders to a halt and pretends, for fifteen minutes, that death is rushing toward it on swept-back wings.

In the moments before Seoul's air-raid drill, the tempo of the city accelerates. Pedestrians lengthen their paces, trotting for an office building or department store. Hawkers in the markets and on the sidewalks wave their arms faster, in wider circles. The city's thick, stuttering current of traffic grows louder and more insistent.

At the first blast of the sirens, pedestrians start running—heels up, shopping bags and briefcases bouncing against their thighs. Drivers slide past one another, jockeying toward the curb. Policemen appear in the intersections and blow their whistles in sharp tattoos, while volunteer marshals with yellow armbands take positions at each corner. The taxis—mostly orange and green Hyundai Ponies—and motorcycles and dingy lavender buses pull to the side of the road and kill their engines. Downtown, the bus doors jerk aside, and passengers scurry into the underground shopping centers and subway stations.

The city is abruptly transformed. In the normally teeming plaza in

3

front of Toksu Palace, a broad, open concourse materializes. A few blocks away, the stillness lends mass and stature to the ancient South Gate. The alleys of Namdaemun Market, naked without the usual horde of shoppers, now reveal their grimy storefronts, their cracked pavement; in the quiet, they grow crabbed and sinister. Farther south, toward the river, underground shelter is scarce. Here, the bus passengers sit impassively in their seats. Shoppers pull themselves up against buildings, while uniformed schoolchildren clutch their book bags in doorways, their horseplay quickly silenced by a marshal. Seoul—13 million strong, the brain of the world's fastest-growing economy—is hushed. From unseen speakers, a single voice addresses the city.

The images belong more to science fiction than to war. There is none of the shrieking panic that comes with a genuine attack, no scooping of children into arms, no heart-bursting dash for cover—only mute obedience and that single, booming voice. Five minutes drag into ten, twelve. An old woman, tattered and disoriented, is hectored into a subway station by one of the marshals; below, people talk quietly or read newspapers or stand sullenly. Another marshal scolds a group of college students who have edged too far up the stairway.

The end comes suddenly. After fifteen minutes, the voice stops. There is a pause, and then the sirens blare again. Immediately, shop doors fly open and people scramble into the streets. Bus engines grind into life. Cars and motorcycles career away from the curbs, and the city reasserts its natural rhythms.

It never appears in the guidebooks, but Seoul's monthly air-raid drill ranks as one of that city's most extraordinary sights: a momentary eclipse of its frantic animation, a self-imposed paralysis. Along with other defenses—the ever-present roadblocks and revetments, the rocket launchers tucked behind billboards, the half-hidden bunkers, the massive antitank walls along the highway running north—the drill stands as a reminder of the city's weird political-economic circumstance, which is that it has become rich and powerful while still, technically, at war. Its glass-shrouded office towers and extravagant boutiques lie a scant twenty-five miles from enemy lines, within range of North Korea's 130-mm artillery; its suburban factories and posh apartment blocks are only seconds from the other side's missiles.

Despite this conspicuous vulnerability, Korea has thrived. In recent years, it has enjoyed one of the world's fastest-growing economies: in 1986, 1987, and 1988, its gross national product (GNP) jumped by 12.9, 12.8, and 12.2 percent, respectively.[1] Growth slowed to a still respectable 6.5 percent in 1989 and appeared to be rebounding in the early months of 1990. And these are only the banner years in what is shaping up as a long-running success. From 1972 to 1983, Korea's GNP grew at an average annual rate of 8.2 percent. Between 1985 and 2000, growth should average between 7.0 and 8.0 percent, while the GNPs of the world's most advanced countries will be stalled below 3.0 percent.[2]

Much of this expansion has been fueled by an extraordinary boom in exports: from the early 1960s until the late 1970s, export growth averaged between 30 and 40 percent and was occasionally much greater. While exports grew at a more modest rate in the 1980s, they were sufficient to create an $8.7 billion trade surplus with the United States in 1988. Korean companies now command large shares of the U.S. automobile, garment, and small appliance markets. One of Korea's automakers, Hyundai, had the best-selling subcompact import in America in 1988; another manufacturer, Samsung, owned 20 percent of the U.S. microwave oven market. By the end of the century, this Indiana-sized nation will be one of the world's top ten traders and have one of its top fifteen economies.[3]

Furthermore, the benefits of this success are filtering down to the country's 42 million people. In the early 1960s, Korea's annual per capita income was a pathetic $90; in 1986, per capita income was around $2,200, and it is expected to break the $5,000 mark in the 1990s.[4] Korea's average urban family enjoys an annual income of $9,200.[5] The country has the biggest middle class in non-Japan Asia, and—assuming that current growth rates continue—its standard of living should approach that of Great Britain by the turn of the century.

Korea's prosperity is miraculous not only because of the nation's wartime vulnerability but also because it has come so quickly, out of so little. Many of the executives who dine in Seoul's fine restaurants can recall weeks and months during which they and their families starved. Or worse: their personal histories embrace the atrocities and wholesale bloodletting of the Korean War. Like their countrymen, they have clear memories of their nation as it was thirty-five years ago, a land of bombed-out rice paddies, leveled cities, stricken people. They can remember that even as recently as the early 1960s, oxcarts were a commonplace on the streets of the capital.

In a single generation, Koreans have rebounded, and they have done so *with a vengeance*: this is a parvenu nation, understandably captivated by its sudden wealth and status, eager to announce its arrival in the boldest terms. It boasts the world's largest steel plant, largest cement plant, largest textile goods factory, largest single dry dock; the tower on Mount Namsan is said to be the tallest in Asia, while a new shopping mall claims to be the world's largest "comprehensive leisure town," incorporating the Orient's second largest department store, which itself boasts the world's largest chandelier, weighing in at 10.5 tons. At sixty-three floors, the Daihan Life Insurance Building is the tallest edifice in Asia. And so on.

THE MANUFACTURED MIRACLE

Evidence of Korea's success—in drab statistics and glimmering chandeliers—is readily available, but shedding light on the reasons behind that success is more difficult. For more than two decades now, in the West, in the socialist and communist nations, in the capitals of envious Third World nations around the globe, investigations have focused on the root causes, the policies and the personalities that explain Korea's brilliant transformation. These studies are often tinged with disbelief, and for good reason; after all, when peace finally came to this nation in 1953, it found little of consequence. No minerals or oil, no capital, no infrastructure, not enough food. The homes were leveled, the factories crushed, the fields trampled.

Indeed, the nation's only resource was its people, and they hardly seemed a wellspring of economic vitality. During the previous half century, Koreans had been colonized, brutalized, exploited, educationally deprived, prohibited from speaking their language, dislocated by the millions through conscription and war and the division of their country, killed, maimed, and terrorized. They were sick. They were impoverished. They had every conceivable excuse for sliding into corruption and despotism, and, at times, they have done just that.

Yet the simple answer to every question about Korea's success is always the people, who have shown themselves to be a resource with enormous powers of self-renewal. From their oldest cultural traditions, modern Koreans have learned a respect for authority and a dedication to family. Out of their poverty, they have learned diligence; out of their fear, urgency. Most important, they have exhibited a jack pine tenacity. As soon as the flames are extinguished, they are quick to set down roots, eking sustenance from the blackened landscape, thriving.

In the aftermath of devastation, the people of Korea set about manufacturing their miraculous transformation. They boosted their national literacy rate to over 95 percent; they put in the world's longest workweek; they were frugal as individuals and as a nation (they have paid off some of their debts to international lenders *ahead of time*). The leaders of Korea's mammoth conglomerates or *chaebol* have invested profits instead of smuggling them to Zurich or New York. The bureaucrats have devised brilliant plans and executed them with precision. In short, this is a triumph of behavior; Korea has not grown rich by finding new deposits of gold or huge fields of oil or by applying a special new technology. Put in the best light, under that colossal chandelier, this country's transformation is the sort of parable that should be read to the children at bedtime.

Sort of. In actuality, the transformation has been more complicated, and darker. Yes, the Korean work ethic is partially founded on Confucian values that emphasize harmony and respect for authority, but those values also support a deadening conservatism, a lack of communication, and a stifling tendency toward autocratic methods—in government and education as well as business. Yes, Korean corporations have become global competitors because of their employees' unflagging capacity for hard labor, but they have also crafted a management style that often exploits those workers, that apes paternalism while subjecting Koreans to abuses shunned in much less developed nations. Yes, the Korean government has engineered much of the miracle, but it has abetted the worst abuses by the corporations, has applied its troops to the bone-breaking repression of dissent, has censored and tortured and murdered in the name of economic development.

Finally, Korea's transformation has been an expression of national will, of a dedication to country and race. But that will has been formed and exercised in a culture that—since its early industrialization—has thought in military terms, that has looked to the military for its organization and its leadership. The Korean way of working (and of managing workers) may be based on ancient Confucian values, but these have been recast in the experience of a desperate and violent modern history. The first result has been a peacetime economy with a sense of mission and stringent controls more appropriate to a nation at war; the second is a population of workers who are neither belligerent nor savage but who have been forged into an aggressive and expeditionary economic force.

Certainly, at times, traditional Confucian elements dominate in the workplace. Many Koreans insist on using these to interpret corporate culture and management style. The image of the family is most frequently applied: one powerful employers' federation explained Korea's lack of modern labor relations by noting the prevalence of "the father-centered," "family-oriented management system" in most small and medium-sized industries.[6] But the paternalism of Korean employers is notably sporadic and often hypocritical. The more apt metaphor is the military, which, like the family, provides strict authority, basic physical needs, companionship, and life-structuring values. The difference is that your commanding officer is more likely to see you as the means, whereas your father sees you as the end. In a truly paternalistic system, Korea's workers would not be so openly sacrificed to the higher good of economic development; they would not be so easily expended in the nation's successful but costly assaults on world markets.

The military metaphor fits, and understandably so. In a society where so many other aspects of life have been contingent on military considerations (or on leaders who have been, for the most part, military men), why should economics, labor relations, and corporate life stand apart?

While it ranks only twenty-third among the world's most populated countries, the Republic of Korea maintains the world's sixth-largest army, and—because the country is still at war—that institution's influence is pervasive. Soldiers and "combat police" are ubiquitous: they can be seen in the streets, patrolling sensitive locations, making spot checks of the packages and briefcases of passersby, confronting strikers and student demonstrators. And when the personnel are not visible, their equipment and preparations are clearly in evidence: every mountaintop seems capped with a radar dish and observation post. On hillsides above the rail lines to the north, piles of boulders are charged with explosives, ready to tumble onto the tracks to stop an enemy advance. At dusk, golf course fairways are strung with cables to fend off North Korean gliders. Along the coasts, wire fences are set with colored rocks in coded patterns; changes in the patterns alert patrols that the fences have been disturbed, possibly by North Korean infiltrators. And the patrols are not the only ones on the lookout; posters in restaurants and other public places admonish citizens to be wary of and immediately report potential spies.

In addition to this persistent background exposure, every Korean male receives an intensive dose of military thinking and behavior during compulsory national service, which lasts from twenty-four to thirty months. This experience is physically rigorous because, unlike U.S. forces, Koreans do not have air mattresses, heaters, or gas generators for hot meals in the field. Soldiers complain that they are undernourished and frequently beaten; from 1980 through 1988, 2,765 soldiers died as a result of suicide or harsh discipline. (This suicide rate was roughly 3.5 times that of the U.S. armed forces.)[7]

For most Korean males, participation in the military begins early and continues virtually throughout life. Military preparedness classes have been required in high schools and colleges, and before 1989, college students were obliged to take part in field exercises during spring break—in uniform, with military haircuts, carrying live ammunition. Following active duty, continuing contact with the military is assured by service in the national reserves until age fifty-five.

It seems difficult to overstate the importance of this nearly cradle-to-grave experience. For Korea's young men, the years of preparation, active service, and reserve duty have been a source of education and training and a model of how the modern world works. It is too much to suggest that this experience is psychologically definitive. But, as a World Bank study noted, "for virtually all of the male labor force, military service seems to have been an important source of skill formation and general experience in an organization having many characteristics of modern industry."[8]

ECONOMIC FOOT SOLDIERS

The military may mimic modern industry, but Korea's industrialists have also observed that modern industry can be made to mimic the military. Indeed, the military model has been transferred to industry with often slavish devotion. A Korean sociologist visiting Hyundai Motor Company's Ulsan plant in 1983 drew numerous parallels to his service in Korea's armed forces:

> Everyday life of employees was tied to factory work. Workers spent most of the day in the factory, wearing the gray Hyundai uniform. They were required to obey the strict regulations of the factory. For example, their hair had to be cut short. Their rank was revealed by the shape of their name tags which were pinned on the left breast pocket. They came to the factory before 8:00 A.M. accompanied by marching music blared from loud speakers. At the factory gates, guard-houses controlled the entrance and exit of workers and guests. The workers . . . had a noon lunch in the company cafeterias which were divided into sections for different ranks of employees.[9]

At times, industry's embrace of military methods can bring comic-opera results. According to an often-told but unsubstantiated story, North Korean agents once warned the officials of a Mideast nation that the "construction" team about to arrive from South Korea was, in fact, a military strike force. The officials were skeptical but sent an observer to the airport to watch as the plane from Seoul landed. To his horror, the supposed masons, carpenters, and machine operators marched wordlessly off the plane, their uniforms spotless and neatly pressed. They arranged themselves in perfect ranks on the sweltering runway and stood at attention. The leader blew his whistle, and the men counted off in crisp, loud numbers. There was another whistle, and the first rank pivoted sharply, marching off toward the baggage claim; at the next whistle, the second rank followed, and so on. The observer raced back to his superiors exclaiming that, yes, the nation had obviously been invaded by South Korea. An alert was sounded, real soldiers were mustered, and many long and detailed discussions of the Korean culture and work ethic ensued before the hosts were convinced that the construction laborers were nothing more than normal, highly disciplined Korean employees.

By and large, though, amusing anecdotes about the Korean workplace are rare. Even though the nation's conglomerates have recently loosened their grip on employees' lives, regimentation of workers remains a grim fact of corporate and factory life. There are the persistent salutes (proffered by steelworkers, shipworkers, and even corporate executives to show deference and respect for a superior) and the ubiquitous uniforms, seen on the assembly lines, in the boutiques and retail shops, in the shipyards, in the offices of banks and travel agents and conglomerates alike. (Even the plainclothes police wear a uniform of sorts: hip-length denim jackets in summer, identical beige or pale blue down parkas in winter, dark blue trench coats in the rain.) Ranks, with distinguishing insignia, are commonly used, and restrictions are placed on workers' appearance and after-hours behavior. Dissent, in and out of the workplace, is brutally repressed. In the worst instances, the military mentality is distorted into pseudopatriotic posturing by the promanagement *kusadae*, or "Save-the-Company Corps," operating under inflated names such as Hyundai Group Vocation Peace Corps to Keep Freedom and Save the State.

Finally, and most important, the military's influence is revealed in the willingness of employers and the government to accept grave social and human costs to achieve economic targets. Korea's housing and social services have been virtually ignored in order to maximize development, and the nation's air and water have become appallingly polluted. Korea also has what is arguably the highest rate of industrial accidents and deaths in the developed world. According to one church group, the first twenty years of Korea's campaign to industrialize produced nearly 2 million deaths and injuries—"four times as much suffering as was caused by the Korean War."[10] Although it seems inappropriate to compare levels of suffering, the fact remains that Korea's economic victories are being built on the bodies of its workers.

THE PRESIDENTS GENERAL

As might be expected, this military culture does not percolate up from the bottom of society; rather, it originates in the highest levels of government. The three presidents who have overseen the republic's economic miracle—Park Chung-Hee, Chun Doo-Hwan, and now Roh Tae-Woo—were all generals before coming to government, and the first two achieved their control of government through the exercise of military strength. (Roh's political career began with the coup that installed his colleague and classmate, Chun, as Korea's dictator.) Although they relinquished their commands, they continued to be loyal to the men, institutions, and ways of thinking that brought them to power; those loyalties necessarily colored their perceptions of the world and their actions, as well as those of their subordinates and, ultimately, the society at large.

General Park Chung-Hee affords the best example. After taking control of the country in 1961, he set upon a program for economic development that had all the hallmarks of a military campaign. Vulnerable targets were identified and analyzed. Trusted comrades— frequently other generals—were enlisted to command important operations, such as the creation and management of Korea's pivotal steel industry. In 1968, half of the generals who had retired in the previous twenty years were employed by the government. One observer noted that "former generals alone (excluding military men of other ranks) made up half the cabinet, one fifth of the National Assembly, two-fifths of all ambassadorial appointments, and two-thirds of the heads of state-run firms."[11] (Two decades later, this practice was still common; a 1988 parliamentary investigation found that in several government-owned corporations, ex-military men filled an abnormally large percentage of management positions.)[12] Meager resources— both public and private—were mobilized to attack specific markets with a single-mindedness that obscured the costs to other sectors of society. And workers became the economic foot soldiers.

Park's approach was perfectly natural for Korea. This was, after all, a nation that had lived under a militaristic colonial master for thirty-six years, during which it was converted into a producer of arms and matériel. This period was followed by years of military administration under the Americans, then more years of civil war. Park applied military thinking to economic development because it was what he knew. Furthermore, in his mind development was not a simple issue of increasing wealth or improving life-style. In Korea in 1961, economics was an issue of vital security, to be addressed like any other threat to the nation's existence. A Fortune 100 company executive with some years experience in Korea explained it this way: "All the techniques and controls are intriguing, but the bottom line is that Korea's development is about survival. It's as basic as a rock fight."

This hazy line between economics and security is likely to become even more smudged if, as one Korean think tank predicts, political and military alliances become less applicable for economic purposes and economic power becomes more applicable for achieving security goals and exerting influence.[13]

Relations with North Korea are an excellent example of how South Korea has applied its economic heft to promote security. Despite constant diplomatic maneuvering, relations on the peninsula remained hostile and unstable for decades after the Korean War. Recently, though, genuine interaction between the North and South seems to be taking place in the form of trade and proposed joint ventures. At the same time, South Korea has been exchanging trade missions and creating economic links with the Soviets, the People's Republic of China, and the East Bloc nations. These countries are being courted because they represent huge potential markets and because, as they fall into a web of economic relationships with the Republic of Korea, North Korea might follow—in short, a sort of reverse domino theory. Eventually, the North's hunger for hard currency and products, the South's hunger for natural resources and markets, and the passionate desire on both sides for unification may settle tensions in one of the planet's most anxious regions.

A WORKER
FOR THE TWENTY-FIRST CENTURY?

Korea's brilliant successes are decidedly not just a function of military organization or thinking. To the contrary, they represent a complex of ancient values and modern history, of management strategies and individual leadership, all of which will be considered in subsequent chapters. Together, these elements have created workers—white- and blue-collar alike—who are driven yet docile, ambitious and afraid, smart but willing to take orders. These factors have not produced *model* workers; Korean productivity is not high by Western or Japanese standards, and quality is only recently a pursuit. But they have forged economic warriors who have captured jobs and markets from workers in other nations.

The Korean transformation has been stunning not only for its successes but also for its continued unfolding. The nation is currently undergoing what appears to be another metamorphosis, this time toward political and economic freedoms. Authoritarianism is becoming less palatable in the office, on the factory floor, and in the streets. In large part, this labor "mutiny" has arisen because Korea is winning its economic war. The generation that now dominates the work force is impatient. The precariousness of their peace is less evident (air-raid drills notwithstanding), and, unlike their parents, they have probably never known the threat of starvation. Their pride demands that they dress and travel and enjoy life to the same degree as their Western and Japanese counterparts. Their discipline, by some accounts, is slipping.

This is not to suggest, however, that Korea's workers are incapable of leading the country into continued prosperity. "The recent problems are very understandable," explained an American management consultant in Seoul. "It's like kids during their first month away at college. The restraints have been removed, there's a very heady sense of freedom, and it takes a little while before they can establish their own equilibrium." But a work ethic that is deeply embedded in the nation's culture is not going to be reversed overnight.

Despite the country's proven ability to accommodate change, many of its most conservative cultural traits remain surprisingly enduring. Sidewalk vendors hawk traditional medicines—the curled shavings of antler horn, a bear's misshapen head and claws—just outside a computer store; biotechnology coexists with arranged marriages. In fact, if the country is to preserve and add to its gains, its greatest obstacle will not be change but the lack of it—in education, in science and technology, in the relaxation of government regulations, in the opening of its markets, in the growth of the much-neglected small businesses that employ over half the nation's manufacturing work force.

There is no guarantee that Korea will be able to balance workers' demands for freedom with its leaders' inclinations toward authoritarianism, or that an equilibrium between change and conservatism will be struck. But these challenges seem unexceptional compared with what the people of the peninsula have already overcome. Assuming, then, that Korean workers continue their astonishing performance into the next century, they are of clear importance for the rest of the world's nations—developed and developing, communist and past communist.

First and most immediately, they threaten the livelihoods of workers and managers in North America and Europe. Already, they have captured some industries. Some Western companies have shut their doors, and some Western workers are no longer at their jobs precisely because of Korean exports.

Second, over a longer term, Koreans could become friendly and even free-spending consumers of Western products. Although their economy has been largely closed to outsiders, change is in the offing. Credit is being deregulated, tariff barriers are falling, free enterprise seems finally to be arriving in what has been an only nominally capitalistic country. As the the fruits of Korea's economic success reach the common man and woman, they have more money for Western goods. It remains to be seen, however, whether Korea's economic and political powers will be willing or able to open their markets (and, thereby, relinquish their control)—and whether Korean customers will choose to buy from the West.

Finally, the Korean model—rigid authoritarianism leading to prosperity and the possibility of democratic freedom—is clearly seductive to other developing nations. When leaders in those nations look at Korea, they see an excellent short-term rationale for concentrating their political and economic control. Korea is, above all, a glimmering advertisement for the benefits of fascism. They also see a nation whose level of development appears to be readily achievable, as opposed to economic giants such as Japan and the United States. Moreover, many of these nations are receiving firsthand experience of Korean methods as more and more Korean companies move their less profitable, labor-intensive industries offshore.

For this reason, especially, Korea's success—perhaps even more than Japan's—challenges the principles and practices that constitute labor-management-government relations in the West. It already has had a direct influence on the fortunes of American corporations and American workers. And, to the degree that its exploitive methods of organizing and managing workers can be grafted onto other nations' populations, it will continue to devil our fortunes for a long, long time.

Given that Korea's workers are important in both the immediate and longer terms, in their own right and as a model, the question naturally arises: who are these men and women?

2
▲▲▲

Meet Mr. Kim

When Kim Kyong-Suk opens his eyes, the sky, seen through a small window high in the concrete wall, is still dark. His young wife, next to him on the thin mattress, stirs. Their child, an infant boy sleeping on her other side, senses the house awakening and turns fitfully.

The floor of their tiny room is warm from the ducts that run under the linoleum, but the room itself is cool. Kim dresses quickly while his wife prepares a meal of cold rice and vegetables, leftovers from yesterday's evening meal. Kim eats, then leaves so he can be at work by 7:45. He must walk a mile to the small factory where he operates a grinder, smoothing welds on rings of metal that—after heat treatment and hobbing and more treatment—will become gears for automobile and truck transmissions.

The work is hard and dirty, but that does not trouble Kim. He is more concerned about conditions in the plant. The owner has been exceedingly inconsistent in his concern for his workers' well-being: on the one hand, he has prohibited smoking (for health reasons) and provided a chapel for his employees (prayer services are held every day). On the other, safety standards are lax. After heat treatment, the radiant gray-hot rings are spread across the shop floor to cool; the slightest misstep could mean ghastly burns, days or weeks of recuperation, lost wages. The company provides no ear protectors against the noise, no goggles. The building is poorly lit, unheated in the winter, and, more important, violently overheated in the summer.

Kim has held this job for five years. Although he likes his fellow workers, he worries that he cannot last long in his present position and knows that there is little opportunity for him to advance in the company. He scans the shop and notes, again, that the workers are all, like him, in their mid- to late twenties, some a few years younger; fifty-four-hour workweeks under these conditions take a toll on older men. Kim may have become more aware of this lingering doubt in the past two weeks; a recent surge in orders from an American manufacturer has kept him at his machine until around nine o'clock at night, even on Saturday.

It is dark and cold as he returns home; his legs ache, and his son is already asleep. Yet Kim is grateful for the overtime. Despite a 15 percent pay raise last year and the possibility of a similar hike soon, the increasing costs of rent, food, and clothing mean that his salary and bonus still barely cover expenses. There is not enough surplus to allow a larger apartment, which means that he and his wife must delay having another child. And, as his parents' eldest son, he knows that he is responsible for their welfare, especially after his father retires in a few years. Pressures are building on Kim to add to his small savings, and overtime is the only solution.

Still, Kim Kyong-Suk and his wife allow themselves occasional luxuries. One is the small Goldstar radio and cassette player that he now turns on, softly so as not to wake the boy. He listens to the music and talks to his wife as she prepares his evening meal.

Mr. Kim is a fabrication, amalgamated from government statistics and encounters at a small factory in southeastern Seoul. Still, he is a fair representation of Korea's manufacturing labor force. Like him, the average production worker is male, young, employed by a small private manufacturer, living in a city. His wages are low, his hours long, his future uncertain. But he is not starving and is, in fact, beginning to taste some of the fruits of Korea's booming economy.

Obviously, this picture oversimplifies much. The Korean work force, notwithstanding the nation's remarkable homogeneity, has a richness and complexity that cannot be captured in a thumbnail portrait. Similarly, the statistical information, although there is a wealth of it, is only partially illuminating. One World Bank report dolefully noted that "some two-thirds of Korea's private, non-agricultural work force belongs to the small-scale or informal economy for which no wage data exist."[1] Many of these statistically invisible laborers are engaged in export-related manufacturing—working out of their homes, making labels or wiring tiny strings of lights or any of a thousand small jobs. And even among Korea's major employers, information about conditions and wages can be highly guarded and contradictory.

Nevertheless, certain tentative observations can be made about the men and women who have forged Korea's astonishing economic transformation.

A SMALL CIRCLE OF FRIENDS

Although it has generated enormous anxiety, the Korean work force itself is far from enormous. The country's economically active population has yet to exceed 17 million. (By comparison, the economically active population is about 60 million in Japan and twice that in the United States.)[2] Unemployment in Korea is low overall (2.8 percent in 1989) but appreciably higher among university graduates, in part because the Korean devotion to education creates more graduates than the economy can absorb.[3] In fact, less than 60 percent of 1987 college graduates found jobs that year.[4]

Roughly half of all working Koreans are employed in construction, finance, retail, government, and other services; another 23 percent are engaged in agriculture, fishing, and mining. The remaining 27 percent constitute the entire manufacturing labor force of Korea, a total of just 4.4 million workers. In other words, a truly extensive study of Korean workers could almost *name* them. (China, in contrast, numbers over 60 million manufacturing workers.)[5] Half of Korea's work force can be found in very small-scale, low-technology, often family-owned operations with fewer than ten employees; because this segment of the economy is frequently ignored by official agencies, data on it are exceedingly sketchy. Among the 2.2 million manufacturing workers tracked by the Ministry of Labor (that is, those working at concerns with ten or more regular employees) the male-female split is roughly sixty-forty. The split between production and nonproduction workers is approximately seventy-five-twenty-five.[6]

Since 1970, three intriguing shifts have marked Korea's manufacturing work force. First, it has more than tripled. Part of this increase is attributable to a population boom that has expanded the pool of economically active Koreans by 67 percent. The rest can be traced to the movement of workers off the land and into the factories; from 1970 to 1987, agriculture's share of total employment dropped from 50 percent to around 20 percent.[7]

Second, the manufacturing work force has changed its areas of concentration. Some industries, such as textiles and apparel, have maintained a relatively constant percent of total employment, but others that were virtual nonentities have become keystones of the economy. For example, the electrical machinery and appliance industry—which produces a great many of the stereos, VCRs, and TVs now in America's homes—has expanded its work force by more than 1,000 percent; whereas it once absorbed only 5.3 percent of all manufacturing workers, it now accounts for 16.1 percent of employment. The manufacture of transport equipment (meaning cars, for the most part) has had a similar growth.[8]

A third shift is also notable. In 1975, less than 46 percent of the manufacturing work force was employed by small to medium-sized enterprises (SMEs, with from 5 to 300 employees). By 1986, the SME share had grown to nearly 58 percent and was predicted to reach 63 percent by 1991. And those figures clearly underestimate the importance of these companies: when the very smallest manufacturing establishments (those with fewer than 5 employees) are included, the SME share of employment was already 64 percent in 1986.[9] This deconcentration of the work force can be traced to the larger firms' increased automation and their desire to push their most labor-intensive (and therefore less profitable and more troublesome) businesses onto small subcontractors and other suppliers.

THE HARDEST-WORKING
MEN AND WOMEN IN THE WORLD

Most discussions of Korea's economic success begin with this: Korean workers log the longest week in the world.

Although the national standard is a 48.0-hour week, the 1986 average in manufacturing was 54.7 hours per week (54.4 hours for men and 55.2 for women). This compares with 47.3 hours per week in Sri Lanka, 46.0 in Japan, 45.2 in Hong Kong, and 40.7 in the United States.[10] Looked at another way, Korea's manufacturing laborers put in an average of 25 days and almost 235 hours per month in 1987.[11]

Korea's workweek reached a peak of sorts in 1986; more recent surveys suggest a slight decline that can be attributed to several factors. First, although this fact is difficult to document, it is generally accepted that Koreans—having reached a basic level of comfort and security—are craving more leisure time. At least as significant have been the sweeping reforms and liberalizations initiated in 1987. These brought higher wages for regular hours (allowing some workers to get by with less overtime) and a more rigorous enforcement of labor laws pertaining to overtime. Before the summer of 1987, employers commonly paid straight wages for overtime work, if they paid at all. Now that the government is enforcing laws on overtime pay, employers find it more economical to add a second shift, thereby reducing workers' hours. If the forty-four-hour standard workweek is gradually introduced, as planned, in 1990 and 1991, Korean workers will have even more time off.

Despite the assumption that Koreans are eager for more leisure time, there are indications that many of them are happy to continue working long hours, especially now that they can expect to be fairly paid for their overtime. In fact, *guaranteed* overtime is often a demand of workers negotiating new contracts with employers. And when the Federation of Korean Trade Unions asked over 7,000 female members what constitutes an ideal job, the strongest response (mentioned by 44.3 percent) was "humanitarian treatment." Only 8.2 percent desired shorter hours, despite the fact that almost a quarter of them worked over eleven hours per day. And just 8.0 percent dreamed of higher wages. [12]

THAT HIGHLY VALUED CHEAP LABOR

Korean laborers not only work long, they also work cheap.

In 1987, the average hourly compensation for production workers in manufacturing was just $1.69, compared with $11.34 in Japan and $13.46 in the United States. Koreans also made considerably less than workers in Singapore ($2.37), Taiwan ($2.23), and Hong Kong ($2.11). And that low Korean wage represents a jump of 21.6 percent over 1986, the result of dramatic pay hikes and currency appreciation. [13] Since then, dramatic pay hikes—90 percent in dollar terms—have put Korean workers on a par with their counterparts in Singapore, Hong Kong, and Taiwan. But even at decidedly higher wage rates, Korean workers remain a bargain, because they are both highly educated and—recent disturbances notwithstanding—highly cooperative. Nevertheless, wage hikes and activism among Korean workers have encouraged the country's corporate leaders and bureaucrats to begin looking for even cheaper labor elsewhere in Asia and in Latin America.

Obviously, the hourly average obscures the more interesting contours of the Korean labor market—the highs and lows, the winners and losers. Here are a few quick (albeit dry) statistical differentials:

• Although manufacturing has driven Korea's economic boom, it is the least rewarding sector of the economy, with its workers making only 85 percent of the average for all industries. In other words, depressed manufacturing wages have made Korean goods much cheaper and more successful in global markets.

• Production workers are particularly poorly paid, making less than 80 percent of the average for all workers; only service workers make less.

• Administrative and managerial workers, in contrast, are highly rewarded; their average earnings of approximately $1,000 a month (in 1986) were fully three times more than production workers made. [14]

• Education is well rewarded in the Korean labor market. When they can find jobs, male college graduates make 140 percent more than those who finished middle school or less. [15]

• Regardless of whether one is white-collar or blue-collar, working in a large company offers the best opportunity for compensation; workers at manufacturing firms with 10 to 29 employees make less than 80 percent of what their counterparts at the largest (500 or more employees) corporations take home. [16]

• Women are paid substantially less than men; overall, the average wage of a female worker is 46 percent that of the average male worker. [17] From 1971 through 1981, male earnings averaged 2.26 times female earnings. [18]

• Korea's private companies, unlike those in some developing countries, offer better rewards than does the government. A college graduate in an entry-level position makes roughly 35 percent more in the private sector than he would in the public sector. [19] Nevertheless, students rank some public enterprises (especially the utilities) as highly desirable employers because of working conditions and the possibility of advancement, especially for women.

Despite these distinctions, the distribution of income in Korea is remarkably balanced, especially by the standards of the world's developing nations. Only 5.5 percent of the population lived below the absolute poverty line in 1988, and an increasing number of Koreans consider themselves middle class. [20] Overall, the republic's level of economic equality approximates—or exceeds, by some measures—that of the United States and some countries in Western Europe. And Korea has maintained that level of equality (with some fluctuations) for the past quarter century. [21]

PRODUCTIVITY

Korean laborers work very hard for very little, but their productivity is nothing to boast about. Officials with the quasi-governmental Korea Productivity Center (KPC) have estimated that Korean manufacturers are fully 40 percent less productive than their Japanese competitors.

Part of this deficiency can be directly attributed to the people; those

intimate with the Korean style of working describe the situation variously, from "They know how to pace themselves" to "Given the chance,
people in Korea will screw off as much as anyone else in the world." In
certain industries, white-collar workers' long hours can include a great
deal of newspaper reading, talking with colleagues, resting heads on
desks, even watching television. Indeed, the emphasis on long hours
may actually impede overall efficiency.

But much of Korea's low productivity reflects the country's reliance
on less advanced technologies. The KPC found that "only 31 percent
of the companies it surveyed in 1986 had any form of automation."[22]
The technology gap is especially broad in older industries, such as
textile making. One study of Korean and Japanese companies with
similar revenues in electronics and textiles found that the Korean
companies had *twice* as many employees. In contrast, though, other
Korean industries, such as steel, regularly set world records in productivity. In 1987, the Pohang Iron and Steel Company (POSCO)
produced 772 tons per employee, compared with 371 tons at USX
and 505 at a major Japanese company, and POSCO's new plant at
Kwangyang produces 933 tons per worker. Overall, POSCO officials
claim that labor constitutes only 6 percent of their total production
cost, versus 23 percent in Japan and 30 percent in the United
States.[23]

In recent years, Korea's productivity has shot up, especially in
comparison with more established industrial powers. The KPC calcu-
lates that Korea's productivity has improved by over 117 percent since
1980, versus 35 percent in Japan; the U.S. improvement has been just
31 percent since 1977.[24] Part of Korea's advances can be traced to
better laborers working more efficiently at better machines. But part
can also be attributed to the employers' flexibility in rapidly adjusting
wages and the size of their payrolls. Bonuses could be cut, wages
trimmed, and workers let go as economic conditions warranted; that
ability, however, was based on an absolute impotence of organized
labor that no longer exists.[25]

The real race today is to increase productivity before labor costs
and the value of the *won* put too much pressure on the price of Korean
goods. The most recent laps in that race have not boded well. Yet there
is optimism among Korean economists, who forecast a robust GNP
growth of 7.2 percent between 1991 and the end of the century, with

improved productivity (from technological advances and increased economies of scale) accounting for nearly half of that expansion.[26]

AGGRESSIVE-PASSIVE WORKERS

While Korea's workers have become an intimidating presence in global competition, they are exceedingly docile in the face of authority. This has been the case in the past and, despite the often traumatic labor unrest since mid-1987, it remains a fairly accurate depiction.

To get a feeling for just how submissive Korean workers have been, consider that, from 1979 to 1984, on average only half a workday per 100 workers per year was lost because of strikes. The figure was 4 times higher in Japan and more than 100 times higher in the United States.

All that seemed to change radically in 1987, when government liberalizations allowed workers to express their deep discontent and engage much more freely in labor organization. In that year alone, 8.2 million workdays were lost in labor disputes—the vast bulk of which occurred in the half year after liberalizations were announced. (In all of 1986, by comparison, just 72,000 workdays were lost to labor actions.)[27] And these were passionate and contested strikes; the statistics fail to describe the eyes raked with tear gas, the beatings, and, in one case, the loss of life. In 1988 and 1989, labor disputes were fewer but longer in duration and often more violent. Following a government crackdown, strike activity in 1990 was down sharply.

This upheaval might seem to be a severe test of the depth of Korea's economic miracle. In actuality, the activism of Korean labor has had distinct limits. First of all, strikes in Korea have traditionally occurred at times of political change and have often reflected political rather than economic passions.[28] Thus, with the extraordinary shift toward democracy that occurred in 1987, a high number of strikes could have been anticipated. Second, a great many of the strikes were able to shut down production with the support of only a small group of employees; by one account, in the majority of work stoppages, less than 6 percent of the work force actively struck the employer.[29]

Finally, the strikes have been directed at the largest employers, where working conditions are usually better. Among the smallest companies, which employ the majority of Korea's work force and where conditions are most grim, 99.42 percent were *untouched* by labor disputes in 1987.[30] As one Korean labor expert put it, "The workers here are still very conservative. The labor laws are a hodgepodge and are generally considered to be lacking in legitimacy, and yet workers try to adhere to them. In the smaller companies, workers accept the reality that there is little chance for better terms and conditions of employment."[31]

In short, while activism is growing, Korean laborers remain decidedly more tractable than workers in other countries.

Although Koreans may be "conservative" when it comes to formal labor actions, they are very likely to register their discontent with their feet. The 1987 turnover rate for Korea's manufacturing work force was 4.3 percent—a higher rate than in the United States and much higher than in Japan. And that rate was low by recent standards; from 1980 to 1984, the turnover rate ranged from 5.0 to 5.6 percent.[32] Koreans also show a very high *inclination* to move, whether or not they actually do so. One study found that, during hard times, Koreans would be more likely than Americans or Japanese to leave their employers for a more prosperous company.[33]

Given that they are in demand, that many employers frequently withhold or underpay wages, that working conditions are often appalling, and that seniority is not greatly rewarded, the turnover among production workers is hardly surprising. In addition to being potentially beneficial for the worker, this high mobility can also be good for the economy as a whole. If workers had been fixed in particular jobs—out of employer loyalty or insecurity about other opportunities—it would have been impossible for Korea's planners to shift from one industrial target to another.

Unfortunately, Korean workers rarely improve their lot by changing jobs, and in many cases they sacrifice the few financial advantages seniority can bring. This fact has not been lost on employers; in one study, a personnel manager expressed dismay that the monthly turnover at his plant was only 2 to 3 percent; a higher rate among unskilled workers would help keep labor costs down without affecting productivity.[34] Of course, as Korean industries become increasingly reliant on hard-to-find skilled workers, high turnover rates will become more worrisome.

A YOUNG WOMAN'S PLACE
IS ON THE ASSEMBLY LINE

Statistically, the average Korean worker is male. Nevertheless (and contrary to certain Confucian precepts, such as "Keep a woman at home and ignorant of outside events"), female workers constitute a critical segment of the nation's labor force. As production workers, they dominate several key export industries, such as garment making and small electronics assembly. From age twenty through twenty-four, they constitute 57 percent of the work force, although they are less than 49 percent of the population.[35]

Women also serve as a striking example of the way the traditional and the modern interact in contemporary Korea. Unfortunately, the modern part for a young woman is too often a day filled with mind-numbing electronics assembly, followed by a night in a rented room, far from her family. And the traditional part is that women do not enjoy an equal voice or equal pay in a society that remains distinctly male controlled. In fact, it is the egregiously low pay women receive that accounts for much of the competitiveness of the export industries they dominate.

That Korean men earn considerably more than their female counterparts is far from shocking; the same phenomenon occurs in societies that have reached the apex of industrial development. In fact, the differential is more easily explained (not to say justified) in Korean society: marriage, followed by child rearing and homemaking, is virtually the only accepted life course for Korean women, who almost always leave the work force when they wed and therefore benefit less from wage increases based on experience. Although this pattern is slowly changing, the career of a female factory worker in most cases lasts just seven or eight years.[36]

The Korean working woman is cognizant that she is playing a temporary role and is therefore less insistent about achieving wage parity with men. One social scientist drew the following portrait of a *yogong* or factory girl: She "works and earns for a specific purpose, one usually family-connected, but she takes an essentially passive view of her earning potential. When it is found, for example, that men in the ceramics plant who do exactly the same work as women earn twice as much . . . the prevailing female attitude is that this is as it should be. Some girls . . . protest not the inequities between male and female income but rather the fact that women workers abroad, in Europe or the United States, are paid eight to twelve times as much for the same work."[37]

As noted, the pay differential between men and women in Korea is pronounced, with male earnings more than double female earnings. Differences are less extreme when college-educated men and women are compared, with men making an average of 1.6 times as much as women.[38] On the bottom of the education scale, however, female day laborers are sometimes paid only a third of what their male counterparts receive.

But male and female Korean workers are separated by more than just their pay scales. Women tend to work longer hours, under more trying conditions, and are "more subject to the whims of employers under the guise of protecting family morality."[39] They are also more likely to be forced into early retirement and are less likely to receive on-the-job training and other tools for career advancement.

The tradition of grossly exploiting women workers can be traced, at least in part, to practices of the Japanese dating back to their occupation and annexation of Korea. Many young women became "indentured factory workers in a system imitative of Japan's, in which, in return for a dowry payment to parents, employers were given *in loco parentis* rights, enabling them to underpay, to discipline harshly, and even incarcerate the girls in dormitories to isolate them from labor agitators. The Japanese police obligingly returned those girls who rashly fled."[40]

But the Japanese merely capitalized on an existing situation in which women were the objects of profound discrimination. Traditionally, and as recently as one hundred years ago, women had personal names only during the period between puberty and marriage; before and after they were known only as someone's daughter, someone's wife. In fact, it was the Japanese who initiated the use of individual names for women and awarded them property rights. Their motives, however, were far from altruistic; one scholar has argued that "the Japanese, as at home, wished to 'alienate' Korean women from the confines of their kin-affiliated households to the extent that they could be exploited, especially as factory hands in the burgeoning Japanese-sponsored economy."[41]

Korean women have a lot of ground to cover before they catch their male counterparts, but here, too, change is coming. And despite the subservient role that women have played, they are far from powerless. They have for some time held leadership roles in labor organization and on university campuses. And the Korean with the largest reported income in 1987 was a woman, fifty-three-year-old Han Young Ja, who earned $7.3 million after a banner year for her company, Sam Yang Chemical. Ms. Han, it would be remiss not to mention, makes tear gas.[42]

THE QUALITY OF LIFE

The standard of living for Korea's workers has improved enormously since 1960. Basic human needs are being better met:

	1960	1970	1980
Crude birthrate (per 1,000)	42.7	30.3	24.0
Crude death rate (per 1,000)	13.4	9.1	6.9
Infant mortality (per 1,000)	78.3	50.1	33.1
Life expectancy (years)	54.4	60.3	66.1
People per physician	3,540.0	2,240.0	1,690.0
Access to safe water (% population)			
Total	12.1	58.0	71.0
Urban	18.6	84.0	85.0
Rural	9.5	38.0	54.9

(Source: *Korea: Development in a Global Context* [World Bank, 1984], p. 99)

In addition, workers are enjoying at least some of the fruits of industrialization:

Ownership per thousand	1960	1970	1980
Cars	0.5	1.9	6.2
Radios	31.2	124.4	392.7
TVs	0.3	13.0	164.4

(Source: *Korea: Development in a Global Context*, p. 100)

Naturally, such development has come at a price. Korea is a densely populated country (425 people per square kilometer, versus 325 in Japan, 110 in China, and only 25 in the United States); in fact, if the figures are adjusted for the availability of arable land, the republic has the highest population density on the planet.[43] And that density is pronounced in cities such as Seoul and Pusan, which are home to 71 percent of all industrial workers. Given that the government has stressed economic growth over social issues, housing is in understandably short supply. And pollution is world class: Seoul's atmosphere has four times as much sulfur dioxide as Tokyo's. Just before the 1988 Olympics, many athletes—even those from venerable smog capitals such as Los Angeles—complained about the difficult breathing in the host city.

Pollution is a problem that Koreans are just beginning to confront: nascent environmental and antinuclear groups are expressing their concerns for the first time, and researchers are starting to reveal the hidden dangers of modern Korean life. The government is clearly not leading any of these efforts, though: when a survey revealed that several Seoul restaurants were serving food with dangerous levels of mercury, reports noted that the republic had yet to establish standards for acceptable levels of this life-threatening contaminant.[44]

When the Korean worker falls on hard times, the state-provided safety net offers scant protection. In 1986, less than 57 percent of the population was covered by government-subsidized medical insurance. Plans are in place to extend coverage, however, and the trend in Korea's development suggests that this and other social-welfare programs will take an increasingly large proportion of the central government budget.[45] It is worth noting that there is considerable room for such expansion of government's role: the World Bank estimates that the republic spent only 7.2 percent of its 1986 budget on housing, amenities, social security, and welfare—a smaller percentage than almost every other country at a similar level of development.

But that is not to say that the republic is deaf to the needs of its people; in one area, education, the central government spent over 18 percent of its 1986 budget, more than the United States, West Germany, or any other developed nation. By 1989, the government was spending 22 percent of its budget on education, and planning to spend fully 30 percent in 2001.[46]

OPENING THE DOOR: EDUCATION

To a degree unsurpassed in the world, Koreans are dedicated to—if not obsessed with—education. There are both historic and contemporary explanations, but the salient point is this: for most Korean children, all their education, all the fourteen-hour days of preparation, all the classes with special tutors (technically illegal but widely used nevertheless), indeed most of their lives narrow inexorably to a single December day when the college entrance exam is administered.

The importance of this state-supplied test is difficult to overestimate. Admission to one of the top Korean universities—Seoul National, Yonsei, or Korea University—can virtually program one's life. Classes will be better, as will the opportunities for overseas study, and, most important, one will meet the right people. Teachers and classmates will define, to a large degree, one's opportunities for success after graduation. In short, the range of the possible is determined by this single, demanding, terrifying ritual.

The cafeteria at Seoul National, on the late afternoon of the test day, is crowded with somber parents from every stratum of Korean society. Furs mingle with cloth coats, rosaries jingle against worry beads. The air is stale, the tables littered with milk cartons and orange peels, the ashtrays smeared with cigarette butts. As the light fades toward five o'clock and the close of the test, some parents grow jittery; others just bow their heads.

Then the young examinees arrive. The first, a girl in a blue pea coat, appears before the test's scheduled conclusion. Her surprised father jumps out of his chair, and she collapses there, her head on the table. She is absolutely still for a long minute. Mother and two siblings stand at her side while father fetches barley tea in a green plastic glass and sets it before her. When she finally lifts her head, her eyes are red and watery but she is not crying.

The students come quickly now, cascading down the steps from the examination buildings, and the mothers arise, arching and craning for a glimpse of their young; some dash out to wait in the frigid December air. Students who have come without their parents wander into the cafeteria, squinting and giddy with exhaustion. Several boys light up "88" cigarettes and inhale hungrily. "I feel dissected," one says. He laughs wildly. "I'm afraid I did very poorly and so I am very depressed."

Similar scenes were repeated at nearly 500 test sites around Korea on examination day, 1988, with 600,000 applicants vying for 140,000 spots at the eighty-one top-ranked universities.[47] Worried about traffic jams with so many students and parents, the government had requested that private corporations and its own agencies stagger their office hours.[48]

Immediately following the test and for several days thereafter, Korea's students celebrated. There were tragedies—two Seoul students drank themselves to death—but there were also stories of tremendous triumph. The top score at Seoul National that year was posted by a young man whose father was a bedridden former street scavenger and whose mother worked as a maid and construction laborer. Having failed to pass the test the previous year, the nineteen-year-old slept only four hours a night for twelve months and attended "cramming institutes" on money his parents earned by making envelopes at night.[49]

It is exactly this sort of possibility, this potential for taking a youngster from dire poverty to a position among the elite, that encourages Koreans to devote 5 to 30 percent of their family incomes to school fees and tuition.[50] Every Korean knows that higher education means better economic rewards for the whole family. And what works for the family works for society, too. Korea's only resource is its people;

for the nation to continue its astounding progress, that resource must be exploited to its greatest potential. Hence, the substantial public investment.

Equally important, Korea gets an excellent return on this investment. Whereas America spends billions to graduate functional illiterates, Koreans are remarkably well educated, even by the standards of the most advanced nations: literacy is estimated at better than 95 percent, perhaps the highest in the world. In a recent test of math and science ability among thirteen-year-olds in Ireland, Korea, Spain, the United Kingdom, the United States, and four Canadian provinces, Korean students won top honors, surpassing American students by a wide margin.[51]

The Korean dedication to education is ancient, but it has increased as Korea has developed: in 1965, only 35 percent of secondary school–age children were enrolled, but by 1985 the proportion had jumped to 94 percent. And although only 6 percent of college-age Koreans were enrolled in 1965, almost one-third were attending just two decades later.[52] Consequently, this still-developing nation has more Ph.D.s per capita than any other country in the world.

The commitment to education has its roots in the Confucian tradition, which emphasizes rote memorization and conformance to moral superiors and established ways of thinking. The first primer in many Korean schools sets out the lesson clearly: in the village, it says, everyone is either older or younger—meaning that relationships are clear and inviolable. That embrace of hierarchy is still manifest, in the near complete control exerted by the central government on all levels of education (public and private), in the emphasis on lecturing and memorization over discussion and analysis, in the classes of uniformed elementary-school students who march through the streets of downtown Seoul chanting "one, two, three, four" (in English, for the benefit of passing Westerners).

Unfortunately, this style of learning stands at odds with what is needed for a progressive industrial society. Modern education—the kind required to pave the way for technological and social advances— demands a constant introduction of new ideas and a constant testing and reevaluation of past knowledge. One of the greatest tasks facing Korea today is the reform of its schools, to encourage inquiry and debate without sacrificing the nation's traditional respect for authority and commitment to academic fundamentals.

THE DAILY BATTLE

There are a number of grim things one can say about Korean manufacturing, but perhaps the most damning is that little attention is paid to the health and safety of working men and women while on the job. This is especially true of the smaller establishments, which employ the majority of workers. In the words of a missionary who has lived among those workers for two decades, "It's a war out there. People are getting seriously hurt every day."

There are statistics to back up these claims. In 1986, Korea had 0.17 deaths for each 1,000 persons employed in manufacturing, 5.5 times the number in Hong Kong and 9.0 times the rate in Singapore; in addition, the Korean number is artificially deflated because it covers only workers in establishments with fifty or more workers, thereby excluding the majority of Korean employers and those most likely to have primitive and dangerous working conditions.[53] Although it is possible to find countries with higher rates of work-related death, Korea's rates are extraordinary given its level of economic and social development. And when the rates for deaths and injuries are considered together, Korea has one of the most tragic records in the world: in Japan, 0.61 percent of all workers were injured or killed in 1987; in Taiwan, the rate was 0.70, in Singapore 0.93; in that same year, a phenomenal 2.66 percent of all Korean workers were killed or injured.[54]

Consider the statistics from any angle and the same picture emerges. Koreans work desperately hard. Man or woman, on the job or in school, regardless of the conditions, the pay, or the hours, they place a value on work that is difficult for Westerners to comprehend. In part, their commitment derives from culture and tradition and is therefore transportable: witness the success of Koreans in alien cultures (Manhattan or southern California, for example) and under extreme conditions (such as the desert construction sites in Libya and Saudi Arabia). But Korea's ascension also comes from the unique structure of its economy, which has been created and refined with one goal: the maximal exploitation of the nation's material and human resources to compete successfully in the global marketplace.

3
▲ ▲ ▲

The Field:
A Profile of the
Korean Economy

High above the noisy, bustling streets of downtown Seoul, sunlight pours through floor-to-ceiling windows. The file cabinets shine, the polished linoleum floors glisten, and the sixteen desks (in four groups of four) are tidy and at precise right angles from the wall. Over loudspeakers recessed in the ceiling, a male voice exhorts the employees to exercise at their desks; music—of the bouncy international aerobics variety—rains down on the heads of the men, several of whom are smoking, none of whom is flexing any visible muscles.

A public-relations official for this, one of Korea's largest chaebol, is attempting to describe the business group without sounding immodest. It is a difficult assignment, because this conglomerate, along with a very few others, pioneered the country's industrial development; its employees could populate a city; and its products have carried Korean manufacturing—and influence—around the world. Furthermore, he notes, "the revenues of our trading company alone equal more than 10 percent of the entire GNP for the nation." A quick glance at the numbers shows a discrepancy. "Yes," he concedes, "the public numbers indicate something less than that. But the truth is that our revenues are actually much more than 10 percent of the GNP." For a moment, no one speaks. "I can't explain the difference. It's too complicated." He laughs softly, a little embarrassed but unmoving. "Anyway, you can believe me. It's much more than 10 percent."

In describing economies, it is sometimes appropriate to refer to their pyramid shape. At the base, there are a great number of small enterprises doing a small amount of business; fewer enterprises are buying and selling in larger quantities, and, at the pinnacle, a very few companies are doing huge volumes. In some countries, the pyramid is relatively flat. In others, the sides are steep.

In Korea, the economy looks like a two-by-four with a spike sticking up through its middle. There are many establishments with few employees doing very limited business and a few medium-sized companies. Then there are a very few, immensely powerful, often family-run business groups or chaebol, the largest of which control fifty or more companies and employ more than 175,000 workers; the top ten of these financial clans account for 12 percent of Korea's employment, 30 percent of its sales, and 24 percent of its value-added. And that power has been increasing since the late 1970s. [1]

In fact, the power of the chaebol may be even greater than these "public numbers" indicate. Korea's conglomerates are far from forthcoming about their real assets and control, and one can assume that—for political and tax purposes—some of their earnings have been artificially deflated. Others may be inflated. The overall dimensions of Korea's major business groups are, after all is said, a source of wonder and speculation. According to one scholar, data are regularly manicured to indicate conformance to corporate or government goals—so much that "outsiders rarely, if ever, know what truly is going on behind the administrative curtains of either public or private enterprises."[2]

Nevertheless, some facts about the Korean economy and its mammoth chaebol can be stated with at least some confidence.

THE OVERNIGHT SENSATIONS

Any overview of the chaebol must begin with their size. They are, by all standards, immense: *Fortune* ranked the Samsung group, with $35.2 billion in 1989 sales, as the world's twentieth-largest company. Daewoo is forty-seventh. Hyundai coyly resists revealing its group revenues but hints that, if it did, the group would probably rank just above or below Samsung. In any case, two of its affiliates made the Global 500 on their individual merits, as did one of Lucky-Goldstar's affiliates.

In Korean terms, the chaebol are beyond immense. The Samsung group's 1989 sales, for example, were equal to a whopping 17.25 percent of Korea's GNP. For a company to have similar clout in the United States, its 1989 sales would have to be $900 billion—more than 7 times the revenues of General Motors.[3] And while Samsung and Hyundai are currently at the top of the heap, they are not alone. The other top chaebol have also shown impressive revenues. Lucky-Goldstar's 1989 sales were estimated to be $25.0 billion, and Daewoo reported $20.0 billion. Together, sales of these top four chaebol were equal to 56.0 percent of Korea's 1989 GNP.

There is a tendency to focus on just these four, but Korea has other large conglomerates. Testifying before a parliamentary audit session, the Bank of Korea offered the following figures on 1987 sales and profits for the top ten chaebol. (The bank appears to have understated these sales severely, but the figures are useful for comparisons.)[4]

Group	Revenue	Net Profit	(As % of revenue)
Hyundai	$16.30	$ .162	0.99
Samsung	14.80	.121	0.82
Lucky-Goldstar	12.06	.127	1.05
Daewoo	8.99	.043	0.48
Sunkyong	5.94	.068	1.14
Ssangyong	3.91	.061	1.56
Hanjin	3.03	(.073)	—

Group	Revenue	Net Profit	(As % of revenue)
Korea Explosives	2.34	(.068)	—
Hyosung	2.29	.018	0.79
Dongkuk Steel	1.81	.048	2.65

(In U.S. $ billion, converted at an exchange rate of 792 won/$1 U.S.)

The chaebol are also massive employers. In 1989, Samsung had 177,000 workers; Hyundai, 167,000; Lucky-Goldstar about 100,000; and Daewoo, 91,000.

The size of these companies is stunning, but it pales next to the pace of their growth. These are young companies: the granddaddy of the chaebol is Samsung, which turned a virile fifty years old in 1988, while the youngest of the top four, Daewoo, has a *founder* who is only a few years past fifty. Koreans like to note that the big Japanese groups, which are somewhat comparable to the chaebol (and are, in fact, represented by the same Chinese ideograph), took a century to reach their present level of industrial might.

The explanations for this hypertrophic growth are complex but can be reduced to several key factors: a hungry and educated work force; the availability of American aid and, later, loans and investments from several foreign sources; and, finally, a government that was eager to support those companies that would, in turn, support its plans for development. And the government had a vast capacity for providing aid and comfort: it could protect foreign loans and investments (often through the physical repression of hungry workers), and it could bestow extraordinary benefits and concessions on loyal industrialists. In sum, the dramatic growth of the chaebol was based on cozy relationships with political leaders as much as on technological, cost, or other competitive advantages.

By virtue of their extraordinary size and their government preferences, the chaebol exert virtual monopolies over certain kinds of products and markets. One study showed that three top chaebol (Hyundai, Samsung, and Daewoo) controlled 90 percent of eighty-eight different markets.[5] Another noted that at one point in the early 1980s, over 81 percent of major commodities were controlled by a very limited number of large corporations.[6] And, perhaps most important in a developing economy where capital is scarce, these companies have monopolized the nation's financial resources. As recently as 1987, the top five chaebol received almost 15 percent of all bank loans in the country.[7] The top thirty conglomerates snared almost a third of all bank loans.[8]

LYING DOWN WITH THE LIONS

Korea's economic transformation came at a time when power in the country was highly concentrated—which is a polite way to say that the economy grew under a succession of ruthless dictators, who were not reluctant to squeeze the business community to achieve what they considered necessary goals.

Since 1962, Korea's economy has been planned in general and in specific; government ministries have identified target industries and markets, regulated interest rates, and provided cheap credit and other inducements. Just as important, the security forces have played an active role in suppressing labor organization; in some cases, the police and intelligence services have been more aggressively antilabor than the companies.

When corporations followed government-initiated strategies, they were usually rewarded or, at a minimum, protected. And if they hesitated to participate or bucked the government's plans, punishment could be severe. Companies were notified of impending tax audits; their credit and access to hard currency suddenly dried up; import-export allowances were canceled. And when the private response was slow or timid, extensive publicly owned enterprises were created. The government has held direct or partial ownership in industries as varied as steel and petrochemicals; in recent years, it also controlled nearly 80 percent of banking and insurance operations.[9]

The upshot of the government's interventions is exactly what one might anticipate: individuals with good connections to powerful people could walk away with lucrative contracts and special concessions. "Managers here like to talk about the entrepreneurial spirit in Korea and about how one guy created Hyundai out of nothing," explained Harry Kamberis, who heads the Seoul office of the Asian-American Free Labor Institute (AAFLI), part of the AFL-CIO's International

Affairs Department. "Well, he didn't create it out of nothing. He created it out of personal contacts with people in power. I've seen the kind of government incentives they have to do things or not do things. The government decides how these guys are going to act."

Sometimes, the corporations earn their favors. In the aftermath of the Korean War, for example, Hyundai's founder, Chung Ju-Yung, contracted to reconstruct a bridge over the Naktong River. The footings had yet to be laid, however, when postwar inflation began to send the cost of materials and equipment skyward. Trapped in his contract, Chung was assured of massive losses but continued working; at times he was forced to draw on the life savings of his family and friends. Eventually, the bridge was rebuilt over Chung's ruined finances. Then-President Syngman Rhee acknowledged that the country owed Chung a debt, though, and new projects—some much larger than the bridge—began to fall to Hyundai. Considerably more savvy, Chung was now able to build bridges (and sign contracts) in a way that would guarantee a profit.

In many cases, preferences were awarded to companies simply because no one else was qualified to tackle the government's projects or achieve its goals. When Park Chung-Hee resolved to push his country into the modern era, he knew he would need the active participation of men with manufacturing and financial acumen, who were a relatively rare breed in the Korea of the early 1960s.

Often, though, the government's comprehensive economic power bred simple corruption. Favors were bestowed on the friends of Korea's leaders—colleagues from the military, former classmates, or home-town pals. A personal relationship was not always sufficient—kickbacks and bribes were often used to encourage government bureaucrats and military rulers—but it was almost always necessary. As a result, the many competent and eager Koreans who lacked such contacts were frozen out of important industries and markets. At one point in the 1960s, for example, a consortium of construction firms known as the Group of Five had such a lock on domestic projects (in part because of their practice of awarding kickbacks of up to 5 percent of the contract amount) that other firms would not bother to bid against them. [10]

Although there are obvious advantages to working with an authoritarian government, the chaebol have also learned that when you lie down with lions, you are likely to suffer an occasional mauling. The government of Park Chung-Hee was particularly inclined to make unrefusable offers; in the most infamous case, Park asked Daewoo's chairman, Kim Woo-Choong, to assume control of an unfinished, deeply indebted shipyard. Kim demurred, but Park announced the takeover anyway, while Kim was out of the country.

Another celebrated instance took place in 1984, during the Chun Doo-Hwan regime. Yang Chang-Mo, chairman of ICC-Kukje—then Korea's seventh-largest chaebol, with 38,000 employees and annual revenues of around $1.4 billion—made a series of financially lethal faux pas: first, he failed to make sufficiently generous donations to two quasi-government organizations with close ties to the president and his family. He then compounded the insult by arriving late for a dinner hosted by Chun, a serious breach of etiquette. (In general, Chun was a stickler for such matters; before one press conference, he demanded that reporters remove their gold rings and keep both feet flat on the floor.)

Yang's punishment for these oversights was swift and devastating. Less than a week after his tardy arrival at dinner, a major bank stopped honoring ICC-Kukje's checks. Other financial institutions smelled a disaster in the making and quickly called in their loans, leaving the group helpless and heavily in debt. To no one's surprise, Yang's appeal for governmental help fell on deaf ears; just two months later, officials began dismantling the group. (In April 1988, Yang filed suit against the government in an effort to regain control of stock that he was forced to sell.)

Although ICC-Kukje paid the highest price for its intimate relationship with the government, the public-private partnership has usually benefited both sides. Recent events, however, seem to suggest that the balance of power has shifted. With democratization, pressures are building to limit the staggering influence of the chaebol; at the same time, democratization has limited the power of government to make unilateral changes in Korea's economic and financial structures. The government is by no means abdicating its control; at the end of 1988, it was still possible to find a story in the English-language press that began, "The government has allowed only two companies to branch out into the petrochemical industry based on an *appropriate* domestic demand for ethylene by 1993" (emphasis added). [11]

Nevertheless, as Korea moves toward genuine free enterprise, its monstrous conglomerates are in a position to snuff out their moderately sized domestic competition, and the government may no longer have the power or the will to oppose them.

EXPORTS

The heart of the government's development strategy—and, consequently, the obsession of every chaebol—has been the penetration of foreign markets. The thinking is painfully simple: in the 1960s, Korea had nothing. Its only chance of survival was to haul in natural resources from one spot, capital and equipment from somewhere else, put them together to make something of greater value, and ship that out to a country that could pay for it in real money. "What a precious thing is one cent of hard currency!" President Park once said. In the early days of Hyundai, its founder forbade the drinking of coffee because it was not grown in Korea and could only be purchased with that precious hard currency, which was needed to buy more raw materials and equipment, to make more exports.

Koreans have embraced this strategy fervently. They even have a national Export Day, which has been celebrated every November 30 since 1964. And there has been plenty to celebrate. In 1989, Korea sold over $61 billion worth of products overseas; just twenty-one years earlier, the country exported only $455 *million*. Wherever you sit, this looks like impressive growth. After several years of persistent and substantial growth, exports plateaued in 1989, but many observers claimed that this was a momentary lull and not the beginning of a trend.

Since the beginning of its export boom, Korea's strong suit has been manufactured goods (rather than raw materials such as fish or rubber or rice); over the years, those goods have taken on even greater importance and now account for 95 percent of all exports. Primary customers have been the United States (39 percent) and Japan (18 percent); primary products have been textiles, garments, and electronics.

Korea's success at penetrating these markets was far from immediate, however. Even though the strategy was adopted in the early 1960s, exports constituted only 10.3 percent of GNP by 1970, and the country's trade balance that year was a grim deficit of $922 million. This situation showed signs of improvement (exports shot up by almost 100 percent in 1973), but the oil crisis of 1973–1974 arrived to relieve the Koreans of any sense of economic security. Because of its near-total reliance on imported oil, the nation was understandably rattled; energy costs skyrocketed, and the overall slowdown in the global economy depressed export growth to a low (for Korea) 14 percent in 1975.[12] Consequently, the deficit in Korea's current account in 1974 was nearly that of the previous four years combined.[13]

Pushed to alleviate this imbalance, the government tried to stimulate exports by introducing a system of general trading companies, or GTCs, in 1975. According to this strategy, designated companies would spearhead the export drive by putting more personnel and resources into overseas sales; in return, they would receive access to bank credit and exceptions from foreign exchange regulations. The package was enough to seduce Samsung and, soon after, four other large conglomerates.

The GTCs were not the answer to Korea's trade imbalance, which grew substantially worse after the second oil crisis in 1979. (Korea's imports outpaced exports until 1986; since then, a trade surplus has become regular.) But they did assume a major role in handling Korea's exports, which continued to grow at double-digit rates for most of the following decade. As of 1987, there were seven major GTCs, with 290 subsidiaries and branches around the world, overseeing nearly half of Korea's total exports.[14]

The GTCs perform trade functions for their own affiliates as well as for subcontractors and other small and medium-sized enterprises (SMEs). At Hyundai, for example, the trading company will provide the SMEs with financial assistance and information on world market trends. It will then act as broker between the small company and a buyer, watching quality and arranging insurance, transportation, and so on—typically through Hyundai affiliates, of course.

Today, exports have grown from their 1970 level of 10.3 percent of GNP to roughly 30.0 percent. At the chaebol, they frequently constitute an even higher percentage of revenues. Hyundai, for example, derives about 60 percent of its sales from exports, while at Samsung exports account for roughly 50 percent of sales. At Lucky-Goldstar, the figure is around 30 percent; at Daewoo, around 25 percent. These figures suggest that several of these conglomerates have been even more successful in penetrating global markets than has the country as a whole; or, to use an alternate interpretation, it means that they are more heavily reliant on exports and more susceptible to American and Japanese recessions, Mideast oil shocks, and the gamut of risks that attend international trade than is the country as a whole.

STRUCTURE: THE OCTOPUS

Korea's conglomerates haven't just grown up, they have also grown out. Over their brief history, they have become widely—if not wildly— diversified, exploiting their economic heft and political connections to overwhelm smaller competitors. Today, their tentacles embrace products and markets of every description, in all parts of the world.

The chaebol are, again, similar to Japan's business groups, with a number of semi-independent corporations clustered around a central company. In Japan, the central company would usually be a bank; in Korea, the same function is commonly served by a general trading company. Because they have not been built around a bank or other financial institution, the chaebol have been beholden to the central government for access to credit—a lever of enormous significance.

But the structure of the conglomerates is considerably more complex. Take Samsung as an example: among this chaebol's twenty-plus affiliates are an electronics company (expected to be the world's fifth largest before the end of the 1990s), a daily newspaper (circulation 1.4 million), a shipbuilding company, a chain of department stores, an aerospace company, a five-star hotel, a medical company, an economics institute, an insurance company, a sugar refinery (with extensive investments in biotechnology), and more. It has production facilities in the United States, Portugal, Mexico, Thailand, England, and elsewhere. It boasts an international web of sales and trading offices. And the Samsung Co., Ltd., the group's GTC, has roughly twenty divisions or subaffiliates of its own.

Much the same portrait can be drawn of the other major chaebol. Although each has its special expertise, the top four are all engaged in a dizzying array of industries. Asked to identify his corporation's major areas of interest, a Lucky-Goldstar spokesman mentioned petrochemicals, electronics, and service. This decidedly broad focus encompasses Korea Mining and Smelting, Goldstar Electronic Devices, Goldstar Semiconductors, LG Credit Card, and the intriguingly named Lucky Insurance, among a total of roughly thirty-three acknowledged affiliate companies. (Korea's Fair Trade Commission, interestingly enough, claims that the Lucky-Goldstar group has approximately sixty affiliates; the discrepancy probably derives from different ownership standards in defining affiliation.)[15]

Another highly diversified chaebol, Daewoo, produces the Leading Edge computer, oceangoing vessels, pianos, T-shirts, components for the American F-16 fighter jet, the Pontiac Le Mans, and several thousand other products among twenty-nine affiliates. And although Hyundai is probably best known for its automobile and construction operations, its twenty-seven affiliates (or thirty-seven, if you accept the Fair Trade Commission's definition) also make electronics (including a personal computer), steel, furniture, supertankers, ceramic tiles, telephones, and apartment complexes. Altogether, the top ten chaebol comprise slightly fewer than 300 companies, institutes, and foundations; within each group, these affiliates have been connected through interlocking directorships and cross-investments.

In part, all this diversification comes from a Korean penchant for keeping hands-on control of all operations. Whereas their Japanese competitors will often job-out the most risky or cyclical work and thereby keep their own employment consistent, Koreans often prefer to keep even the smallest operations under the corporate wing. At Hyundai, for example, the obsession to integrate in all directions has occasionally reached absurd proportions. The group once announced plans to manufacture its own work gloves for employees, claiming that supplies from smaller vendors weren't adequate. (It eventually backed down under pressure from the government and those small manufacturers, but did so reluctantly.) This tendency toward "absolute" diversification has been widely decried, because it makes the big companies vulnerable in economic downturns and hurts the smaller companies that provide a large share of the annual 500,000 new jobs needed for Korea's expanding labor force.

Some conglomerates are more inclined to use subcontractors, however. Samsung claims to have about 20,000 of them, of whom 5,000 are considered significant.[16] And as that group moves toward more technology-intensive industries, more and more of its labor-intensive activities—with their lower profits and uppity workers—are destined to be fobbed off on these small and medium-sized suppliers. In what may be a preview of a significant shift in the makeup of Korean conglomerates, Samsung has announced its intention to hand over production of several low-profit electronics lines to small and medium-sized companies.

Other changes in chaebol structure are also occurring. First, as Korea's economy as a whole moves toward more technology-intensive products, the role of the GTCs is changing. "Their function is most important in selling low-tech products," a Samsung spokesman noted. "They can't sell high-tech products because they don't have the know-how. They are generalists." In addition, the small domestic producers, who once had to rely on GTCs for information, contacts, and services, now have the sophistication to run their own overseas operations.

Consequently, GTCs are placing more emphasis on triangular trade and overseas joint ventures, particularly in resource development; Hyundai's trading company, for example, is involved in Yemen's Marib oil field and Australian coal mines. The GTCs are also pioneering the movement of many Korean products to lower-wage countries, such as Indonesia, Costa Rica, and Bangladesh.[17] And they are striving to open new markets, especially in countries where barter and other trade techniques must be used to overcome hard-currency problems.

Perhaps most important, the GTCs are seeking to establish themselves as importers now that Korea is opening its markets to foreign-made products. In an interesting twist, they may even import products from their own overseas production facilities. "Let us say an OEM [original equipment manufacturer] client in America wants Korean-made VCRs," explained a Samsung manager. "We will handle the export from Korea to the United States, and we will then import VCRs from our plant in Thailand to satisfy the Korean domestic demand." This, he predicted confidently, will be a common practice in the future.

The second change in Korea's chaebol structure comes from new fair-trade laws, which are threatening to restrict and realign the giant conglomerates. To be sure, the current and rather extreme level of diversification is not likely to diminish. (After all, to whom does one sell a troublesome or unprofitable shipyard, if all the other major conglomerates already have one? And will the government, despite its professed desire to embrace true free enterprise, allow a simple shutdown and the massive displacement of workers that that would entail?) Nevertheless, the trade laws, which are being phased in, will affect chaebol growth and operations in the future. In particular, a conglomerate's ability to invest in new companies, or cross-invest within the group, will be curtailed. Intrachaebol discounting and subsidizing are likewise prohibited, although controlling this activity may prove difficult; research by one government agency found no significant level of such activity, but an official conceded that it could be "hidden in highly complex bookkeeping."

The chaebol are somewhat shy about expressing their opinions on this issue. When asked, they usually display sudden interest in the idea that the new fair-trade laws might affect their operations. At one chaebol, repeated questions on their impact brought (a) a confession of ignorance, followed by (b) inappropriate laughter, and finally (c) an anxious request to "please move onto another page of your notebook." At another, the official position on the new law was clearly negative: "Korea's business groups are not highly capitalized," the spokesman said, "and we need more if we are to compete globally."

MANAGEMENT STYLE

The techniques used to organize and motivate Korea's workers are discussed at length in later chapters, but several points should be made here.

First, management science is a relatively new concept in Korea. According to Park Young-Ki, professor and director of Sogang University's Institute for Labor and Management, "Until very recently, there was some theory but no practice. It was alien to Korea."[18] He added that in the entire country, there was no degree program in industrial relations until the 1988–1989 school year. One Western labor observer privately noted that this makes perfect sense: "Why try to understand the subtleties of a phenomenon that you can control so completely with brute force?"

Second, Korea's huge and frequently monopolistic businesses tend to concentrate authority in the hands of a few individuals. One survey found that in 80 percent of the companies studied, the stock was held by ten or fewer people. These are often the men who founded the chaebols and their families, and they are not passive: the owners of Korea's conglomerates are typically the managers. As might be expected, the bureaucracy can be quite flat. At Hyundai, for example, the heads of the twenty-seven affiliates all report directly to the group chairman.

Although it may be odious to Western sensibilities, such centralized power is traditional in Korea. Even today, political authority is profoundly focused. Only the president and members of the National Assembly are elected; other officials, from cabinet ministers to local mayors, are appointed. (Efforts are under way to introduce more local rule, however.) Most decisions are made by bureaucrats in Seoul or, if they are made locally, by a huge (17 percent of the work force) civil service whose loyalties are clearly to the central government.[19]

At the corporate level, the concentration of power has several ramifications. For one thing, it allows companies to operate with a high degree of secrecy or, at least, obtuseness. This is witnessed in the references to public numbers, confusion over "highly complex bookkeeping," and the overall observation that no outsider can really divine what intrigues are operating within a chaebol.

Companies are also more likely to be seen as the extension of individual personalities. Koreans respect the accomplishments of their successful entrepreneurs and remain loyal to them, regardless of formal definitions of control. A Daewoo manager explained that, in fact, "the Daewoo business group is not a legal entity. Our founder, Kim Woo-Choong, is the legal chairman of certain companies that are affiliated with each other. But Chairman Kim's influence does not come from that. When banks think about lending money, they do not think in terms of business groups. They think of personalities, of companies under the control of Kim Woo-Choong or [Hyundai's] Chung Ju-Yung."

From a managerial standpoint, tight control permits the conglomerates to be very responsive to fast-breaking opportunities or problems despite their extraordinary size. That responsiveness is not lost when Korean companies locate outside Korea. Asked about corporate decision making, an ex–vice president of Hyundai Auto Canada replied,

"You're talking one guy—S. Y. Chung." Currently chairman of the Hyundai group, Chung (who is a brother of founder Chung Ju-Yung) is a previous president of Hyundai Motor Company and continues to take an active interest in that affiliate. The former executive also noted that Chung does not hesitate to use his authority: "I rode one time with him in a car and I said that our grills and headlights, which were silver, would look sharper in black. A week later, we got the OK to do that."[20]

But this emphasis on authority also means that communication between employees, even those who work side by side, can be truncated. "In Korea," explained a Westerner with several years experience in a Korean-American joint venture, "decisions require top-level approval. They are forced up the line of command and require lots of manhours. In fact, there's a prohibition against communication across department lines." It is perhaps no accident that a similar style of "stovepipe" communication exists in the Korean military, which has formed the thinking of so many young Korean males and guided the development of the nation's economy.

A third major characteristic of the Korean management style—and one closely linked to the emphasis on authority—is that, like their counterparts in Japan, the chaebol are very paternalistic toward their workers; every attempt has been made to graft the Confucian father-child bond onto the workplace. Accordingly, corporations frequently provide food, lodging, recreational facilities, schools, scholarships, and medical care for employees and their families. In Korean paternalism, however, the emphasis is on control as much as care: the "father" of the corporate family is very much in charge of his children.

That control can be exercised in petty matters, as at the Hanjin group, where stewardesses from Korean Air were forbidden to wear blue jeans, even when they were off the job. It can also interfere with basic human rights: some employers have forced their workers—under threat of discipline or dismissal—to take part in company savings plans, to stay within the company compound after work, to attend religious services in company chapels on their own time. Many of these abuses have existed in the chaebol, but they are more likely to be found in smaller companies.

There is a clear contradiction between the paternalism and the abuses of authority in Korean companies. That has led Park Young-Ki to suggest that "the paternalism of Korean companies is fake." In a

true family, Park noted, "fathers look after their sons without precondi-
tions. Here, the employers are pretending, and the more they pretend,
the more this falsity is transparent."

Of course, like everything else in Korea, the management style is
changing. The broadening of civil liberties since June 1987 has
influenced worker expectations, making strict authoritarianism less
acceptable. At the same time, increasing competition and the advancing age of the chaebol founders has accelerated the push toward
professional management. Finally, pressure from the government is
encouraging the business groups to make public offerings of some of
their affiliated companies. Nevertheless, concentrated authority—in
the boardroom and on the assembly line—will continue to be the rule
for the immediate future.

FINANCING: ADDICTED TO DEBT

Korea's corporations are not afraid to borrow. Among large companies,
the debt-to-equity ratio averages 5.1:1.0, but at some of the largest
conglomerates it is even higher. Samsung, for example, had a 7.0:1.0
ratio in 1987, while Daewoo's was 6.6:1.0. At Hanjin, the seventh
largest chaebol, the ratio was 14.0:1.0, an altitude at which oxygen
begins to thin.[21] The existence of these debts is hardly surprising. It
takes capital to build a world-class economy out of ashes in just a few
decades. And, the chaebol argue, Korea's relatively underdeveloped
consumer credit system means that more debt must be shouldered by
manufacturers.

The government is now pushing Korea's chaebol to lower their
indebtedness by raising money in the equity market. This strategy
serves at least three functions: it reduces the debt-to-equity ratios, it
encourages local securities companies as they begin to be established,
and it puts more control of the chaebol into the hands of the average
citizens who have built and maintained them. In fact, the government
has directed that with every public offering, 20 percent of the shares
up for sale (usually about 30 percent of the company) must be set aside
for employees.

Korea's chaebol—clannish in mentality when not actually run by a
single family—are less than enthusiastic about going public. Among

the twenty-seven affiliated companies in the Hyundai group, for example, only ten are publicly traded. The rest are still under the control of founder Chung Ju-Yung and his family. At Daewoo, only nine of twenty-nine companies are public.

A number of reasons are usually given for this reluctance. In the first place, the chaebol are worried that the value of their companies will not be sufficiently recognized; in the second, they view any loss of control as a grave danger. They argue that their efforts to pursue long-term investments will be jeopardized by stockholder pressure for short-term profits. Proponents of broader ownership claim that these fears are exaggerated. Even when a chaebol's affiliated company is publicly traded, they note, individuals are limited in the amount of stock they can hold. Consequently, management has little to fear from aggressive or interfering stockholders, and the business group can be assured that a publicly traded affiliate will stay within the flock. The chaebol's greatest loss, say their detractors, will be the ability to pay a kickback or hide profits without the interference of pesky regulators or stockholders.

Despite chaebol resistance, the trend toward public offerings seems inexorable, if only because the equity markets are one of the few financing options available. Limits on foreign investment are already in place, and domestic loans to the top business groups are regulated to guarantee at least some funds for the nation's small and medium-sized enterprises.

PROFITS

Despite their bulk and enormous revenues, the chaebol appear to be content with relatively small profits. According to one 1987 report, "236 major listed [publicly traded] companies posted net profits of less than 1.6 percent of turnover."[22] Other figures show that among the top five chaebol, the best performer had net profits of a little over 1 percent of revenues.[23]

Taken at face value, these figures may be indicative of either the burden imposed by heavy debt service or the government's pressure to hire as many workers as possible, thereby minimizing social unrest and, unfortunately, productivity and profits. Of course, low profits may reflect nothing more than a patient growth strategy. At Daewoo, to pick just one example, 1987 sales were around $13.5 billion and profit was just $37 million. These figures might raise eyebrows in other nations, but Daewoo chairman Kim had already indicated that expansion and diversification—not profits—were his primary goals. "If we wanted to make money, we'd just have 2,000 McDonald's around the country," he said. "When per capita income reaches $5,000—that will be the time to go for profits."[24] This sort of attitude is easily adopted when corporate ownership is narrowly held. If the family—or the founder himself—deems it necessary to keep profits low to finance growth, who is there to argue or complain?

But these low-profit figures should be considered with less naïveté. Skeptics suggest that the chaebol enjoy real if not stunning profits, which are hidden, sheltered, or simply underreported to reduce taxes. They support this claim, first, by pointing out that 1987 profits at the country's *smallest* manufacturers (the most labor-intensive, least auto-mated, and least likely to get credit at decent rates) were 3.3 percent of sales.

Second, they note that Korea's complicated tax system allows con-siderable latitude in reporting profits, and its high tax rates encourage corporations to exercise that freedom. (It is doubly desirable to claim a poor return—or even better, a loss—on any investment made at the government's urging. In that way, the company saves the immediate taxes *and* flags itself as worthy of an extraordinary tax break or concession from a sympathetic regime.)

Another frequently cited indication of chaebol profits is the con-glomerates' extreme reluctance to seek equity financing, even when such a decision means they must forgo low-cost government loans and borrow at usurious rates from private sources. One very rational interpretation of this behavior is that these companies find it more economically advantageous to borrow at high rates and retain the capacity to avoid or evade taxes.

A final source of suspicion comes out of Korea's traditional business practices, wherein large profits (a 50 percent net return is considered a real possibility) are the expectation and risk is acceptable in pursuing such a goal. Given that the chaebol are often graced with low-risk, government-backed, low-interest loans, they should be able to accept lower profits, but it seems unlikely that the meager returns often cited would satisfy even one's own family.[25]

BIG GUY, LITTLE GUY

Any discussion of the Korean economy or its workers inevitably concentrates on the chaebol, for obvious reasons. They are monstrous, rich, powerful, and often ruthless. Despite their spare linoleum hallways and drafty factories, despite the blandly uniformed receptionists and overeager, blue-suited assistant managers, something like glamour touches them.

But the chaebol are only half the story. Korea's small and medium-sized enterprises (those with fewer than 300 employees) employ around two-thirds of the manufacturing work force. They produced over 38 percent of the nation's manufacturing output in 1986, and that proportion should climb to 44 percent by 1991. They have also played an important role in Korea's growth-through-export strategy: in 1987, the SMEs, either directly or through the chaebols' GTCs, supplied 38 percent of the nation's overseas sales.[26]

In many respects, the chaebol and the SMEs work hand in glove; the conglomerate offers international trading experience, marketing savvy, and even financing, while the SME provides the manufacturing muscle. Through all of this, though, the chaebol is in clear control. It has the customers and the money, and the SME needs both. "These small companies have trouble getting loans," a Samsung official confided, "so we can charge them a rate that is slightly above market."

On the other side, each SME has only its workers, and Korea has a great many other small suppliers with this identical resource. Harry Kamberis of the AFL-CIO's Seoul office put it like this: "All the SMEs have much the same raw material and other costs. They basically compete on the level to which they can effectively exploit their workers." Indeed, working conditions at the SMEs are bad, almost universally worse than at the chaebol. Few of these small operations are unionized, and the abuses can be appalling by Western standards. This is true in electronics assembly and especially in the garment industry.

Lip service is paid to upgrading the SMEs and softening the spike-and-board-shaped economy into a pyramid, but actual commitment is limited. Out of over 200,000 such enterprises, the government agency created to help SMEs serves only about 3,000 annually. While some of that agency's programs provide valuable assistance in training and productivity improvement, at least one concentrates on and awards financial support to shift labor-intensive operations overseas, to even lower-wage countries in Southeast Asia.

And when the programs try to protect SMEs from the chaebol, teeth are noticeably missing. One program, for example, sets aside approximately 200 products exclusively for SME production, but these are usually low-tech, labor-intensive, and generally unattractive to the chaebol anyway: the list currently includes wristwatch cases, manhole covers, and tofu. When the items actually have some economic importance—printed circuit boards, for example—the chaebol protest that they cannot get consistent quality or adequate volume and need permission to make the product themselves.

That kind of swinish behavior, combined with a genuine sense of fairness among Koreans, has fueled a growing antichaebol sentiment. Even the government-funded Korean Development Institute has come down on the conglomerates, pointing out "a number of negative side effects" that can arise when an enormous proportion of a nation's political and economic power is concentrated in the hands of a few families; these side effects include "misallocation of resources, monopolistic control of markets, and increased barriers to entry," as well as "a problem of equity."[27]

STRENGTHS AND WEAKNESSES

Although Korea's economy is robust and has been so for several decades, it remains exceedingly vulnerable—a "house of cards" to some observers—and its chaebol "are said to be among the worst financially structured corporate bodies in the world."[28]

A primary source of concern is the domestic market; it has been growing at an impressive rate (accounting for roughly half of 1987's nearly 13 percent GNP growth), but Korea's internal consumption remains too small to relieve the dependence on overseas markets. A recession in the United States, which accounts for almost 40 percent of all Korean exports, could be devastating. At the same time, a continued rapid increase in domestic spending could reduce household savings and eliminate funds for capital investment or research. It would also threaten to increase inflation, which has been onerous and volatile in the past. The 1980 rate hit 29.0 percent; although inflation in 1989 was a more manageable 5.0 percent, prices surged early in 1990.

Second, like Japan, Korea is heavily dependent on imported natural resources. Approximately three-quarters of its energy must be brought into the country, and that dependency is growing.[29] The costs are staggering: as recently as the mid-1980s, roughly a third of all foreign currency earned annually from exports went to pay for energy purchases abroad.[30] Korea has made significant investments in nuclear power since it was battered by the oil crises of the 1970s, but another oil crisis would still act as a heavy brake on the economy.

Finally, Korea is not yet a stable country. It is continuing to see rapid change in all respects—economically, politically, and socially—and these movements must be successfully accommodated if the nation is to continue its advance. Some of the more unsettling economic changes have been noted. The political changes are perhaps even more dramatic. How could this country *not* be beset by extraordinary political dilemmas: it is trying to balance the Confucian inclination for hierarchy and control with its first exuberant taste of freedom. It is attempting to develop democratic institutions without practical experience in democratic behavior. And it remains desperately eager to embrace, in fact merge with, North Korea—a nation with which it has been at odds for four decades.

But Korea's social transformation is probably the most heady. Industrialization, urbanization, and the recent liberalization have eroded much of the traditional framework of Korean society. Extended families are breaking down. Respect for older generations is less automatic. A homegrown pornography industry—unthinkable before 1987—is thriving, with lurid ads adorning every bus stop. (Some of the details have yet to be worked out, however; an English-language poster for one soft-core film promised "fantastic narcism!") The government has identified these social concerns as a threat to the economy, and with reason: if it is to avoid social upheaval, Korea must begin to grapple with critical shortages in housing, terrible pollution, rising expectations for leisure time (and recreational facilities where that time can be enjoyed), and the question of public assistance for those who are not caught in the Confucian net of social responsibilities.

These are serious challenges to Korea's continued prosperity, but they are by no means insurmountable. Investment in better housing, for example, would be at once socially beneficial and a boost to the domestic economy. And while much has been made about the need to divide better the benefits of their country's transformation, Koreans are aware that they live in a highly egalitarian society—wealth distribution is on a par with that of some Western nations and well ahead of most other developing countries. (Indeed, wealth is somewhat suspect among many Koreans; the nation has laws against private yachts and private tutors, and the government once admonished well-heeled citizens for having overly ornate house gates.) Less than half the work force pays taxes, and top income brackets pay considerably. Now, as the government begins to emphasize social issues, equality should improve even more.

MEA CULPAS ALL AROUND

The preceding chapters have presented a thumbnail sketch of Korean workers and the corporations for which they toil. This overview fails to capture the richness of Korea's economic culture, but it does describe, broadly, certain characteristics of the country's troubling success.

Troubling? Well, yes (except perhaps in the eyes of certain international lending institutions), because Western workers have lost jobs to Korean workers and Western corporations have lost markets to Korean corporations. And because Korea's success has cast doubt on Western, particularly American, standards of education and the value that the West puts on labor—its work ethic, in other words.

Korea, for its part, has been trying to make itself less troubling. On the one hand, it is inclined toward justifiably touting its success; on the other, it seeks to placate protectionist Korea-bashers—a curious mix of chest thumping and breast beating. Korea is trying to reduce its subsidies, to deregulate, to open its markets—ever so slowly—to the West. Most important, it is eagerly striving to balance its trade surplus.

Even if Korea begins to behave like the more developed Western industrial powers, though, it would remain the most unnerving Asian nation. Japan's triumphs have been spooky to an overconfident and insular America, but we can sedate our anxiety by recalling that it was an industrialized country well before World War II. Now, after years of reconstruction, it has simply regained its rightful place in the planetary order.

But *Korea*? This was a bombed-out backwater, a pathetic dump of a country that had been snatched back and forth between serious Asian powers like a rag doll between quarrelsome children. And it has practiced a crude, almost feudal style of management grounded in fear, physical repression, and the compliance of a poor and traumatized people. If Korea could come from nothing, abuse its workers and *succeed*, could challenge Japan and the United States, then anything could happen. If Korea could come this far in a few decades, why not India, China, Indonesia? This is a rationale for paranoia that Japan has never offered.

India, China, and Indonesia—as well as other developing nations—are clearly studying Korea's triumph. They are delving into its ancient culture and recent history, its sociology and management style. They are inquiring into the charismatic personalities who have guided its passage into the modern world. And they are probing the dark heart of Korea's economic miracle, which is that humiliation, suffering, and horror have set the pilings for this astonishing construction.

PART TWO

▲▲▲

A Superficial History of Korea and the Korean Economy

4

▲▲▲

The Hermit Kingdom:
Korea Before 1876

Scrambling up the side of Mount Namsan, south of Kyongju, one is easily lost. No matter: backtrack to the last 1,000-year-old rock carving of the Buddha and veer to the left this time, stumbling onto a wider path. Up again, past more ancient statuary, more bas-reliefs and shrines. Dilettantes are soon jaded: this one is only 600 years old, that one too weathered.

At the summit, though, one's interest is immediately revived. Below, to the north, the grass-covered mounds of the royal tombs rise from the flat plain of the city. To the east, golden rice paddies as venerable as Namsan's Buddhas shine in the sun. Past them, the road climbs another mountain toward Pulguk-sa Temple (built in 528), with its stone terraces and its teal- and coral-painted beams, and, beyond the temple, the Sokkuram Grotto, with its gorgeous, white granite Buddha.

There is more to Kyongju—pleasure gardens and ancient observatories, ruined palaces and a bloated bell that got its voice from a child thrown into the molten metal—all of it thrown together to form an open-air primer on Korean history. Kyongju also represents the nation's political triumphs, because it was the capital of Silla, the first kingdom to unify the peninsula; it was the place where the people of Korea became Koreans. This was a monumental accomplishment, and it happened a long time ago; when North America was a wilderness and Europe was in chaos, Korea had a thriving and unified culture.

For that reason Kyongju is a monument to the triumphs of the Korean people and also to their tragedy, because what they had is the terrible definition of what they have lost.

GEOGRAPHIC DESTINY

More than that of most countries, Korea's fate has been predestined by its location. Dangling off the muscular body of Asia, squeezed hard between the sophisticated and aggressive cultures of China, Japan, and Russia, it has tempted invaders from all directions. Koreans have fought among themselves as well. The result has been a long history of war and revolution, but out of the tumult they have forged a bold and productive culture.

The pinnacles are well documented: the world's oldest example of woodblock printing (created sometime before A.D. 751) is Korean, and the nation can date its use of movable metal type to 1234, almost two centuries before Gutenberg was born. As early as 1392, a government agency was in place to oversee the production of books.[1] Later, in the mid–fifteenth century, King Sejong created Hangul, an extremely precise and yet accessible alphabet, especially in contrast to the Chinese writing that had preceded it. Ancient Koreans were advanced in metallurgy, astronomy, and meteorology. They also manifested great talents in architecture and religion. Indeed, it is said (most frequently by Koreans, who do a poor job of veiling their pride in this regard) that Japan's governmental, religious, technological, and artistic traditions are all founded on imports from Korea. A register of Japanese families in 815 suggested that one-third of the nobles were of Korean descent.

But the emphasis here should be less on arts and science, more on the invasions and infighting. (It is possible that Korea became known as the Land of the Morning Calm simply because those hours contrasted so strongly with the blood and chaos of the rest of the day.) Not surprisingly, the list of Korean achievements has its military entries—

from the early (1377) establishment of a government superintendency to cast cannons and make gunpowder to Admiral Yi Sun-sin's invention of the world's first ironclad warships, the turtle ships that were used to wrest the sea-lanes from invading Japanese in the mid–fifteenth century.[2]

Even the myth of Korea's creation has a distinctly invasionary flavor: at the dawn of time, Hwanung, the son of the Divine Creator, descended to earth with 3,000 companions and declared himself ruler of the universe. Hwanung's magic created the first woman (from a bear and twenty pieces of garlic), who bore the founder of Korea, Tan'gun, who was then overthrown by another invader, this time from China.

Although there is probably not a great deal of precise historic truth in this legend, it does underscore the importance of foreign armies in Korean history. Beginning in the earliest days of ancient Korea, tribal groups on the northern end of the peninsula had to contend with Chinese aggression. This danger of attack led to military alliances that ultimately resulted in the first Korean kingdom, Koguryo, which was formed around the first century A.D. Koguryo was renowned for its warrior aristocracy, which protected the kingdom from Chinese forces and enriched it with captured land, animals, and people.

In the third and fourth centuries, two other tribal kingdoms—Silla and Paekje—arose in the south. Along with Koguryo, they ruled the peninsula during the (predictably named) Three Kingdoms period, a time marked by tremendous cultural growth. A national academy to teach Confucianism was established, Buddhism was introduced (in 372), and the arts flourished. This period also brought taxes (on cloth and grain) and corvée labor, which required the free peasantry to bend their backs to the building of fortifications and irrigation works—improvements that, in theory, would benefit the entire society. This period escapes being labeled a golden era, though, because the three kingdoms were engaged in constant and bloody conflict with one another and, on occasion, with China. At one point, Sui China attacked Koguryo with a force in excess of one million troops; the assault failed, however, and is thought to have played a role in the downfall of the dynasty. Undaunted, the subsequent Tang dynasty also threw itself into Korean affairs.

Out of all the secret alliances, double crosses, and sneak attacks, Silla emerged triumphant in 668 (though it did pay tribute to the Tang).

The peninsula luxuriated in a brief era of peace and growth. A National Confucian College was formed in 682, and the principles taught there eventually led to the creation of a state examination system for the selection of government officials. Buddhism thrived, while the "Flower of Youth," a paramilitary organization for the sons of Silla's elite, helped to develop a cohesive and well trained warrior aristocracy. Most significant, the Silla kingdom marked the first time that the peninsula was politically and culturally united—a condition that held (albeit tenuously) until the end of World War II, almost thirteen centuries later. And it was a particular kind of unification, one that would be echoed in present-day Korea. Kyongju, like modern Seoul, drew a large percentage of the country's total population (15 to 20 percent), and the development of local power outside the capital, again as in modern Korea, was "rigidly and almost continuously discouraged."[3]

Eventually, beginning in 768, revolts and infighting among the aristocracy undermined the Silla kingdom. Fractious nobles used their great wealth to create personal armies, then used those armies to assume more wealth and power. Meanwhile, the common people suffered. Those who failed to pay their debts were forced into slavery; heavily taxed farmers could not make a living and were driven off their land. Rebellions swept over the nation, and law and order disintegrated; peasant insurgents called "grass brigands" were ubiquitous, while the Red-Trousered Bandits grew so powerful that they controlled huge areas and were credited with driving a queen from her throne in 896.

Among the rebel leaders was a deposed Silla prince, Kungye, who was so embittered that he insisted his followers refer to his former homeland as the "nation of the damned." He was subject to occasional bouts of paranoia and a recurring need to rename the territory he ruled; he also claimed that he could read other people's minds. Despite these eccentricities, Kungye laid the groundwork for a powerful new kingdom that dwarfed Silla and a reemerging Paekje. After his death (at the hands of his subjects), Kungye was succeeded in 918 by Wang Kon, who renamed the state Koryo (a contraction of Koguryo) and founded a nation that would stand for 450 years.[4]

The Koryo state brought new cultural strides—notably the establishment (in 992) of a national university that included technical colleges specializing in law, calligraphy, and accounting; numerous private academies for the education of the elite were also opened. In addition, Koryo's rulers instituted a civil-service examination that opened government positions to a broader class of applicants. Yet despite these civilizing influences, chaos was a fact of daily life. Palace intrigues, assassinations, military revolts, peasant and slave uprisings, and harassment from Mongol tribes on its northern border undercut Koryo's stability. In 1170, military and civil officials engaged in a power struggle that ended "in Korea's only pre-1961 successful military coup against civilians," which was followed by a century during which power shifted among ten warlords from six families.[5]

In 1231, during this century of military rule, the Mongols invaded; they spent the next quarter century pillaging the length and breadth of the country. The final truce required that the Koryo pay tribute (including gold, horses, falcons, young women, and eunuchs), that the crown prince live in Peking as a hostage until the death of his father, and that he eventually marry a Mongol princess. The Mongols also pressured the Korean government to introduce, at the end of the thirteenth century, a Neo-Confucianism that stressed ritual and the importance of familial bonds. The humiliations of this absolute surrender, combined with the Mongols being ousted from China in 1368, severely weakened the Koryo dynasty. That, in turn, brought internecine battles, more confrontations with the Chinese (including an army of brigands known as the Red Turbans), and plenty of opportunity for a rising warrior, Yi Song-gye, to display his political and military talents. After installing and dismissing two evidently inadequate monarchs, in 1392 he finally elevated himself to the throne, moved his capital to Seoul, and founded a dynasty that would last for half a millennium.

THE YI DYNASTY

The first centuries of the Yi dynasty were relatively peaceful. Korea paid tribute to China and allowed eager Japanese merchants limited trading privileges at three southeastern ports. Within the country, the powerful, landed aristocrats (called *yangban*) who had supported Yi's takeover launched a takeover of their own, reforming administrative laws along Confucian lines. Naturally, these reforms assured that the yangban became firmly entrenched in the nation's civil and military operations.

The economy of the Yi dynasty was based in traditional agriculture. Peasants tilled the land, served in the military, and answered periodic calls for corvée labor, during which they worked on major projects such as palace construction, wall building, and mining. (They also paid exorbitant taxes; at times, the burden grew so overwhelming that many of them were forced off the land and whole villages were abandoned as their inhabitants turned to banditry.) Handicrafts were imported or produced in the villages or government factories. The government's interest in manufacturing was thorough, in large part because it was the primary customer for manufactured products. At one point early in the Yi dynasty, roughly 6,300 skilled crafts people were on government rosters, making weapons, utensils, paper, and other goods.[6]

The Yi dynasty also instituted an expanded examination system— called by one scholar "the most enlightened system of bureaucratic recruitment anywhere practiced in the world of that time"—which meant that more and more yangban were eligible to serve in the government.[7] The number of available positions, however, remained relatively static at around 1,000.[8] This excess of would-be administrators led to intense infighting among bitterly opposed factions, membership in which was "foreordained and forever," with affiliations passed from generation to generation.[9] Ironically, while the factions were ruthlessly and often violently contesting one another's interpretations of Confucian fine print, Confucian "unaggressiveness" was being invoked to sap the strength of the military. Officials "took quiet but persistent steps to see that civilian dominance was secure. . . . Military honor and prestige drained away," causing "centuries of appalling military weakness."[10]

Meanwhile, Korea's neighbor across the Strait of Japan had been suffering through the era of Warring States. Now unified under Toyotomi Hideyoshi and equipped with Portuguese muskets, the Japanese threw themselves against the enervated Koreans, with the ultimate design of taking on the Ming dynasty in China. They were astonishingly successful; they overran Korea in about a month, beginning in April 1592. Although the ironclad turtle ships of Admiral Yi Sun-sin inflicted heavy casualties on Japan's fleet and played havoc with efforts to reprovision troops on the mainland, it still took four years of Korean resistance and, ultimately, help from the Chinese before the invaders were finally driven out. And they reinvaded the following year.

During their years of domination in Korea, the Japanese destroyed many of the nation's temples and palaces, kidnapped its scholars and crafts people, and drained the nation in other ways. Even though the Japanese forces were repulsed at the close of the sixteenth century, their actions against Korea softened the nation up for yet another conquering nation from the north. Manchu invasions in 1627 and again in 1636 overcame Korean resistance and were a first step in the Manchu conquest of Ming China. A tributary relationship was established, and Yi princes were given over as hostages.

Painfully aware of its vulnerability, Korea tried to pull itself under a shell of xenophobic policies. Contact with all nations (except tribute relations with China and a Japanese trading post in Pusan) was circumscribed. This was perhaps not so much the beginning as the apotheosis of Korea's isolationism. Foreign relations had been curtailed during previous periods, but self-protection now reached paranoic fervor: "Resources lay consciously undeveloped lest they attract foreign avarice; the mining of gold and silver was discouraged lest it lead to increased Chinese exactions of Korean products. . . . Warnings against foreign contact became a conventional theme in government councils."[11]

The next 250 years of the Yi dynasty were peaceful and productive. Manufacturing gradually became privatized, government control waned, and individual artisans—often with financial backing from merchants—began to sell their wares for cash. The introduction of new farming practices, such as the transplanting of rice seedlings, brought a dramatic increase in production (because land could bear a crop of barley while the rice was young) along with a decrease in labor requirements. Even with these advances, though, millions went without sufficient food. In 1812, one province alone counted 900,000 starving peasants; another had 700,000. The following year, 920,000 residents went hungry in a third province.[12]

Notwithstanding the restrictions on foreign contact, Korea was gradually exposed to Western ideas, often through Catholic missionaries who traveled down from Peking. Despite its growing popularity and its clear challenge to the existing Confucian order, Catholicism was tolerated until 1785, when King Chongjo declared it heretical and prohibited its practice in Korea; the following year, laws were decreed that banned the importation of any books from China. The impetus for this crackdown was a papal ruling (delivered, in fact, almost four decades earlier) that cautioned Catholics against ancestor worship. Conversions continued, however, until the Catholic Persecution of 1801, when a number of prominent converts were killed or banished. Not long thereafter, a less xenophobic faction came to power, and Catholicism was permitted; French missionaries arrived in 1836 and 1837. But, as the seesaw of factions continued, another persecution took place in 1839, followed by another relaxation and an influx of missionaries. The number of converts soon reached 20,000.

The priests, of course, were not the only strangers to visit Yi dynasty Korea. Between 1832 and 1866, English merchant and naval vessels had entered Korean waters; French warships had appeared and left, rather abruptly; Russians, Germans, and Americans had all made military or mercenary assaults on Korean soil. These forays alone probably would have been enough to make the nation's leaders apprehensive, but they were also aware of the problems foreigners were causing in China, which from the beginning of time had been the greatest power on the continent. The Opium Wars of 1839–1842 and the occupation of Peking in 1860 did little to enhance Westerners' reputation as beneficent trading partners.

As a result, the father of the young King Kojong, known as the Taewon'gun or prince regent, set upon yet another bloody persecution of the Catholics in 1866. These executions were different both in magnitude (over 8,000 Koreans died) and importance, because they constituted part of a broader campaign to create a national consciousness, to assert royal authority over the aristocracy, to rid the peninsula of pernicious influences, and to retreat from a world that had suddenly become large and perilous.[13] Korea embarked on a policy that earned it the title of the Hermit Kingdom. Interaction with Western nations was forbidden, and Westerners who attempted to ignore the policy suffered the consequences. In 1866, an American trading ship, the *General Sherman*, boldly sailing upriver toward Pyongyang, was attacked and burned, losing all hands. A Russian diplomatic mission was turned away. Even contact with the Western-tainted Japanese was strictly regulated. The Chinese, alone, were considered safe.

Of course, Korea in the late 1860s could not be as perfectly secluded as the Taewon'gun desired. Contacts with Japan did occur, and Catholic missionaries still slipped over the border from China. In other words, the Hermit Kingdom was probably more open to foreign influences than is modern-day North Korea. And, in any case, the Taewon'gun's policy succeeded for only a short time; no one seemed content to leave the hermit alone.

Indeed, the first step in the isolation policy, the Catholic Persecution of 1866, brought about a quick reaction from French forces in China. After very limited successes—and some notable defeats—in the battlefield the French retreated. Five years later, American forces tried to use the destruction of the *General Sherman* as a pretext for forcing open Korea's ports. These efforts, too, came to naught, but within Korea, forces were building for more contact with the West. That fact, plus the young king's desire to take a more active role, as well as fractional fighting, led to the ousting of the Taewon'gun in 1873.

Two years later, the final blow to Korea's isolationist policies came with the *Unyo* incident, when a Japanese naval ship was sailed into Korean territorial waters for the express purpose of drawing fire from Korean defenders. This, in turn, gave the Japanese sufficient pretext to land an emissary, who pressed demands for a treaty that would ultimately give the Japanese access to Korean products and markets. The Koreans conceded, and the Treaty of Friendship (also called the Kanghwa Treaty) was signed on February 26, 1876.

The preceding is an admittedly superficial rendering of Korea's early history, but it serves two purposes. First, it provides an outline of crucial events. Second, it serves as a backdrop for a discussion of some of the traditional social principles that underlie Korea's political and economic performance in the twentieth century, including the Korean style of management.[14]

CONFUCIAN AUTHORITARIANISM

Koreans—indeed, most people of East Asia—view power and authority in a much different light than do most Westerners. An easy way to approach this difference is to note that Westerners think of themselves as progressing out of a dim and barbaric past into a glorious future, whereas Asians posit a golden past and see a future fraught with dangers and brutality. Put simply, when Westerners want to describe utopia, they write science fiction; Asians, in contrast, write history. As a result, Westerners have tended to oppose the concentration of power of bureaucrats and officials who might block their access to imminent opportunities. Asians are more likely to view the consolidation of power as a necessary first step in achieving basic security. Of course, the events of the past 500 years have reinforced the notions of each group; during that time, the West has been blessed with relatively strong governments and institutions, while Asia—including, certainly, Korea—has found itself in periods of warlordism, brigandage, and utter anarchy. [15]

Given the world view that dominates in East Asia, it is hardly surprising to find ethical codes, such as Confucianism, stressing moral leadership and harmonious civil relations. Evidence of Confucianism or Confucianlike religions in Korea has been traced back to the sixth century B.C., but this tradition probably didn't play a substantive role in the culture until much later. It became especially important around the end of the thirteenth century, when the government introduced elements of Neo-Confucianism that were family and ritual oriented, largely to counter the influence of Buddhism; a century later, with the founding of the Yi dynasty, Neo-Confucianism achieved preeminence over Buddhism.

An extensive discussion of Confucianism would be out of place here, but several basic themes should be noted. Above all else, it is crucial to point out Confucianism's promotion of hierarchical social relationships, which has in turn bred an acceptance of authority, an inclination toward elitism, and strong family ties.

Five basic bonds are stressed; in Korea, these have typically been arranged in the following order of importance: father-son, ruler-subject, husband-wife, elder-younger, and friend-friend. Note that three of these relate to the family, and the most important is the duty owed the father by his son. The ranking of these bonds can be significant in defining the character of a Confucian society. When Japan annexed the peninsula in 1910, one Korean scholar maintains, it went to great lengths to emphasize the relationships between ruler and subject to enfeeble Korean culture and strengthen ties to the empire. [16]

Regardless of which bond comes first, a hierarchy of relationships constitutes the skeleton of Korean society. As noted in Chapter 2, one of the early lessons in Korean schools points out that every person is either older or younger than every other—an extremely simple indication of status and social rank. Even today, it is common for Koreans to ask each other, within a few moments of meeting, what their ages are, so as to determine who is due the greater respect. It is said that even twins are not equal; the firstborn, being older, is the superior. [17] The application of such hierarchy to the workplace is obvious: there has been little confusion over who makes decisions in a Korean office or factory and who carries them out.

The elitism of Confucianism has, at times, reached extreme proportions in Korean culture. The landowning gentry or yangban of the Yi dynasty came to represent the worst of Japanese feudalism and Chinese notions of aristocratic superiority. The yangban married only within their class and lived apart from commoners in special villages. They abhorred the idea of working in agriculture, commerce, or any productive activity, because such practical pursuits were the province of the lower classes; the only proper functions of a yangban were public office or scholarly endeavors. While few actually had positions in academia or government, they freely milked the peasantry to maintain a life of extraordinary leisure and privilege. They were often carried about on tippy, one-wheeled palanquins, whereas a commoner was forbidden to ride a donkey in the presence of a yangban unless he was en route to "his own wedding or his grave." [18] These Confucian attitudes clearly acted as a brake on Korea's economic development during the Yi dynasty and, even as recently as the 1960s, the decision to pursue a career in business "was neither easy nor obvious." [19]

Some yangban elitism still exists in Korea. "I've seen people slice a golf ball right into a caddy, and they never express any regret or concern," said one diplomat. "They blame the caddy for being so careless that he got in the way of this elevated person's ball." (On the subject of golf and class distinctions: perhaps the worst job in Korea belongs to the young women at Seoul's crowded driving ranges, who squat in the narrow spaces between golfers, teeing up balls while the clubs of the well-to-do hum through the air around them.)

Preoccupation with status and hierarchy can also be seen in the Korean language, which includes several levels of formality, with different grammatical suffixes and different vocabularies. One is required to "speak up" to one's superiors and "down" to those of lower status. In short, every time a young executive speaks to a supervisor, he unavoidably acknowledges his inferiority and, if Confucian traditions are to be recognized, the fact that he is willing to defer to the superior's wishes. These status levels can grossly impede attempts to learn the Korean language. American businessmen note that their subordinates are required to speak "up," while they are expected to speak "down"; consequently, one must learn to understand a level of Korean that one does not speak, and speak another that is rarely heard.

Koreans tend to be deferential and law abiding—excepting some rather Mediterranean notions about traffic—even when status relationships aren't clearly articulated. One study in the late 1960s found that half of those waiting for a bus during the morning rush hour would stand in line if others were doing so; fully one-third said they would line up regardless of what others were doing.[20] Twenty years later, people frequently line up in Seoul's modern subway stations, only to squirrel and jam their way into the overcrowded cars.

This is not to say that Korea's Confucianism breeds robotic conformance, however. The sense of moral "rightness" that underlies much of Confucian teaching sets a difficult standard for governments. Those that fall short—through corruption, mismanagement, or any other ethical failure—are considered illegitimate in the eyes of the people and are often subject to vehement protest. This tradition can be traced back to the dissent of Confucian scholars during the Yi dynasty; more recent practitioners—typically students—have brought down regimes in 1960 and 1987.

Despite the Confucian emphasis on order and the elevated importance of the modern military, Korea's history shows little glorification of soldiering. Even though the nation's past is rife with battles, Korea never attempted the conquest of another nation by military force. And although it has several striking victories to its credit, Korea has found few military heroes to celebrate; the most highly regarded is Admiral

Yi, who performed his exploits in the fifteenth century. To a large
degree, this lack of status for the military can be traced to the Confucian emphasis on education and public administration. Although
soldiering was marked by considerable pride and acclaim during the
peninsula's early history, later practices—including the use of hired
foreigners and slaves, the shift in function from warrior to public
laborer, and the opportunity for peasants to buy their way out of
service with bolts of cotton—contributed to the demise of the military.[21]

It is frequently noted that Confucianism is not theistic, which is to
say that it is rooted very much in the here and now. As such, the
argument goes, it both encourages and reflects the Korean inclination
for pragmatic rather than ideological or religious solutions, which in
turn accounts for the country's open-mindedness and flexibility. (Consider, for example, how the government has mixed free enterprise and
a heavily planned economy.) Of course, this observation falters in the
face of a profound emphasis on ideology in Kim Il-Sung's North Korea.
If Confucianism's pragmatism was a deeply rooted factor in South
Korea's success, how could it have been so thoroughly supplanted in
the North?

Some observers have gone so far as to suggest that Confucianism
has *not* been a dominant factor in Korea's industrialization; rather,
Koreans' "attitude of obedience to authority . . . [is based] on the
militaristic training and mentality inherited and buttressed over the
years." If Confucianism has had a lasting effect, "it has maintained its
influence only because reinforcement came again and again from the
successive militaristic cultures of Japanese colonialism, the war, and
the rise of the military in the political arena."[22] Others add that Korea
could not really begin modernizing until the passing (or at least
corruption) of Confucianism's extreme conservatism. And, indeed, its
influence has been waning for decades.[23]

In sum, the true contribution of Confucianism to Korea's industrial development is debatable. Its conservatism and antibusiness
elitism clearly impeded growth. At the same time, though, its
stress on hierarchical relationships allows a strong sense of co-
hesion in the family, the workplace, and the society in general, and
its emphasis on education helped to create a highly literate work
force. Finally, although militarism and a deeply rooted fear of insta-

bility surely play a part, Confucian traditions have also inclined Koreans toward authoritarian control.

YOU AND ME AGAINST THE WORLD

By stressing bonds to family, country, and friends, Confucianism spins a web of personal relationships around each individual; in this web, one finds happiness, belonging, and safety.

Much has been made of the especially strong grouping instinct among Koreans, of the "we-ism" that pervades their lives. Once again, the language is an excellent indicator. One uses plural possessive pronouns: it is "our" house and "our" car; it is not "my" house, regardless of ownership. When the landlord refers to a tenant's child as "our" baby, it is more likely to be a verbal reflex rather than an expression of affection or patrimony. Of course, the impetus for forming social bonds is familiar to anyone who has ever joined a computer club or a bowling league. What is perhaps exotic to Western sensibilities is the degree to which Koreans cling to these groups.

The first loyalty is to family and kin, but other social ties play a valuable role. Koreans are quick to establish nonfamily connections by inquiring about upbringing, because having a home region in common is almost as good as a blood relationship. Next most valuable is a common educational background—and the value is genuine. The 1961 coup that installed Park Chung-Hee, for example, was largely engineered by members of the Eighth Class of the Korean Military Academy; afterward, noted one observer, "Every Eighth Class member, whether or not he actually took part in the coup, became a powerful person."[24]

These regional and alumni connections are eagerly cultivated. Within a conglomerate, an employee may belong to a group of Yonsei University graduates, a group of former Taegu residents, and perhaps a special group of Yonsei graduates who grew up in Taegu. Such groups provide a sense of belonging within the huge and sometimes impersonal chaebol. They also provide a means of informal, lateral communication and thereby act as an antidote for the severely hierarchical or "stovepipe" organization that characterizes many of these companies.

This desire for family and other group connections is part of the broader tendency among Koreans to personalize relationships that Westerners might be inclined to leave on a more formal or professional level. Traditionally and today, Korean business is based more on a handshake than on a contract, more on the *kibun*, or mood, than on any legal sanctions. In a pinch—and Korean history is nothing but a long series of pinches—a contract becomes an empty document, whereas a personal relationship engages the integrity and responsibility of all parties. Consequently, extensive time and resources go into establishing and preserving one-on-one relationships. Conversely, Korea has only about 1,500 licensed attorneys in the entire country. This number excludes tax and patent attorneys as well as legal scriveners and other personnel, but even if one adds them, along with all the secretaries, receptionists, and assorted gofers, it is still a minute legal community by Western standards.

People in the United States and Europe may see this inclination toward grouping in a rosy light, and understandably so, because it brings clear emotional and economic benefits. But it also leads to a tendency, indeed a nearly constant tick, to categorize people as insiders or outsiders, as "us" or "them"—and this is hardly an unalloyed good. The drawing of sharp distinctions between groups creates serious problems for Koreans, mostly because, in a contentious world, loyalty to one group often means hostility toward others.

This us-them taxonomy underlies much of the vicious factionalism that has marked Korea's history, from before the days of Silla to the harangues in the current National Assembly. Regional factions are particularly strong and divisive. People from one area are thought to be arrogant, while those from another are considered misers. People from one region are called stone heads, others potato eaters. This hostility stems both from ancient prejudices and from the inclination of modern leaders to support their own kind with economic development, while the home regions of opposition leaders have been ignored. Some corporations are known to favor applicants from Cholla province; others are prejudiced against Cholla and biased toward applicants from Kyongsang.

But factionalism in Korea has not always been so comprehensible as crude regional prejudice. Paradoxically, it may come from the lack of other, more natural divisions within the population: "Compactness of territory, absence of ethnic, religious, political, linguistic, or other basic sources of cleavage . . . have created a society in which groups are artificial. . . . Grouping is hence an opportunistic matter concerned only with access to power for its members, and, because other differences are not present, each group tends to be distinguishable from the others only by the personalities of its members and by their relationship to power at the time."[25]

In the past, factional strife has threatened to atomize society. During one period beginning in 1575, for example, the court was split between two groups; the victorious of these soon split into two subfactions, the victorious of which split into greater and lesser subsubfactions; the lesser of these then split into two sub-sub-subfactions, while the greater managed to fracture itself into *six* sub-sub-subs. One scholar noted that these "factional conflicts, carried out with uninhibited ferocity, had a certain elegance since they were rarely justified by either policy or ideological argumentation. They were like sporting events in that their purpose was only to produce winners and losers."[26] This incessant wrangling, while not so important during the days of an elite and nonprogrammatic government, can be crippling in modern-day Korean government—yet it persists. Indeed, President Park Chung-Hee noted that some factions created during the Yi dynasty were still operating during his regime.[27]

Another facet of this ingrained us-them categorization has ominous overtones for modern Korea's relations with other nations. Because of their homogeneity, Koreans are comfortable making racial distinctions that would make most Westerners blanch. The manifestations are frequent: one hotel displays a miniature of Admiral Yi's famous turtle ship, describing the vessel as "a landmark of national integrity and racial excellence." Workers striking against an American-owned insurance company brandish a sign protesting "the superiority doctrine of white people"—written, pointedly, in English. Many foreigners also claim that Koreans are excessive in their devotion to race and racial purity. According to one Western diplomat, " 'Mongrelization' distresses them. They can't understand how English and German people can intermarry, much less blacks and whites." In the planet's complex, multicultural, multiracial economic future, these attitudes could produce serious tensions or, at a minimum, misapprehensions.

Korea's narrow and extreme group loyalties can be dangerous and counterproductive, especially when they are not ameliorated by broader loyalties to the corporation or the society as a whole. Family ties, for example, have led to rampant nepotism in government and industry. This is probably less the case in larger corporations and chaebol (excepting, of course, at the highest levels, where corporate leadership has tended to stay in the family), but it is generally pervasive. After all, every other employee will be trying to find jobs and promotions for his brothers and sons and nephews, who will then act as spies and supporters during the intrigues and minicoups that mark Korean office life; to fail to do likewise would put one at a serious disadvantage. Similarly, regional and alumni affiliations can promote favoritism and corruption. One sociologist has suggested that the influence of Western individualism has exacerbated this tendency, creating a kind of "self-centered collectivism," in which "any illicit measures may be justified if they are for the welfare of the family-kin group."[28]

Staunch loyalty to the group also reduces individual options for making compromises or conciliatory gestures. Affiliations are so pronounced that the "divide between friend and foe becomes exceedingly vivid and is not amenable to change. Conflicts take on the long range and uncompromising perspectives of family feuds. There cannot be the kaleidoscopic realignments typical of the coalition politics of interest-oriented political systems."[29] This difficulty in achieving compromise was never more manifest than in the 1988 presidential election, when the two opposition leaders—who controlled a majority of the electorate—could not resolve their differences and thereby handed the presidency to their mutual nemesis, Roh Tae-Woo.

Nevertheless, the stereotype of the intransigent Korean is overbroad. Few countries in the world are as densely populated as Korea; the people live in extraordinarily close quarters, and millions of tiny compromises occur every day. And while the nation has been undergoing a period of national labor unrest, negotiations are being conducted and contracts are being signed.

Despite their willingness to join in and pledge their loyalty to various groups, Koreans have a streak of individuality that seems to set them apart from other peoples who have been influenced by Confucianism. In fact, research conducted in the mid-1960s showed Koreans to be more individualistic than their counterparts in either the United States or Japan.[30] (They were also more frugal, more aggressive, and more materialistic.) And although loyalty to family and nation has spurred much of Korea's development, loyalty to the corporation is not pronounced. As noted earlier, worker mobility is high, and, when better opportunities arise, both production workers and managers are inclined to follow them.[31]

THE FORCE OF HAHN

Centuries of invasion, humiliation, dependence, and deprivation have created in the Korean psyche the emotion called *hahn*, which has been described as "a complex of emotional states, including a sense of grief, grievances, grudges, hatred, rancor, regret, remorse and revenge."[32] A similar concept, represented by the identical Chinese character, occurs in other Asian cultures: in China the meaning is closer to pure hatred; in Japan, it means remorse. In English, one might talk of a chip on the shoulder or perhaps an inferiority complex. Finding an identical cross-cultural parallel is not important. What matters is that hahn—or, more accurately, the desire to be freed from it—can be a sharp spur.

It is an ancient obsession. In addition to centuries of military embarrassment, even the most benign cultural exposure could contribute to the Korean sense of inferiority. The introduction of Confucianism, for example, created "aspirations for acceptance and anxiety about unworthiness which have made [Koreans] audacious in carrying out enterprises that test and prove their worth."[33] In modern Korea, hahn has been attributed to the dictators and industrialists who suffered under colonial humiliations, as well as the workers and students who have been repressed and beaten by the hahn-filled dictators and industrialists. One also detects a sense of hahn within the changing Korean family, as sons—and especially their wives—start to resent the seemingly limitless impositions of their aging parents. By some accounts, Korea is a land in which seething frustrations eddy around every Confucian obligation.

One could probably overstate the influence of this emotion, but it would be foolish to ignore it. Hahn is a source of deep passion. It can be used to justify almost any action. And it explains in part the transparent joy that Koreans find in their world-class achievements.

Just as Calvinist Europeans sought financial success as a proof that they were among God's elect, Koreans have pursued it as a denial of their fears of unworthiness or inadequacy.

Korea's distant history was certainly full enough of deprivation and degradation to instill in its citizens a deep, emotional hunger for economic triumph. But if the people managed to retain some equanimity before 1876, their association with Japan, first as a protectorate and then as an annexed arm of the empire, supplied enough hahn to drive them forward for many, many decades.

5

▲▲▲

Korea's Modern Memory, 1876–1945

"The Japanese were brutal colonialists," explained the priest, a long-time resident in Korea. The grounds of the Secret Gardens in Seoul were encrusted with a thin sheet of ice; light snow was piling up on the pine boughs and the ribbed roofs of the Palace of Illustrious Virtue. "It was forbidden for people to use their Korean names, or to speak the Korean language," he continued. "Families were forced to go to Manchuria or to Japan to work." He pointed to a plaque, with details in Korean and English. "And the Koreans do not forget easily. All the signs at the historical sites are like this one. They give the date of construction and the date of rebuilding, after the original building was burned down by the Japanese in the sixteenth century, or the nineteenth century, or whenever. They are always very explicit about that—*by the Japanese.*"

The theme is frequently repeated. Earlier in the week, over ginseng tea, the director of the Korean Management Association had put it differently. "It isn't necessary to motivate Koreans," he said. "We are all alike. We all understand that we must work hard, very hard, if we are to survive. Ironically, we owe much of our success to the North

Koreans. But also the Japanese. We are eager to work hard, because we want to beat the Japanese."

And a few days later, at the Hyundai auto plant in Ulsan, a young manager betrayed a passion that could not have been born of personal persecution, that could only have come through cultural memory. "We are poorer than the Japanese," he explained earnestly. "Our technology is less advanced. If we are to beat them, we must work harder. When they work eight hours, we must work more. Much more."

> Our modern history has been a record of failures, national ruination and confusion. Our masses, the creators of history, lacked autonomy and were characterized by flunkeyism and subjected to the control of foreign powers.
> —President Park Chung-Hee[1]

OPENING THE DOOR: 1876–1910

The importance of the 1876 Kanghwa Treaty was threefold: first, it signaled the end of the Hermit Kingdom. Second, it declared Korea to be a sovereign state (which made the point that it was *not* part of China, regardless of what the Chinese might think), and, third, it gave Japan extraordinary privileges in Korea, including the right to trade in certain ports and the establishment of Japanese legations, subject to Japanese law, on Korean soil.

Soon, other foreigners were descending on the peninsula. Treaties of commerce were signed with France, the United States, and many other Western nations. "After the Korean-American Friendship Agreement of 1882," Park Chung-Hee would later write, "various European nations concluded friendship agreements with Korea, and the situation of Korea at that time was similar to a piece of meat eyed by a pack of hungry dogs."[2] Japanese commercial activity was especially hectic. Just a few months after the signing of the 1876 treaty, the first Japanese bank was established. In 1885, major Japanese transportation companies moved into the port cities; among the ships entering Korean ports in 1893, fully 72 percent were Japanese.[3] Having taken control of the sea routes to Korea, the Japanese began to concentrate on land transportation, eventually building the railroad between Pusan and

Seoul. (It is an indication of Japan's presumptions that it dispatched engineers to Korea for initial railway surveys without receiving any consent from the Korean government.)

The actions of "the Japanese" were often actually those of the Japanese government. For example, an American had originally captured the concession to build the Seoul-Pusan railway but failed to raise sufficient capital. He then offered the rights to the Japanese government, which pressured two zaibatsu—Mitsui and Mitsubishi—to take on the job. Moreover, the government put up four-fifths of the cost and provided guarantees to investors.[4]

This approach—government pressure on the private conglomerates, sweetened by assurances of financial return—marks one of Japan's early uses of private industry to achieve foreign policy goals. A similar strategy had already been used to achieve domestic goals, including development and modernization (especially of the military) during the Meiji Restoration—examples of what would later be called "Japan, Inc." Several decades afterward, this strategy was transplanted to Korea and pursued with increasing vigor until the fall of the empire after World War II. After that, it served as a model for postwar development in Korea by Koreans.

The Japanese obsession with Korea was both economic and strategic. The economic allure was self-evident. Korea was a plum for the picking—blessed with bountiful rice paddies (mostly in the south), rich in natural resources (in the north), populated by men and women who were vulnerable to the military technologies that the Japanese had already acquired from the West. But the peninsula's strategic importance was even more compelling. Korea's proximity made it a constant threat to Japan's security; it was, in the words of Japanese Prince Yamagata, "a dagger pointed at the heart of Japan."[5] Now Western powers were moving into East Asia, by ship and by the Trans-Siberian Railroad, threatening to take this dagger in hand. If Japan was to retain its independence and be considered a world power, it could not allow foreigners to control the destiny of its close neighbor.

Motivation notwithstanding, the Japanese and other foreign influences were a force for modernization on the peninsula. But as such, they also rocked the traditional values and organizations of Korea. In 1894, the accumulated social, economic, and religious pressures exploded in a massive uprising of peasants who were believers in a new and indigenous religion, Tonghak. After losing two important battles to Tonghak rebels, the central government appealed to China for help and received a contingent of 1,000 soldiers; unbidden, the Japanese arrived with 7,000 more. The rebels were defeated, but the Japanese, rather than withdraw, began to exert their strength on the Korean government. China decried this interference in Korea's internal affairs, and hostility mounted. Finally, convinced that an armed confrontation was inevitable, the Japanese launched a sneak attack on Chinese forces in July 1894, and the Sino-Japanese War was under way.

The Japanese won a quick and decisive victory and, just as quickly, set about trying to modernize Korea. Abuses such as slavery and child marriage were eliminated, the government was reformed, and the monetary and tax systems were improved. The civil examination system and class distinctions were abolished, much to the distress of many traditional Koreans. But Japan was soon to find that the Chinese were not the only other power in Asia. Russia now began to work its influence in Korea, supporting Queen Min in her effort to curtail Japanese influence. The Japanese answered by engineering her assassination, but their power was again undercut when Korea's King Kojong fled to the Russian legation in Seoul, from which he ruled for a year, returning to the palace in early 1897.

For the next seven years, Russia and Japan played a waiting game in Korea, both claiming to recognize Korea's status as a sovereign nation. Meanwhile, Korea's rapid modernization continued: the first smallpox vaccinations were given, a postal system was inaugurated, and elementary schools appeared in Seoul. The economy grew more sophisticated as Koreans formed trading companies and merchant associations to help themselves compete against the foreigners.

The standoff between Russia and Japan grew increasingly edgy. Russia moved into Manchuria, then began to push across the Yalu River. Japan protested, negotiations resulted, and the two nations began horse trading over which large chunks of Asia should fall to whom. The talks broke down, however, and, in February 1904, the Japanese relied once again on the advantage of surprise: they launched another sneak attack, this time on the Russian fleet in Port Arthur. As the Russians scrambled to defend themselves, an army of Japanese moved into Korea; the following year, when the Russo-Japanese War ended, Japan's control over the peninsula was a fait accompli.

Despite this political chaos, industrialization managed to put down its first slender roots. The Yi dynasty government had taken the lead in introducing and operating new industries, producing textiles, paper, pistols, and other goods in small factories on state property; state standards dictated what would be manufactured and to whom it would be sold. The government also oversaw the disciplining of workers and set the meager rate of pay.[6] But the benefits of wide-scale industrialization were largely ignored: As one scholar noted, the "Confucian gentleman's disesteem of worldly goods, fortified by the desire to ward off foreign jealousy, curbed economic activity and placed the little there was under strict surveillance."[7]

On the social scale, merchants and peddlers belonged to the low end of the ranks of commoners, beneath farmers. Peddlers had a longstanding relationship with the government, serving as spies, postmen, and extralegal goons; by some accounts, they were inclined to defend royal interests with more ferocity than did the government's own troops. Consequently, merchant business, which in other countries helped to build "a respectable patrician aristocracy as the spearhead of diversity and private interest," translated into something altogether different in Korea: "meanness, gangsterism, and covert collaboration with the government to destroy private interest and, when it appeared, liberalism."[8]

Despite these pejorative opinions about the function and status of business, upright private citizens gradually became interested in commercial activities, establishing independent manufacturing enterprises with the support of the government. The first large textile plant, built in 1897, was a joint venture between the government and private owners, with later plants being operated as completely private operations. Chinaware and tobacco-processing factories also were established, the former the first attempt at an export industry.

But these optimistic endeavors had little chance against the onslaught of foreign capital that was then entering Korea. Western European powers were active in railway construction and mining, while the Russians built a match factory and embarked on lumbering and mining ventures. The Americans, too, were busy in rail and power-plant construction and the operation of a gold mine. (Today, the Korean slang for *gold*, which can be loosely romanized as "no-touch-ae," is supposedly a corruption of the mine owners' command for workers to keep their hands off the rich ore.)

Despite the cosmopolitan flavor of this exploitation, the dominant political and economic power was Japan. After their victory over Russia in 1904, the Japanese extorted a treaty from Korea that established Korea as Japan's protectorate; it is said that because Korean ministers refused to ratify the document, Japanese officers had to affix the Korean government seal. Soon, Japanese citizens were installed in key bureaucratic positions (indeed, by 1907, over 40 percent of all Korean government officials were Japanese).[9] They censored the newspapers, took firm control of the police and security forces, and disbanded the army. This last activity was shamefully easy. Centuries of indifference to and distrust of the military had reduced the armed forces to just 6,000 "largely demoralized men."[10]

All this took place with the tacit acceptance of the American government (as a way to staunch Russian expansion and as a quid pro quo for Japan's acceptance of American interests in the Philippines) and the active lobbying of a substantial number of Koreans, who were members of the Ilchin-hoe (Advancement Society). This group has been portrayed as a Japanese front organization or, alternately, as "one of the only instances known to political science of an anti-nationalist mass movement." Given that, at its peak, it numbered nearly a million members, it was clearly more than a facade established with the connivance of a few quislings.[11] Moreover, the appeal of Japan is easy to understand: it was more modern than either Russia or Korea, it had strong cultural ties with the peninsula, and it was a winner, having recently triumphed over the substantial forces of both China and Russia.

In addition to its military and governmental activities, Japan furthered its penetration of the Korean economy. By 1908, Japanese citizens in Korea were operating seventy-nine manufacturing concerns with an average of forty-one employees each; Koreans owned only six manufacturing operations with a *total* of just ninety-two workers.[12] Also that year, Japan established the Oriental Development Company, one of several state-chartered "national policy companies" created to achieve government goals—the Japanese version of the East India Company of Britain.[13] The company was offered land (indeed: by one account, it acquired 73,500 acres in its first eighteen months of operation) for its agricultural efforts and a guaranteed annual subsidy. Oversight of its operations was retained by the Japanese-controlled government; while Japanese and Koreans were both allowed to own shares, Japanese held 99 percent of the stock, and the major stockholders were government agencies.[14]

Finally, in August 1910, Japan did what it had wanted to do all along; Korea was formally annexed, terminating the Yi dynasty's slow decline and Korea's many centuries as a distinct political entity.

MODERNIZATION UNDER THE GUN: 1910–1945

The Japanese were not benign colonial masters. To the contrary: over the course of their reign, they methodically crushed all resistance, worked forcibly to reshape Korean culture into a Japanese mold, underpaid their Korean workers when they hired them at all, grabbed land from Koreans through an array of ruses, monopolized natural resources from gold to lumber, and expropriated the bulk of the rice harvest—a policy of exploitation and abuse rarely rivaled in the annals of colonialism.[15] No effort was made to dress up their repression as something gentler or more beneficent. Instead, as a sign of their authority, all Japanese—including bureaucrats and elementary-school teachers—were required to wear swords. For thirty-six years, the theme was constant: "stern, centralized, bureaucratic administration without constitutional or popular restraint, its high-handedness justified in Japanese eyes by its efficiency."[16]

In the beginning, Japan's designs on its new territory were simple: keep it unindustrialized and therefore a source of raw materials and agriculture and a market for the goods produced by Japanese industry. To enforce this strategy, the colonial government restricted non-agricultural investments among Koreans and Japanese.

Resistance from the Korean people was constant but far from effective. Nevertheless, toward the end of the first decade of colonial rule, a group of religious leaders promulgated a declaration of independence. The March 1 Movement of 1919 pressed for a termination of Japan's economic domination and the opportunity for Koreans to develop their own modern industry and improve their standard of living. The Japanese overreacted; in the orgy of violence that followed, some

7,500 Koreans were killed and—by some reports—another 50,000 injured. The movement was utterly suppressed, although it did bring about a few superficial changes in Japanese policy. Nevertheless, for decades to follow, it stood as a powerful symbol of the Korean desire for sovereignty; it also reflected an early connection between industrial development and national independence.

The restrictions on investment in Korea were abolished on April 1, 1920, in part to give vent to capital reserves that had been piling up in Japan, which had profited as a supplier in World War I. And Korea was an alluring site for investment: wages were roughly half those in Japan, and workers could be pushed to labor more than ten hours a day.

As a result, the nation went through a spurt of modernization. Koreans took an active part, and the raw number of Korean-owned factories grew rapidly over the next decade. With rare exception, though, these were exceedingly small ventures, in part because Koreans lacked entrepreneurial experience and, to a larger degree, because their status as an occupied people made it difficult to find capital at favorable terms. The Japanese, in contrast, entered Korea in large numbers, with considerable experience, backed by government loans. They clearly dominated the economy, and that dominance grew over the next two decades, so that, in 1940, Japanese companies accounted for 94 percent of all capital investment in manufacturing industries in Korea. Virtually all the important heavy and energy industries were Japanese-owned.[17]

While political resistance was ineffective, the Korean people made efforts on several fronts to exercise their limited economic power against the Japanese. A "Buy Korean" movement attempted to undercut Japanese activities and support Korean-owned enterprises. At the same time, a few prosperous Koreans tried to establish enterprises. Although most of these were founded by small-time entrepreneurs angling for a profitable niche, the landowners and merchants that constituted Korea's "old money" invested in several textile mills during the 1920s—mills that would compete directly with the Japanese.

Some Korean historians like to depict such actions as springing from purely patriotic motives; other scholars are less sure, noting that when "profit and social goals coincide, there is always room for skepticism as to the prime mover."[18] But anyone operating according to normal capitalistic incentives would be loath to compete directly with an entrenched, experienced, successful company that had the blessing of an extremely powerful and proactive government. In short, this was a risky business, with little chance for the windfall profits that usually stimulate such endeavors, suggesting that these early Korean industrialists either were acting out of patriotic motives or suffered from gravely misplaced optimism.

For example: the establishment, in 1919, of the large Kyungbang Limited textile company was widely seen as a patriotic gesture. First, its creation and stock offering (among the nation's first) came on the heels of the March 1 demonstrations. Its trademark comprised eight stars (representing the eight provinces of Korea) and the central symbol from the Korean flag. (Such a display of Korean nationalism would never have been approved by the Japanese, but an inquiry into the trademark was conducted by uninformed officials in Japan and Kyungbang's founders apparently were artful dissemblers.) Additionally, the operation of the factory seemed designed to counter Japanese hiring practices; it hired only Koreans, whereas many Japanese industrialists hired only their countrymen. Kyungbang's marketing stressed that its goods were made by and for Koreans.

Koreans also engaged in strikes against colonial industrialists, and this should probably be construed as a final front in the nation's economic resistance (although it is difficult to say that the strikes were aimed at broad colonial issues rather than specific factory-level complaints). The Japanese at first tolerated a limited number of labor disputes, but the growth of such activity (in 1931, there were 205 strikes involving more than 21,000 workers) and the rising militarism of Japan brought a crackdown.

Toward the end of Korea's second decade as a colony, two events—both external to Korea—had a sweeping effect on its economy. First, a depression in Japan resulted in greatly increased economic controls. Capital fled to Korea, attracted by the natural resources in the north and the south's cheap labor. The colonial government also tried to stimulate this investment by providing "encouragement funds," land, tax breaks, and access to raw materials.[19] Paradoxically, then, Japan's economic woes accelerated Korea's industrial development; the second event, Japan's imperialistic exploits in Manchuria, determined the direction that that industrialization would take.

Substantial Japanese capital had gone into peaceful investments, such as a hydroelectric facility and a huge fertilizer plant (the latter began production in 1930 and has since been cited as the genesis of Korea's modern industrialization).[20] But after 1931, much of the capital went into industries that could support Japan's efforts to establish a greater military presence on the Asian mainland. The first such investments were in heavy industry. Steel and machinery grew fourteenfold between 1931 and 1937, and the chemical industry grew eightfold during that period. Overall, heavy industry as a proportion of total factory production more than doubled (from 23 percent to 50 percent) between 1930 and 1940.[21] Obviously, not all the industries that were developed at this time had a strictly military application: cement, textiles, and shipbuilding were necessary for a peaceful economic expansion as well. But strategic considerations were preeminent. Even the fertilizer plant that supposedly kicked off Korea's modern industrial era was eventually converted into an ammunition factory.

More important, this rapid development offered limited benefits to the people of Korea. Industry remained extremely concentrated and in Japanese hands: in 1942, three Japanese companies controlled 59 percent of all direct investments in Korea.[22]

During the late 1930s, Japan's colonial policies became even more rigid and humiliating. Extraordinary efforts were made to impose Japanese culture on the Korean people: schools were forced to quit teaching Korean history and language; Japanese became the required language at home and in school; Korean-language newspapers were shut down; and Korean writers were forced to write in Japanese. Koreans had to take Japanese names—"an unbearable insult" to these family-obsessed people—and were compelled to perform Shinto religious practices.[23]

In the last years of the colonization, as the war heated up, Koreans experienced exactly the sort of nightmare that had prompted Yi dynasty efforts to create the Hermit Kingdom. Japanese holidays were placed on the Korean calendar, with special attention to observations that stressed the ruler-subject bond between Koreans and the emperor. Young Korean men were conscripted to work in Japanese mines and munitions plants and fight in the Japanese military; hundreds of thousands went to Japan, others to Manchuria. Young women were also pressed into supposedly volunteer units as "comfort girls" for Japanese soldiers.[24]

At the very end, the Japanese war machine cracked, seized, then fell into shambles; Korea's colonial economy fell after it. Factories stopped running, and salaries were not paid. The people of Korea, burdened now more than ever, could at least rejoice at the promise of eventual liberation; pamphlets detailing the Allies' plans for a free Korea (somewhat misrepresented) had already circulated. But liberation—as they would soon discover—would be fraught with its own trials and terrors.

THE JAPANESE LEGACY

The sheer *importance* of Japan's annexation of Korea is never denied and rarely overestimated. The damage worked on Koreans, as a nation and individually, is beyond debate. Yet other aspects of the colonial experience—such as Japan's contributions in social and economic modernization—were sufficient to confound neat judgments.

The deleterious aspects of Japan's tenure were appalling and dramatic, and, whatever else, they argue forcefully for a condemnation of the colonial administration. The Japanese drained Korea of its food and natural resources; they starved and enslaved its people; they overran and otherwise suppressed Korean business (with the subsequent destruction of the country's emerging managerial pool, although later triumphs seem to belie this); and they introduced a distorted form of industrialization, concentrating development in industries that were strictly military or strongly reliant on the military as a market.

The day-to-day brutality of this regime is clearly manifest in the conditions under which Koreans lived and labored. Three-quarters of the population were poor farmers, half of them starving; there are numerous accounts of these rural poor sustaining themselves by eating roots, grass, and tree bark.[25] While this situation can be partially blamed on a slight decline in rice production in the 1920s and 1930s, the determining factor was the doubling of rice exports to Japan during the same period.[26] Those who worked as tenants on the large farms of Japanese landlords faced a doubly precarious situation; not only were they overburdened with taxes and rent payments but they could also be kicked off the land for, among other things, damaging the owner's prestige or complaining about the rent.[27] Many farmers eventually fled, either to become "fire-field people," who practiced slash-and-burn agriculture on uncultivated lands, or to settle in the cities, where they attempted to find work in the factories. Unfortunately, the lot of urban workers was not appreciably better than that of the farmers. Almost half of all factory workers and more than one-third of all miners put in more than twelve hours per day, at wages that were half what their Japanese counterparts made in the same factories. And not everyone was lucky enough to be abused; unemployment reached 15 percent in 1931.[28] (During this period, Japanese workers fared much better in the labor market; although they represented less than 3 percent of the population, they made up 17 percent of the male work force in manufacturing in 1940.)[29]

But while they permitted these extraordinary deprivations, the colonial administrators also brought about changes that were exceedingly beneficial for Korea. The Japanese provided the capital and organization necessary to bring Korea into the modern era, and the economy responded with strong, steady growth; between 1910 and 1940, the manufacturing sector grew annually by more than 10 percent.[30] In tandem with this development came the necessary evolution of a basic communications and transportation infrastructure, a significant expansion of the educational system (although only a few Koreans were able to acquire advanced education), and a well-run agricultural extension service. And the greatest bequest—at least in terms of raw potential—was probably the manufacturing facilities and equipment that the Japanese left behind when they retreated.

There are other ambiguities, as well.

• On one side of the ledger, to their shame, the Japanese extracted natural resources and much-needed food from Korea; on the other, this process gave the citizens of the former Hermit Kingdom their first lessons about operating in the world marketplace. It stretches the point to say that the Japanese introduced an export orientation, but they did expose Koreans to "the existence of external demand for their produce," and several Korean firms engaged in overseas trade, not only in Japan but also in Manchuria, Vietnam, and Thailand, and had plans to move into the Philippines and the United States.[31]

• On the one hand, the Japanese destroyed Korea's native industries at the time of initial occupation; on the other, some economists maintain that these were primitive and economically inefficient operations.

• On the one hand, the Japanese are often credited with exposing Korean workers to the machinery of a modern industrialized society, allowing them to learn by doing or by example; these lessons were so effective, the argument goes, that Korean workers were able to operate the plants immediately after the Japanese left at the end of World War II. There is obviously some truth to this, but Koreans were obliged to learn their lessons from afar; few were allowed to rise into the managerial ranks. A year before the end of the war, fully "95 percent of gainfully employed Korean men and 99 percent of the women were laborers."[32] Furthermore, the primary recipients of Japanese on-the-job training were probably other Japanese, who dominated the skilled labor force.

• Perhaps the most ambiguous bequest was Japan's introduction of the organizational and management techniques that are prerequisites for any modern manufacturing operation. Unfortunately, Korea's first exposure to modern management came from Japanese capitalists who were themselves heavily influenced by the militarism of the Meiji Restoration, who had come to Korea with the clear intention of exploiting it and its people, and who gradually turned their efforts to industries that were designed to satisfy the demands of an imperialistic military. As managers, then, their legacy was one of brutal efficiency, ruthless repression, and an indifferent exploitation of workers.

Politically, too, they taught the Koreans how the bureaucracy and security forces could be used to mobilize—indeed, manage—an entire nation. By appeals to patriotism and survival, by censorship of dissenting opinions, by the inculcation of militaristic values (in, for example, the required high-school training classes), and by unrelenting and totalitarian social control, the Japanese had stirred the Korean people into a frenzy of prowar activity. The lesson would not be lost on observant Koreans, including president-to-be Park Chung-Hee, who was then a young officer in the Japanese army.

Finally, it bears repeating that the Japanese predations against Korea, beginning with the Hideyoshi invasions at the end of the sixteenth century and continuing through World War II, have inspired the Koreans with a complex of emotions—call them hahn, call them economic patriotism, call them fear and vengeance, call them envy and desire—that has motivated them in a way that the most desperate poverty or extreme physical insecurity could not. Koreans universally recall the years of Japanese occupation with great bitterness. (As of 1989, it was still against the law in Korea to sing Japanese songs or show Japanese films.)[33] Many Koreans make a personal point of detailing the dangers posed by their (once again) powerful neighbor. They are unified in their will to be as economically potent as their former masters. They see it as their destiny and their duty, a matter of pride and survival.

As one Korean expert has pointed out, Japan's colonial actions— "perhaps especially those which were most unforgivable—created in Koreans a fierce desire to modernize and to equal, if not overtake those who had enslaved them. . . . Contemplating the results of the ruthless Japanese hand one wonders whether alien colonial regimes, if developmental, are successful modernizers in proportion to their intensity, especially when what is intense is cruelly disciplinarian, creative of the maximum in outrage."[34]

6

▲▲▲

Liberation, Sort Of

She says: Before World War II, my family had a lot of money and land.
A lot. Even after the war, we had something left.

But the Korean War was different. When they came from the North,
we put all our valuables down the well and ran away. When we finally
came back to our home, there was nothing left. The house was destroyed, and when we went to the well, it was empty. Everything was
gone. My grandfather thought it was our neighbors.

Those were hard days. I was a young girl, and I had known what it
was like to have some things. Now my family had nothing. I got
married and had children, and my husband had nothing. We lived in a
small room, and I would cook outside, under a small roof. Our part of
town had water only in the middle of the night, so I had to get up in the
dark to do our laundry. It would be winter, and I would be outside
boiling the laundry in the middle of the night, with my baby daughter
tied to my back. Oh, it was very hard then.

A BRIEF VACATION FROM HELL

Korea came out of World War II on its knees.

It had been battered and exploited by a brutal—and ultimately desperate—occupier. Its economy had been bent to two purposes: the accumulation of wealth by avaricious Japanese colonials and the provisioning of the Japanese military. Korean efforts at development had been crushed by the sheer weight of Japanese capital; most of the nation's large industrial enterprises were owned by colonialists, and as the empire fell into disarray in the last days of the war, these mainstays of the Korean economy did likewise. Production lines broke down, and spare parts grew scarce. By 1945, manufacturing production was less than 20 percent of what it had been in 1940.[1]

Liberation from the Japanese, while it marked the end of a particularly hideous nightmare, meant even greater economic hardships—at least in the short run. Reconstruction was understandably onerous, given the distortion of the economy toward war-related activities, the irrelevance of even those industries following the war, and the loss of Korea's major trading partner; it would be some time before exports to Japan would reach prewar levels. Furthermore, the thousands of Japanese who had overseen the day-to-day administration of government and industry quickly fled the country; as a parting gesture, they flooded the economy with currency in the final weeks before the U.S. occupation troops landed, bringing on hyperinflation.

Finally, Korea's liberators divided the country along the thirty-eighth parallel, thereby severing the bonds between family members and friends that formed the fabric of Korean life. The division also neatly separated the country's economy into unbalanced halves, with agriculture and light industry in the south and the natural resources and heavy industry in the north.

The manufacturing operations vacated by the Japanese were in various states of disrepair, but they were still extensive and extremely valuable. Indeed, these abandoned facilities have been called "one of the largest 'turnkey' projects in history."[2] The colonialists left behind over 2,500 businesses and industries, not to mention huge tracts of land and a modern infrastructure. Some Korean workers took over operation of the plants immediately after the Japanese departure (suggesting that they had paid close attention during the days of occupation and exploitation), but they were eventually relieved of control by the U.S. Military Government, which had been charged with governing southern Korea until reunification could be worked out. In that capacity, the United States eventually oversaw the bulk of its former adversary's lost industrial wealth.

These were difficult days and the challenge was enormous. Soon after Japan's surrender, the Korean population swelled with freed political prisoners and more than 3 million Koreans who'd been drafted for work in Japanese factories throughout that nation's empire.[3] Both of these fiercely anti-Japanese groups turned their anger toward those Koreans who had collaborated with the colonialists, particularly the police and some businessmen. And this already volatile political and economic situation soon deteriorated. Conditions became increasingly chaotic; in the view of one conservative newspaper, the people were "suffering more than they ever did under the Japanese rule."[4] In the three years after the Japanese defeat, Korea was rocked by labor disputes (including a general strike that involved over 300,000 workers), a bloody peasant revolt, and an abortive, Communist-led uprising in the army.

Unfortunately, much of this discontent can be traced to the stewardship of the U.S. Military Government under Lieutenant General John R. Hodge, who was selected for the Korean command simply because he was positioned on nearby Okinawa at war's end, at a time when the rapid movement of Soviet troops into the north put a premium on speed. (One scholar noted that "Hodge was very possibly the first man in history selected to wield executive powers over a nation of nearly twenty million on the basis of shipping time.")[5]

The Americans' management was heavily colored by a lack of direction, an ignorance of Korean affairs, and a tolerance of former Japanese collaborators, some of whom were eager to take advantage of the opportunities that arose in the confusion of this early reconstruction. Some Japanese operations were taken over by the government and others were leased to Koreans, but most were held by the interim government's Office of the Property Custodian, with control delegated to a small group of lucky Koreans, many of whom proceeded to sell off inventories and other assets; in general, these "public" industries were marked by overhiring, inefficient operation, and insufficient data. No basic inventory of former Japanese properties existed until 1947, shortly before the end of the occupation.

The results of U.S. policies were disappointing, to say the least. According to some sources, rice hoarding by profiteers led to a reduction of consumption immediately following liberation, despite a bigger harvest. Furthermore, inflation cut workers' real earnings to well below pre-1945 levels.[6] Two and a half years after liberation, merely 20 percent of previously Japanese industrial operations were in either full or partial operation.[7] And industrial output in 1948—despite millions of dollars in U.S. aid—was only 14 percent of what it had been in 1938.[8]

These were also the early days of the Cold War, and that mentality greatly influenced the military's administration. They were unprepared for and intolerant of the welter of movements and political parties that were clamoring for power, especially those with leftist or labor orientations. The Americans also attempted to hold off on critical political and economic decisions until a unified Korean government could be formed; inertia and confusion set in, and Korea's ancient tendency toward strident factionalism began to assert itself. In the north, meanwhile, power was being consolidated under Kim Il-Sung, a former anti-Japanese guerrilla who had received training in the Red Army.

In 1947, the United Nations established an elections commission to guide Korea toward self-determination. Denied access to the north, the commission went ahead with preparation in the American zone. Several months later, in 1948, the portion of Korea below the thirty-eighth parallel went to the polls to select an assembly. That body picked as its chairman and then president Syngman Rhee, an experienced leader who had served as premier of a government-in-exile in Shanghai (although he was later impeached by that body). Now seventy-three, Rhee was staunchly anti-Communist, archly conservative, and a skillful politician. Like many of the technocrats who would follow him, he managed to combine a liberal American education (he had a Ph.D. from Princeton) with a career as a ruthless autocrat.

The post–World War II years were especially trying for Korea's industrialists. Despite the predations of the Japanese occupiers and their chaotic retreat, some indigenous businessmen had persevered.

Those individuals—many of them small-time entrepreneurs of relatively low status—would eventually form the nucleus of Korea's economic transformation. But they now had to scramble for raw materials
and markets, negotiate the undirected American administration and,
later, the graft-ridden Rhee regime, and, through it all, avoid the
suspicions of their countrymen. Those who had succeeded during the
Japanese occupation were required to explain their prosperity. Even
the brother of the founder of Kyungbang Limited, one of the acknowledged pioneers of Korea's nationalistic industrial development, was
harassed by his workers. In 1949, he was arrested for pro-Japanese
activities during the occupation, although the charges were eventually
dropped.

In addition to the other traumas afflicting the Korean people, the
division of the nation was a source of profound sorrow, one that
continues to haunt the Korean psyche. The desire for reunification has
not wavered in almost a half century. In 1988, the Korean Political
Science Association found that 88 percent of South Koreans still
looked forward to a time when the two halves of the nation could be
rejoined. A very vocal group of South Koreans—mostly young and in
the minority—fault the United States for the division of Korea. History
may place the responsibility; the point is that the economic and
psychological disequilibrium caused by the division had tragic and
unavoidable consequences.

WAR AND RECONSTRUCTION: 1950–1960

The People's Republic of North Korea, under the leadership of Kim Il-
Sung, attempted a unilateral reunification of the Korean peninsula on
Sunday, June 25, 1950. Troops moved south across the thirty-eighth
parallel and achieved a string of quick victories, wresting control of
Seoul just three days later. The United Nations, acting with astonishing alacrity, came to South Korea's defense. A combined force from
America, Britain, France, and thirteen other nations entered the fray;
they were beaten back to Pusan, then managed to turn the tide—
largely as a result of General MacArthur's dramatic amphibious land-
ing at Inchon—and pushed the aggressors far into the north. Chinese
troops entered the war, drove back the U.N. forces, and recaptured

Seoul. A U.N. counter-offensive reliberated the South's capital and brought the front line back close to the original thirty-eighth parallel. The troops bogged down, but the fighting remained persistent and bloody. Negotiations commenced. After two years of haggling, on July 27, 1953, an armistice was signed, the 2.5-mile-wide demilitarized zone was established, and hostilities—excepting the occasional terrorist act—ceased. No treaty has been concluded, however; technically, Korea remains at war with itself.

The ultimate cost of this futile exercise was staggering: the republic's forces had over 400,000 casualties, while the predominantly American U.N. forces suffered an additional 160,000 (including 54,000 American deaths on and off the battlefield).[9] Most estimates put civilian deaths in the South at over 1 million, with another 1 to 3 million dead in the North. On both sides, millions were displaced; between 2 and 5 million North Koreans fled to the South during the war.

The war also left an already shell-shocked economy in shambles: Seoul, which had changed hands four times in twelve months, was in ruins, with over 80 percent of its industry, public utilities, and transport destroyed.[10] Throughout the country, a third of all housing was lost; 43 percent of manufacturing facilities were ruined or damaged; 41 percent of electrical generating capacity was rendered useless; coal production fell by 90 percent.[11] By one estimate, approximately one-fourth of the republic's wealth was destroyed.[12] In short, the material legacy of the defeated Japanese was utterly squandered. As a final abuse, at the same time that the Korean War was destroying the country's economy, the resources needed to prosecute that war brought on severe inflation; prices for some commodities doubled every six months.[13]

The armistice created an opportunity to rebuild, but decades later one wonders where the Koreans could have found the spiritual capital for such an undertaking. The nation had been occupied, exploited, drained. Its culture and language had been suppressed, its people made ignorant by limits on their education and the grind of sheer poverty. And the few shards of a society that remained after the Japanese occupation and World War II they took from themselves in a bloody and futile civil war.

Furthermore, the Rhee government had become a sad model of authoritarian mismanagement. Politically, it mimicked the Japanese colonial predilection for censorship (including even the Voice of America), repression, and corruption. Economically, Rhee's tenure was marked by shortages, high inflation, and stagnant growth. The economy wound down, and farmers were again reduced to eating grass. Thousands moved into urban areas, especially Seoul, only to find unemployment and an explosion of street crime. Rhee was obsessed with maintaining control over the smallest details of the economy; according to reports, he personally approved every foreign exchange allocation over $500.

Korea's entrepreneurs quickly learned that, in an atmosphere where bribery and corruption were pervasive, they stood to gain more through government favors and other nonproductive manipulations than through the creation and running of competitive businesses. Because success depended so heavily on connections with the regime, these entrepreneurs were branded "political capitalists." In return for generous campaign contributions and kickbacks, they were granted access to hard currency (which meant they could import and monopolize scarce commodities), access to abandoned Japanese property, loans, tax favors, bank credit, and lucrative construction contracts.[14] During this period, the United States was virtually the sole means of support for South Korea, and the primary recipients of its aid were Rhee's cronies. Large corporations—the forerunners of today's chaebol—began to emerge, dominating one industry after another. Indeed, they so unabashedly availed themselves of opportunities that later regimes would demand an accounting of their gains under Rhee's administration.

Meanwhile, for the first time in its history, Korea had to contend with a "liberated" labor force. Under Japanese colonial rule, workers had no right to organize. Now, they loomed as a political and economic force. The government responded by establishing laws that detailed labor rights and established a mechanism for the resolution of disputes. Obviously, these documents could not be based on decades of Korean experience and negotiation; instead, they were empty imitations of similar bodies of law in other countries and, as such, were wildly out of touch with the reality of labor relations in Korea. By most accounts, they were drafted without any expectation that they would be enforced. The primary purpose of these laws was propaganda: they were designed to counter portrayals of North Korea as a workers' paradise.

The upshot was tragic: because existing labor law was recognized to be empty of meaning, it created an institutional void. Even after subsequent amendments, employers and workers shared neither a basic understanding about rights and responsibilities nor a mechanism for working through conflicts. Following the aftermath of the liberalizations of 1987, the lack of such fundamental labor policy has at times been crippling and continues to endanger Korea's economic and social fabric.

The Rhee administration did bring its share of benefits and improvements. While it was dedicated to unrestrained capitalism, it established techniques of economic control—regulating access to hard currency, for example—that were later used to guide the country toward genuine development. Rhee also introduced a rudimentary planning apparatus. Furthermore, by 1960, primary education and adult literacy were virtually universal—an astonishing triumph under the circumstances. Postwar reconstruction was completed, and the economy turned to supplying domestic needs.

But Rhee's most significant feat may have been the creation of an effective and modern military. With substantial U.S. aid and technical support, Korea's army and air force were built up sufficiently to discourage another invasion from the North. Despite being dominated by "refugees and those who came from rural and indigent families," the military began to emerge as a political and economic force, eventually becoming "the most technically and scientifically advanced sector in Korean society." At a time when bullock carts could be seen on the outskirts of Seoul, the military was flying and repairing jet fighters, operating advanced telecommunications equipment, and, by some reports, controlling nuclear artillery. Its officers went overseas in large numbers, where they were conditioned to think in terms of utilitarianism, efficiency, discipline, and esprit de corps.[15] The lower ranks, too, learned from their experiences in the armed forces. For Korea's peasants, military service was the gateway to modern industrial life.[16]

The military's emergence also reflected the lack of leadership in the larger society. With the mass migration after World War II, the Korean War with its own mass migrations, an encompassing program of land reform, and other sweeping changes, Korea's traditional power structures were seriously undermined. As the class structure was similarly crumbling, the military officers, who would have been considered lower-class citizens under a traditional Confucian system, began to acquire status and prestige.

Of course, many of the senior officers participated in the corruption and kickbacks of the Rhee regime, but their juniors remained idealistic if not puritanical, and their inclination to reform grew as the behavior of Korea's older political and military leaders deteriorated. In just a few years, these younger officers evolved as polar opposites of the traditional Korean aristocrat: in place of his conservatism, they were modern; against his bitter factional loyalties, they asserted their sense of a new Korea, finally freed from foreign domination; his love of ritual and abstract learning was countered by their pragmatism and technical proficiency. They also introduced Korea to many of the principles of modern management that—along with lessons from the Japanese occupation—would later guide the nation's industrial growth.

In short, Rhee fostered a military culture that promised stability, modernity, technical improvement, and a means for the poor and ambitious to advance; in return it required dedication, discipline, and sacrifice in the name of one's country and family. Without intending to do so, Rhee turned the soil from which the warrior worker would arise.

Rhee did one other thing to promote the emergence of a new industrial order in Korea; he threw the country into such economic and moral disarray that the military's idealistic young officers had an unequivocal reason to act when the right opportunity pressed itself upon them. Their ascension began in the spring of 1960, when the people of Korea, after twelve years of acquiescence, finally rose up against Rhee. In the face of blatant attempts at ballot rigging in the March elections, protests broke out. Police fired on a demonstration in Masan, leaving 100 protesters dead or injured. Several weeks later, at a similar rally in Seoul, police again fired into the crowd, this time killing 150 demonstrators. The subsequent outcry—and the refusal of troops to shoot any more unarmed protesters—made it clear that the regime had lost its legitimacy. Eight days later, Rhee resigned, bringing to a ragged close the administration of Korea's first elected president. An interim government was installed, but its lack of direction and the continuing street demonstrations only underscored, at least in the minds of junior officers, the gross incompetence of the nation's

civilian leaders and the moral weakness of the military's senior officers. Only they, it seemed, possessed the discipline, the ethical purity,
and the qualifications to run the government. And they were needed:
with the civilian government faltering, anarchy in the streets, and a
murderous, Chinese-backed regime to the north, South Korea's future
was clearly imperiled.

THE MIRACLE REGIME: 1961–1979

Rhee was replaced by the ineffective Chang Myon, who was himself
toppled within nine months in a coup engineered by a group of junior
officers. At the head of this junta was Park Chung-Hee, a forty-three-
year-old major general of rural background, Japanese military training, and questionable personal history—among other things, he had
reportedly taken part in an earlier, abortive Communist coup attempt.
He was also, in the words of one Korean, "a man of great hahn," who
was acutely troubled by his country's suffering at the hands of Japanese
colonials, American administrators, and corrupt civilian leaders. Ultimately, he would become as tyrannical as his predecessor, but he
contrasted with Rhee in important ways. First, the two leaders differed
in goals: Rhee was charged with building a nation out of the ashes of
the occupation and two wars, whereas Park was obsessed with the need
to lift his country out of its desperate poverty.

They also differed in style. Rhee's administration was marked by
corruption, waste, and divisive political intrigues; he was inclined to
achieve his ends through "political parties, youth groups and cronies."[17] Park, in stark contrast, was a man of authority, vision, and
action. He was single-mindedly dedicated to national development, he
was accustomed to modern problem solving through bureaucratic
channels, and he got results. He quickly imposed his military mentality on the populace at large. Corporations were directed and deployed
as though they were so many divisions, while Korea's ragged army of
workers were drilled in the need to sacrifice and follow orders—or
suffer the dire consequences.

Despite his preeminence, Park by no means acted alone. He was
backed by his colleagues in the military, who represented the most
advanced sector of Korea's still-backward society. He had the support

of educated and ambitious young bureaucrats, who had marked time during Rhee's administration, watching with frustration as the Japanese used exports to rebound from their wartime devastation. He had American advisers and, at the outset, American aid.

Most important, he had the tacit support of the people, whose needs and desires he so clearly reflected. He recognized that they had become disgusted with corruption in government, where, in his words, predatory businessmen threw bribes to officials "like a rabbit flung before the starved lion."[18] He was also an experienced military leader who could deal effectively with the threat from the north. But his primary insight was that Koreans desperately wanted an improvement in their economic circumstances, almost without regard for the cost. In 1962, shortly after his rise to power, he stated that it was an "undeniable fact that the people in Asia today fear starvation and poverty more than the oppressive duties thrust upon them by totalitarianism . . . the Asian peoples want to obtain economic equality first and build a more equitable political machinery afterward. . . . The gem without luster called democracy was meaningless to people suffering from starvation and despair."[19] And, finally, he underscored the direct connections between freedom, national security, and economics: "A sound development of democracy and national power . . . over Communists are ultimately dependent on the success or failure of economic construction."[20]

Unlike many other leaders in developing nations, Park was able to support his rhetoric with action. His strategy, put simply in a 1967 campaign slogan, was "construction first and distribution later."[21] In practical terms, this meant achieving rapid economic growth through promoting exports, delaying improvements in the lives of Korea's workers, but continuing to buttress national security. Because Korea was impoverished—without capital, technology, or resources—it was necessary to extract the greatest return from every investment; consequently, Park emphasized manufactured goods over farming, large corporations over their small and medium-sized competition, and certain geographic regions over others. In achieving his ends, he was never hindered by ideological niceties. Instead, he took freely from capitalism and socialism, mixing free-market mechanisms with distinctly authoritarian interventions. The result has been euphemistically labeled "guided capitalism." It is in fact a splendid working model of fascism—both in the technical, economic sense of the word (private ownership of the means of production, with comprehensive social, political, and economic control exercised by a totalitarian government) and as commonly applied (an epithet for hyper-authoritarianism). The point is that from the earliest days of his regime, Park was clearly in charge and willing to use any techniques that would work.

He demonstrated his authoritarian methods early on. Among the military regime's first acts was the Law for Dealing with Illicit Wealth Accumulation, which brought the arrest of ten of Korea's most prominent business leaders and threats that their supposedly ill-gotten assets would be seized by the government. Eventually, the businessmen were ransomed with heavy fines, but the incident established the primacy of the government over industry and Park's willingness to reinforce that relationship with brute force.

Park surrendered to public pressure, resigned from the military, and in 1963 held elections, which he won even though opposition candidates garnered 53 percent of the votes.[22] After that near-catastrophe, Park's economic advances solidified voter support for a landslide victory in 1967. By 1971, however, his popularity had slipped, and his margin of victory (over Kim Dae-Jung) was sufficiently narrow to suggest that he was losing control; in response, he declared martial law and rewrote the constitution. In subsequent years, Park became increasingly autocratic, using imprisonment and torture to quash all opposition. He ruled through a series of emergency decrees, which were vigorously enforced by the military and police. Among the most notorious of these was the Ninth Emergency Decree (in May 1975), which made it a punishable offense to criticize either Park Chung-Hee or his policies, including the Ninth Emergency Decree.

While Park's rule was frequently marked by the nightstick and torture table, less dramatic means of control were also employed. First among these was central planning, which had been introduced to Korea in the early 1950s with limited success. Under Park, however, ambitious five-year development plans became the software that drove the economy. In the first plan (1962–1966), exports were promoted, but the real stress was on improving the balance of payments; during the course of that plan, however, exports began to soar past expectations, and the bureaucrats awoke to their true potential. In the second plan (1967–1971), the use of exports to achieve industrialization was emphasized. In the third plan (1972–1976), the push to export was reiterated and refined. In the past, exports had come from pumping up light industries that had arisen naturally out of domestic demand; now Park turned toward heavy and chemical industries, which, from the outset, were constructed with an eye toward serving international markets.[23]

Implementation of the five-year plans was achieved through a variety of sophisticated techniques. These included the erection of import barriers and, in the mid-1960s, fiscal and monetary reforms. Targets were established for export industries and markets, and government ministries tracked the performance of the overall economy and individual corporations in achieving those targets. By 1966, exporters could count on preferential treatment regarding interest rates and taxes. But one tool stood out among all others: "the government's control of commercial bank credit has been the single most important source both of the government's influence over the private sector and [the] chaebol's capital accumulation," wrote one scholar.[24] By regulating the price and availability of credit, the Park regime was in a position to approve or disapprove new ventures and provide a lifeline in difficult periods. In short, it held a stranglehold on the chaebol.

Of course, this capital did not originate with the government. In the late 1940s and 1950s, Korea relied almost exclusively on American aid. Coincident with Park's ascension, however, the United States began to move from handouts to loans. Park saw no reason to pin his economic security to one source; he threw open the door to loans from a variety of sources, and Korea's indebtedness skyrocketed, tripling between 1965 and 1967. By 1971, it had increased tenfold.[25] But unlike other developing nations, Korea made good use of its borrowed funds. Some undertakings failed, but, in the words of one observer, "At least you can see where the money went." And some money did find its way to well-managed export-oriented industries and the necessary infrastructure to sustain them.

Foreigners were also encouraged to make direct investments in Korea, with incentives that included a five-year holiday from income taxes and promises that profit and principal could be repatriated. This direct investment was modest—most external funds continued to come

as loans—but it is worth noting that the Japanese responded enthusi-
astically. Relations between the two countries were normalized in
1965, and over the next decade Korea's former oppressor became its
most important source for loans and investment capital, as well as its
most significant trading partner. Japanese accounted for 39 percent of
all direct foreign investments between 1967 and 1971; from 1972 to
1976, Japanese activity jumped to 71 percent.[26] In 1973, Japan
accounted for 95 percent of the total direct foreign investment in
Korea.[27]

The reemergence of extensive Japanese influence in Korea, despite
the bitter memories of occupation that remained just two decades after
Japan's ouster, seems quite remarkable. Yet both parties had powerful
motivations. For Japan, especially now that its military was crippled by
the surrender agreement following World War II, Korea remained a
security risk. Japan was also eager to move its most labor-intensive and
polluting industries off of scarce Japanese land. For their part, the
Koreans were in dire need of capital and technology; in addition, as
debt increased, it became preferable to accept direct investment
rather than more loans. In some cases, the Japanese made huge
investments that ran counter to what would be considered normal
economic wisdom. A good example was the Japanese decision, in
1969, to back the massive Pohang Steel Project with over $120 million
in grants, loans, and deferred credit payments, after the project had
been rejected as unworkable by an American and European consortium.[28]

Park's other economic interventions were even more direct; a key
element in his strategy was extensive government investment in public
enterprises. These included electricity and water projects, as might be
expected, as well as mining, construction, and manufacturing. By
1972, this sector constituted over 9 percent of the gross domestic
product, putting it on a par with India and probably ahead of Italy and
the United Kingdom, countries with much more vocal socialist constit-
uencies. These enterprises grew considerably more rapidly than the
overall economy and stimulated growth in other sectors.[29]

All Park's grand designs and their masterful execution by his
bureaucrats would have gone for naught if Korea's workers had resisted
their subordinate and unrewarded role, but they were never given
sufficient leeway to assert their rights or desires. While most aspects of

Park's economic management contained a mix of carrot and stick, the handling of labor was almost all stick. Shortly after taking power, the military regime froze wages, prohibited all labor disputes, dismantled some unions, and arrested unionists.

Genuine labor activity continued but was hampered by the government-controlled trade federation and the flood of impoverished (and therefore exceedingly docile) workers coming in from the country-side. Subsequent laws further undercut labor's position, by prohibiting disputes at foreign companies or in strategically important sectors (in 1968), by limiting collective bargaining (1971), and by emphasizing the role of factory-level or enterprise unions over regional or central-ized union organizations (in 1973 and 1974).[30] Strikes became vir-tually illegal. Although technically they remained a legal possibility, the complicated procedures made "striking by the book" impractical. At the same time, the government failed to enforce labor laws that protected workers' few rights. When strikes did occur, most were caused by an employer breaking provisions in labor law or the union contracts that were negotiated.[31]

The reasons for dealing so harshly with labor were manifold. First, union activity was associated with leftist or Communist ideologies, which ran distinctly counter to the mentality of those who had fought against Kim Il-Sung and his Chinese allies. Second, as Park began to emphasize direct foreign investment over loans, it was especially important to demonstrate a secure labor environment. And last, for Korea's export-oriented industrialization to continue, the nation's la-borers would have to work longer and for less than their competitors in other countries. In short, cheap labor was among the most potent of Park's economic weapons. As an American study noted, "The mainte-nance of strict control over organized labor has undoubtedly been a factor favoring high profits and the reinvestment of earnings. The costs of such a policy have obviously been a serious repression of civil rights and, no doubt, in some cases an exploitation of workers by unscrupu-lous employers."[32]

Park's legal and physical repressions quieted labor; the successes of his regime were sufficient to defuse any other broad-based opposi-tion. Large segments of society were clearly troubled by events, but these worries were muted by the booming economy. And it was boom-ing: during Park's tenure, the Korean economy expanded fivefold.[33]

The average annual increase in manufacturing jumped from 11 percent between 1955 and 1965 to 24 percent between 1965 and 1975. Exports grew (from 1962 to 1976) at a world-beating average annual rate of 42 percent. As a percentage of GNP, exports soared from only 3.3 percent in 1960 to 6 percent (1965) to 38 percent (1975). And the Koreans were not just trading in rice and kimchi: by 1976, 90 percent of all exports were manufactured goods, including electrical machinery, appliances, and footwear.[34]

On the individual level, private consumption tripled.[35] And the benefits were felt by all strata of society. Park's regime achieved "a sustained annual real increase in income of roughly 10 percent both for the country and for the poorest 40 percent of the population."[36] Perhaps most important, Park brought a sense of stability after decades of chaos. Most Koreans were willing to trade individual liberties (which they had, after all, rarely tasted) for a measure of predictability in their political and economic lives.

Korea's industrialists—faced with charges of illegal profiteering and then large fines—had a rocky start under the military regime. But among the results of Park's strategy was a staggering growth in their position and wealth. In some cases, these blessings came out of political favoritism; in most, however, access to credit and the award of lucrative contracts reflected a chaebol's willingness to march to the five-year plans and a record of efficiently using resources.[37] Indeed, the desire to punish profiteering was ultimately squelched when Park recognized that the only force capable of tackling rapid industrialization (in the words of one scholar) "happened to be the target group of leading entrepreneurial talents with their singular advantage of organization, personnel, facilities, and capital resources. They had to be handled with care."[38]

And what loving care they received: between 1965 and 1975, the size and assets of these "inside" chaebol mushroomed. As the plans moved toward heavy and chemical industries, huge investments were needed; these, in turn, called for "centralized policy intervention and preferences on a scale which couldn't be even imagined" when the economy was based on light industry. Big corporations (those with more than 500 employees) increased in size, diversity, and power. They exerted monopolistic control over more markets and contributed a growing percentage of the value-added in the economy.[39]

At the same time, however, the conglomerates began to show that they could exist without relying solely on government benisons. Worried about their growing power, Park took steps in 1975 to limit their growth and force them to go public. But these campaigns were not vigorously pursued, and the chaebol continued to expand. Indeed, after 1975, "it became difficult for newcomers to amass enough financial and human resources to compete with already established chaebol."[40] The chaebol, therefore, were relatively assured of market control.

Because of the intimate relationship between industry and government, the parallel between Korea and Japan is obvious. But most observers agree that whereas there may be a "Japan, Inc.," with bureaucrats and entrepreneurs sharing the decision making, the power balance in Korea is clearly tilted toward the government. Some suggest adapting the corporate analogy thus: "the President chairs a policy board composed of ministers, with businessmen as operationally independent managers or production units." The performance of these managers is critical, "but they are emphatically not members of the board."[41]

This is lively imagery, but when the administration is military in its origins and methods, when the society is obsessed with national security and views economic success as a tool for achieving that security, then the military remains the better metaphor. And increasingly during the Park regime, Korean industry came to be influenced by military thinking. As the economy boomed, the chaebol were in need of bright managers with an understanding of authoritarian efficiency and an appreciation for modern management techniques. Inevitably, they turned to former officers, who wound up overseeing the former soldiers now toiling in the factories. They managed them, quite naturally, with the same effective techniques they had employed in the military.

The Park regime also had its share of vivid nonresults. Despite its initial zeal for reform, it did not profoundly change Korean society and, in fact, eventually fell into its own patterns of graft and corruption. The "elite structure remained pretty much the same as before, with the exception that now a large batch of retired military men suddenly found a channel for upward mobility" into the political, bureaucratic, and economic arenas.[42] In many respects, the military culture fostered by the Park regime constituted a return to the authoritarian and brutally efficient methods first introduced by the Japanese rather than a substantive new departure. But because the movement was homegrown this time, it was better able to work itself into all aspects of political and bureaucratic life and, ultimately, to insinuate itself into the entire society.

In sum, Park Chung-Hee reinvented the warrior worker using many of the repressive and authoritarian methods of the Japanese. But instead of pursuing wartime production, Park sought to make production itself the battlefield. In staging his strategic assaults—first on light industry, then on heavy and chemical industries—he marshaled the human resources of Korea's bureaucrats, industrialists, and laborers. Under the perfect excuse of dire national security, he dispensed with human rights and worries about unfair concentrations of wealth and power. He orchestrated the Korean economy as though it were a vast military exercise and Korea's workers as though they were conscripts. And, in return, he gave them victories and spoils beyond their wildest imagining.

Not all Koreans were willing warriors. Censorship became pervasive, and opponents—including politicians, religious leaders, and students—ran the risk of being arbitrarily imprisoned, viciously tortured, and killed. As the nation's economy continued to expand, workers' expectations rose. They began to join with students and other activists, demonstrating for better wages and the ouster of the government-appointed officials who dominated the labor federation. But it was Park's own men who ultimately brought his downfall. On the night of October 26, 1979, Park was shot to death by the head of the Korean Central Intelligence Agency, Kim Chae-Kyu, during an argument over dinner at the presidential quarters. Kim, who was the architect of extraordinary repression, claimed—apparently without irony—that he was trying to restore Korea to democracy.

THE CHUN YEARS: 1980–1987

In the months following Park's demise, Korea went through a spasm of optimism and political activity. Park's prime minister, Choi Kyu-Hah, assumed control of the government and indicated that he would con-

sider reforming the constitution. At the same time, however, Major
General Chun Doo-Hwan, then head of the powerful Defense Security
Command, began consolidating his position. In December 1979, he
abruptly arrested a number of his superiors in connection with the Park
assassination and quickly became the de facto head of government,
although Choi remained as a civilian figurehead.

As the nation's optimism collapsed, protesters—especially
students—took to the streets. Strikes became rampant: according to
one report, "between January and April 1980 alone as many as 848
strikes actually occurred"; this compares with annual rates of around
100 strikes during the last decade of Park's reign.[43]

The escalating disorder, especially among students, unnerved the
new government, so much so that it dissolved the National Assembly,
banned all political activities, and shut down Korea's colleges and
universities. Opposition leaders, including Park's nemesis Kim Dae-
Jung, were arrested.

Demonstrations occurred throughout Korea, but those in Kim Dae-
Jung's hometown, the southern city of Kwangju, were the most protracted and the most bloody. After ten days of virtual anarchy in May,
during which government troops killed and maimed bystanders and
demonstrators with equal abandon, the death toll was between 200
(according to the government) and 2,000 (according to human rights
watchdogs). And many thousands more were injured.[44]

The massacre at Kwangju only hardened Chun's position. Kim Dae-
Jung was sentenced to death (a sentence later commuted to life imprisonment), and repression remained widespread and brutal. Then,
just a few months later, the general dispensed with appearances and
installed himself as president, following the obligatory rigged election.

During the early days of his rule, Chun's actions appeared to
indicate a liberalization. Martial law was lifted, public debate seemed
more open, and a new constitution was enacted with provisions that—
at first glance—appeared to support workers' rights to unionize,
bargain collectively, and strike. But those freedoms were severely
curtailed by subsequent labor laws that hamstrung the government-
sanctioned Federation of Korean Trade Unions (FKTU), shut down its
regional offices, and limited workers' rights to organize or lead unions.
Only in-house unions were allowed, and then only in enterprises that
had more than thirty workers. This latter provision assured that ap-

proximately 80 percent of all Korean businesses, including the worst factories and sweatshops, were exempted. Finally, third parties—such as international labor organizations, students, religious groups, even the FKTU—were forbidden to participate in negotiations. During this same period, a number of labor leaders were removed from the streets and given a special course in "purification education" by the military; quick learners were graduated in just two weeks, while the slower students took a full half-year to master the material.

The FKTU was never known as a tenacious proponent of workers' interests, but following the 1980 laws it became little more than a lapdog, and membership dropped off sharply. Without a strong voice, workers under Chun were subjected to the worst kinds of abuse by managers. Companies would ignore worker demands or restrict their negotiations to the most malleable factions. They "often bank-rolled general union conventions and bribed delegates" in order to get preferred candidates elected.[45] Any worker who became vocal about his or her disenchantment or who tried to organize fellow workers was likely to be dismissed or, at a minimum, harassed by hired goons or promanagement workers. Griping workers were beaten with pipes, kidnapped, sexually abused. A favorite technique was to hog-tie and blindfold activists, take them on long car rides, threaten them, slap them around, then dump them at the edge of town.

They were also likely to be blacklisted by the Agency for National Security Planning, formerly the Korean Central Intelligence Agency, which would vet workers for companies; computerized lists of workers with a history of political or union activism were (and, in 1990, still were) made available to corporations. Obviously, listed workers would find it difficult to find work under their own names, so they were obliged to falsify work applications, using forged or borrowed papers. Frequently, they were exposed and arrested for their misrepresentations.

The government also took an active role in strikebreaking. In a renowned case involving a plant operated by an American company, the Control Data Corporation, the government stepped in and arrested strikers *after* the company had resolved their complaints. The government also blocked Control Data from rehiring some of the activists, claiming that they were too radical and could not be allowed to mingle with the workers.

The Chun years were marked by a generalized concern that workers might be contaminated by university-bred radicalism. Consequently, all former college students—committed organizers and unemployed liberal arts graduates alike—were banned from taking factory jobs. Of course, economic necessity drove many of these graduates into the factories anyway, where they became so-called disguised workers— men and women who had been forced to lie on their work applications. This set of circumstances gave the corporations the best of all possible worlds: it allowed an upgrading of the work force and it silenced potentially unruly elements, because anyone who was overly vocal would invariably be investigated, discovered to be a university graduate, and punished. Because they had falsified their documents, these workers could count on being fired and were likely to spend time in prison.

Police custody is probably an unlovely experience in most countries of the world, and Korea is no different. But during Chun's administration it was distinguished by the particular brutality bestowed on those who had been caught organizing against the government's labor policies. The lucky detainees were pressed into the army for extended periods of "purification," while the unfortunate were subjected to beatings, rape, electric shocks, cigarette burns, and water torture.

While labor and students were increasingly oppressed, Korea's business groups continued their astonishing growth. Like Park before him, Chun began his regime by getting tough with the chaebol. In the weeks before his installation as president, he took strong actions designed to reduce their excessive debt and, not incidentally, their power. The conglomerates were forced to divest real estate and subsidiaries, limits were put on their credit, and external auditing was enforced. But after an initial period of enforcement, Chun—like Park before him—backed off, and the chaebol enjoyed renewed good fortune, eventually achieving their current world-class size and diversity.

At the same time, the business groups were rehabilitated in the eyes of the public. First of all, the industrialists were generally lauded as effective operatives—if not the prime forces—behind the economy's seemingly unstoppable expansion. Second, and more important for Korea's future, the government began to concede its inability to control every aspect of the economy. Some liberalization of economic controls had already begun in 1979; 1980's terrible performance added further incentive to change. During that year, GNP growth *dropped* by 5.2 percent; simultaneously, inflation shot up to 29 percent, and current account deficits swelled.[46] The government acknowledged that its meddling may have had adverse effects. In particular, one study noted the investment in heavy and chemical industries, "which substituted bureaucratic judgment for market tests, was costly, and left scars on the economy."[47] In the future, the government promised, there would be a greater reliance on market mechanisms. This, of course, was sweet music to the chaebol, whose mammoth size was an extraordinary advantage in normal free-market competition.

Chun (or, more accurately, his bureaucrats) recognized that Korea was entering a third phase of industrialization. It had already tackled the difficult transition from an agricultural economy to one based on labor-intensive manufacturing. Now Korea was shifting to capital- and technology-intensive manufacturing. That meant it was entering the society of mature nations, where dictatorial interventions and heavy-handed protection of markets were less acceptable. But at the same time that he was being pressured to reform and open up Korea's economy, Chun knew that he had to stabilize it after the trauma of the second oil shock.

Like a good general, he moved steadily but cautiously against his targets. "In contrast to the liberalization experiences in South America," noted a World Bank study of Korea's transition, "there is little urgency or drama to this effort. The Government is withdrawing slowly . . . in the policy areas of domestic finance, import barriers, and direct export promotion."[48]

One area from which the government was decidedly *not* withdrawing, however, was the very significant manufacturing input of labor. Here, too, pressure was building from international organizations, but Chun chose to ignore it. After all, cheap labor had been the key weapon in his country's development, and, despite the shift toward capital-intensive industries, it would remain crucial for decades to come. If he needed to provide stability for the economy, what better place to do it than in the control of wages, which would in turn curb inflation and improve the competitiveness of exports. As the World Bank pointed out, "wage control policies, such as mandated reductions in the rate of growth of public sector wages and moral suasion in the case of private sector wage settlements, helped reduce nominal wage growth from about 21% in 1980–81 to an average of 8.5% during 1984–85."[49] In this case, "moral suasion" has a fairly specific meaning: government officials would announce a target increase, which the dependent chaebol would accept. Workers might protest, but, faced with the eventuality of dismissal and arrest, they, too, usually rolled over.

The results of Chun's stewardship were as stunning as those of his predecessor. Aided by external factors—a drop in oil prices, low international interest rates, and economic recovery in Korea's overseas markets—the economy again boomed and developed such momentum that not even the chaos of his departure would derail it. Per capita GNP grew from $1,589 in 1980 to over $2,800 in 1987. The growth in exports was not as stratospheric as under Park, but given that the economy had matured, the increases were equally impressive. And by 1986 they were sufficient to provide Korea with its first-ever positive trade balance. As the economy matured, it became more sophisticated, with investments in semiconductors, aerospace, and biotechnology. Finally, and perhaps most dramatic, Korea under Chun virtually wiped out its net international debt.

Ultimately, though, Chun will be remembered for being more Park than Park. He permitted several periods of relative political liberalization, and the nation began to move toward more economic freedom, but his regime was generally more repressive and corrupt than Park's. (Some Koreans privately refer to Chun as "our Marcos.") Even if his transgressions had been slightly *less* than his predecessor's, he would have measured up poorly against the rising awareness and expectations of the people. Koreans were growing weary of the recurring demands that they sacrifice for national and economic survival, of the lack of civil freedoms, of the increasing wealth of the nation's elite. A booming economy and a climbing standard of living had not brought stuporous satisfaction to Korea's people; rather, they began to raise new demands for noneconomic improvements. A mutiny was brewing in the early months of 1987.

It did not matter that Chun was relinquishing his authority, at least insofar as he was stepping down from office and effecting the first peaceful transfer of power since the republic's birth. What mattered to the people of Korea was Chun's attempt to terminate debate on constitutional reforms and, for all intents and purposes, appoint Roh Tae-Woo as the next president. And it mattered that he failed to rein in his security forces, whose capacity for offhanded violence was shocking even to jaded Koreans. Street demonstrations became especially impassioned following the death of a young student activist under gruesome police torture—an incident that proved a turning point in public sentiment against Chun's leadership.

Those were two keys to the massive protests that broke out in the spring of 1987. Presumably, Chun could have called on the security forces to quash the demonstrations, and, indeed, the streets of Seoul were frequently thick with pepper fog. But various forces conspired to still Chun's hand from further violence. The United States indicated that undue force would be unacceptable. The Korean military was reportedly anxious about propping up so unpopular a president.

And, ironically, Chun was inhibited by the approach of the 1988 Summer Olympics, which had been shaping up as a splashy testimonial to the extraordinary successes achieved under his administration. Chun and his organizers (including Roh, who headed the Olympic committee for several years) had envisioned the games as a gala coming-out party, a chance to draw undivided global attention to Korea's self-made miracle. The world's press would ride in Hyundai taxis, stay at Daewoo's luxurious Hilton Hotel, watch replays on Samsung television sets, call home on Goldstar telephones. They would marvel at the performance of Korea's own athletes, no longer hampered by poverty and disease. (One popular English-language book on Korean culture had surmised that the nation's poor showing in the 1964 Tokyo Olympics was the result of poor coaching and "the physical limitations caused by intestinal parasites.")[50] Around the world, billions of viewers would be exposed to the Korean talent for getting the job done right, on time, within budget. It would be expensive, unnerving, nit-picking work, but it would dispel at last any notion of Korea as an inferior nation, a former colony, a supplicant to others' power and grandeur.

The world did come to Seoul, and, for the most part, it left duly impressed. But for Korea, the most important outcome of the Olympics took place over a year before the opening ceremony, while some of the venues were still under construction. When the glare of pre-Olympic attention first fell on the peninsula, there were the inevitable stories about Korea's brilliant economic successes. But other stories dwelled on the less savory aspects of Chun's administration: the repression and the horrible working conditions that lay behind those successes, the rioting students and the sympathetic workers and middle class, the oft-mentioned threat of North Korean attack. People looked at the up-heaval in the Philippines and fretted that Korea was on the cusp of similar chaos. There were worries about sabotage, commando raids, athletes sprinting through billowing clouds of tear gas. Opposition leader Kim Young-Sam drew parallels between the coming Olympics and the 1936 games in Berlin. And, finally, there were intimations—always vehemently denied—that the games might be canceled.

Nothing could have been less palatable; even the suggestion that the games might not take place was unbearable. It was a point of pride. It threatened to redouble generations of hahn instead of dispelling it. And there was the money, too—billions of dollars invested in organiza-tion and new construction. The games would have to be held, and that is how they came to be the perfect lever against Chun's authority. If he tried to increase repression, the world would turn away, the games would be lost or compromised, and his regime's legitimacy would be irrevocably destroyed. If he loosened his grip, the voice of the people would be heard, and then, too, his regime would crumble.

Amazingly, then, the death of a single student activist and an international sports contest were among the most significant events in Chun's fall from grace. And because of the government's overarching powers, that political demise had repercussions throughout the soci-ety. Above all, it unleashed decades of anger and resentment within Korea's long-suffering army of workers.

7

▲ ▲ ▲

Mutiny

The combat police and their plainclothes counterparts, the grabbers, stand four deep on the cold steps of Samsung's headquarters, near Seoul's old South Gate. The police have donned gas masks, and the screens of their shining, black helmets have been lowered into place. They stand shoulder to shoulder in the evening dusk, their drab green ranks intermittently accented by small red fire extinguishers clipped into jacket pockets; one brand, Firejet, shows a housewife dousing a flaming pan. The grabbers have slipped on shin protectors, making their street pants balloon like jodhpurs.

Twenty-five yards down the block, the vendors are packing up their bananas and leather goods and magnetic shoe inserts and, reluctantly, surrendering the busy sidewalk. Witnesses to the turbulence of the past eighteen months, they are now, in late 1988, too savvy to risk their stock (and their skulls) in what could be a serious riot. Word is out that some 20,000 unionists have already convened at a rally across the river; soon they will be bused to Samsung headquarters, to show support for that group's striking shipbuilders and to protest the company's fiercely antiunion policy. More police are coming now, jogging heavily up the street to positions behind the main building.

The first union bus, when it comes, is filled with singing, waving teenage girls. They are wearing white headbands, but otherwise the scene seems more like a high-school picnic than a massive labor rally. The young men in the next bus seem only slightly graver. Gradually, the numbers swell into the thousands, a mix of young and old; more buses arrive, with buses of combat police behind and alongside them. In the rush-hour traffic, they jockey with trucks, city buses, and passenger cars to drop their loads and find parking.

Despite the show of government force, the protesters are allowed to approach the building, to fill up a street on the south side, to sing songs and chant their slogans. Speeches are rasped out of a bullhorn. Commuters slow their pace and stare, while Samsung's office workers watch from above, drifting from their desks, then returning. Occasionally a window brightens with the flare of a cigarette being lit.

After about forty-five minutes, the sky has turned black and the singing has grown less enthusiastic; the night's cold is settling in. Then, from a terrace on the second floor, someone hangs a fire hose over the edge and sends a frigid spray over the demonstrators. The taunt lasts only a moment, but the chanting now comes with redoubled vigor. A young man suddenly heaves a hammer into a huge, inch-thick plate-glass window; it shivers and cracks but does not shatter. A similar tremor runs through the massed police, but they, too, hold their formation.

The protesters now push the limits even further. In clear view of the police, they build a pile of signs and Samsung appliances—a refrigerator, hot plate, and washing machine—and set them on fire. Thick black smoke billows up, brilliant orange light jumps across the face of the building. With the blaze, the tension ratchets up a notch. All the talk about democratization notwithstanding, everyone knows that the police and the strikers remain at fixed and opposing poles. Animosities are real and armistices tentative. Anything could happen.

This time, nothing does. The fire burns down and the protesters reboard their buses. Ninety minutes after the first youngsters arrived, the street is empty except for the burnt-out metal casings of the appliances, a small pile of burning signs, and a few soldiers warming themselves before it. The oldest—a thin, pockmarked man—points to the flames, smiles, and says "Beautiful" in English.

The five radical unionists on the couch are fussing with their nails or giggling or staring shyly at the floor. Quick to laugh, dressed in jeans and brightly colored jackets, hair cut short and stylish, they do not seem a hard lot. But in their early twenties, these women are already seasoned veterans of two exacting economic campaigns. In the first, the launching of Korean goods into the world marketplace, they are late recruits. In the second campaign, to win basic workers' rights from Korea's employers, they are the shock troops. For their efforts, they have been harassed and threatened and finally fired from their jobs at a small electronics company on the outskirts of Seoul. They have stood up to their male managers in verbal confrontations and in pitched battles; during the worst fracas, one supporter lost an eye. Several of these young women have been roughed up, and they have photographs to prove it.

Here, in the offices of the Federation of Korean Metalworkers' Trade Unions, the president of the union and several of her rank-and-file detail their grievances. They claim that they are obliged to work an average of 120 overtime hours a month, sometimes laboring around the clock, and they are not paid overtime rates for many of those hours. They are forced to attend religious services, which often include a speech by the company president, an ex–police chief who insists that the workers call him Father. Some of these services feature a video-tape of the miraculous feats accomplished by the woman who owns the factory, a faith healer who now lives in Los Angeles. The air on the assembly line is polluted. Television cameras constantly spy on the workers—they claim there is even one in the women's toilet—and they are subjected to body searches when they leave the premises. When they tried to form a union, they were attacked by promanage-ment thugs with the collaboration of a corrupt union official from the district office.

What of all the talk about a new, democratic Korea?

"I've heard all the speeches," the president replies through a translator. "But my own life hasn't felt any democratization. After this long dispute, there isn't any help for us. Even the opposition political party doesn't help." She concedes that the unions and the churches—the traditional centers of labor support—have backed the strikers, but "there has been nothing from outside, from the society in general. People outside are busy and have their own concerns. They can't be bothered with other people's problems."

Are the workers worried? "No. We are fighting for justice, so we have no anxiety. We do have problems. Right now, because we are blacklisted, it would be impossible to get another job. We could move to another region to avoid the blacklist, but we don't want to do that. We'll go back to our factory one day."

The labor expert's office is a few blocks from the National Assembly, on a high floor with a panorama of the boulevards below. Today, in the parking lot next door, the cream-and-green buses of the combat police—ten or twelve of them—are idling next to one another. The police themselves are in front of the Assembly building, forming human barricades on three sides of a small group of protesting workers. The proportions, as usual, are about four police for each demonstrator. Viewed earlier, the rally had seemed a modest and understated affair: a few bullhorns, the typical headbands, the chanting punctuated by clenched fists thrust into the winter air. But now something has changed: the chants are growing louder, the protesters are moving, and other bullhorns, presumably those of the police, are casting strident commands.

In his office the labor expert does not prick up his ears, does not even comment on the noise. Asked who is demonstrating, he describes the circumstances but never rises from his couch. "This is an everyday phenomenon down here," he explains with a smile. "We don't even pay attention anymore."

THE MUTINY OF THE WARRIOR WORKER

Since liberation from the Japanese, Korea's work force had been among the world's most docile; strikes were so rare—about 100 annually—that the Ministry of Labor did not bother to collect data on them.

But Korea's silent workers were by no means content. They were being exploited, they knew, and they had few legal channels for improving their lot. One labor expert had described the situation succinctly: "Businesses simply reject unions. Since our laws are not consistently enforced by the Ministry of Labor, violating them poses no great threat to industry. . . . In other cases, union officials are 'kept.' That is, companies pay their salaries, provide them with automobiles and drivers and there are other perks. . . . This is absurd. Where is the fairness? Naturally, workers don't respect the law of the agreements their representatives negotiate."[1]

Inevitably, workers' frustrations boiled over. In 1985, labor unrest increased sharply. It held steady during the next year, and then, in the last half of 1987, it exploded.

Political events precipitated the explosion. In June, Chun Doo-Hwan declared that his party's nominee (and sure successor, given that the votes would be cast by an electoral college controlled by that party) would be Roh Tae-Woo, a retired army officer who had stood at Chun's side during his violent rise to power. Infuriated by the prospect of another autocratic regime led by another former general, almost a million students and middle-class citizens locked arms in the streets in several weeks of massive demonstrations. To his credit, Roh quickly recognized that he would not be able to lead the nation without submitting to a bona fide ballot. So on June 29, 1987, he announced a platform of reforms that included the direct election of the president and other liberalizations, including increased freedom of the press.

That date marks a watershed in Korean history. The country's political and social climate changed virtually overnight, but nowhere was the change more dramatic than in the conduct of labor relations. In the aftermath of Roh's speech, Korea was swept with an unprecedented wave of strikes—more than 3,600 in a half year, with 2,552 disputes in August alone—affecting 70 percent of all corporations with more than 1,000 employees. During these heady months, Korean workers formed approximately 1,400 new unions, as compared with the 2,600 unions that had existed before the June 29 speech.[2] Union membership jumped by 38 percent over the previous year.[3] Workers demanded, among other things, better pay, more time off, safety equipment, the abolition of sexual and occupational discrimination, the abolition of morning physical exercise, better food at lunch, and more freedom in choosing their clothes and hairstyles.[4]

Roh's call for an open election may have stemmed from a genuine conviction that he stood to capture the majority. Perhaps he assumed that his friends in the military would intervene if the opposition were to mount a serious threat. Or perhaps he was savvy enough to foresee how his opponents would eventually split the electorate, handing him a victory with only 37 percent of the vote. In any case, the campaign that began on June 29, 1987, ended with his presidential inauguration in February 1988; this constituted the first peaceful transfer of power since 1947, when the Republic of Korea was founded.

The election of Roh Tae-Woo did not, however, bring an end to the strikes and demonstrations. During 1988, labor disputes were fewer in number but, on average, nearly twice the duration of those the year before. And in the early months of 1989, unrest was back on the upswing: the Ministry of Labor reported that strikes were up 55 percent over the year before.[5] Furthermore, Korea's long-established union federation, the Federation of Korean Trade Unions, was being challenged by new unions and union federations. As each tried to outdo the other, demands escalated, bargaining positions were held more tenaciously, and the turmoil seemed destined to grow.

A TASTE OF ANARCHY

Roh had already set himself apart from his predecessors by announcing his program of liberalizations. In the early days of his administration, he further distinguished himself by resisting the many temptations to assert his new power in grand and intimidating fashion. Instead, his government's response to the continuing labor unrest was to sit on the sidelines, virtually abdicating its authority in industrial relations. Officials were fearful of being associated with the now-disgraced Chun administration and being branded "antidemocratic," so they refused to enforce laws protecting either workers or management. In the words of one expert, Korea was "in a state of anarchy with respect to labor disputes." With one exception (a railway strike), Roh steered clear of labor problems during the first year of his administration.

But after its years of policing labor-management relations, the government's decision to downplay its role left an enormous void. On one side, unions grew increasingly active and increasingly radical. On the other, corporations felt abandoned by the government, which meant they had both a need for protection and an opportunity to act with impunity. Often, they mustered a "Save-the-Company Corps" or *kusadae*, composed of promanagement workers and, sometimes, hired thugs. Such groups had been a fixture in Korean labor relations for many years, but they became especially important to employers in the wide-open days after June 1987. Their tactics varied from factory to factory: some employed direct force, which is an antiseptic way to describe rock-throwing, pipe-swinging mayhem; some relied on the traditional authority afforded male managers in factories where women workers predominate; and some propagandized workers with speeches and video presentations.[6] But while methods differed, in every case the kusadae had one goal, which was to smash the unions.

Hyundai, one of the most virulently antiunion of all Korean business groups, was involved in several of the ugliest incidents during this period. In May 1988, a labor organizer was kidnapped as he left a meeting with Hyundai company officials at a Seoul restaurant. He surfaced again several days later, after he had agreed to write a letter of resignation to the company. What separates this incident from those that took place before mid-1987 is that the activist was able to take his complaint to the authorities and get results. Several weeks later, the Seoul police pinned the kidnapping on two Hyundai executives, who were then arrested. (Management's negotiation-by-abduction tactic was reciprocated some weeks later, when employees at Hyundai Heavy Industries briefly took the chaebol's founder, Chung Ju-Yung, as a hostage in order to press their demands for higher wages and an independent union.)

Of course, Roh's pointed inaction was only part of the trouble during this chaotic period. Even if the government had exerted its authority in a discreet and evenhanded manner, the resolution of disputes would have been hampered by the lack of negotiating experience. After decades of management's near-absolute dominance, neither labor nor business had learned the most elementary lessons about negotiation and compromise. Business was inclined to stonewall, while some labor leaders were pursuing political agendas rather than improvements in wages or conditions. The mediators who were available were generally inexperienced and distrusted by labor, because they had previously resolved disputes "on the basis of political expediency or otherwise corrupted criteria," rather than on their true merits. [7] And finally, even with the most reasoned actions on the part of labor, management, and government, the hodgepodge of laws and regulations still needed rationalization.

In addition, the old unions were limited in their ability to represent workers, largely because they were so tainted by their collaboration with the Chun regime. (The FKTU was severely compromised; this was especially so after it miscalculated the balance of power and came out in support of Chun in April 1987, just as the people of Korea were dispatching him.)

Even if there had been a fair government, overseeing experienced negotiators dealing with legitimate unions, Korea would have encountered some degree of labor upheaval, simply because acceptable strike behavior or "the rules of the game" (as it was incessantly called) had to be worked out.

For example: One of the most important and vigorously contested ground rules has been the "no work, no pay" principle. As strange as it may sound to Western ears, Korean employers have commonly paid laborers while they strike. "They'd even feed them," noted one American familiar with Korean labor practices. "You'd stand outside a factory and the strikers would be brandishing signs and even clubs. But when the lunch whistle would blow, they'd put down their gear and go eat. Afterwards, they'd go back outside and pick up where they'd left off."

Depending on who is doing the interpretation, the practice of supporting strikers is said to have derived from (1) the employers' realization that strikes were often tied to political rather than industrial or personal issues; (2) a genuine paternalism (which recognizes that underpaid workers need minimal support during a strike); or (3) the understanding that cutting off a poor man's wages would quickly turn a political strike into a personal matter. During the upheavals of 1987, however, several chaebol could not resist observing that strikers had little financial incentive to settle their grievances and return to work. Accordingly, these employers attempted to enforce a "no work, no pay" rule—to the rather predictable furor of the unions and their supporters.

Eventually, the "no work, no pay" rule will probably become standard, but this dispute about disputing, like many others in Korea's evolving labor-management environment, may take years to be resolved.

Of course, Korea's brief period of anarchy played nicely into the hands of hard-line antiunionists in business and government. Roh Tae-Woo probably had no choice but to back off somewhat and let Korea's workers assert their power. But by thoroughly removing government participation, he gave the middle class a very unsavory taste of unbridled labor activity. Eventually, both business *and* the unions were calling for government intervention as a face-saving way to break deadlocked negotiations. Meanwhile, the costs of the mutiny—in reduced production, services, exports, and overall stability—were keenly tracked and reported.

All of this set the stage for a massive and irrefutable reassertion of government authority. Intimations of that reassertion came at the end of 1988, when Roh announced that illegal strikes would no longer be tolerated. But the government waited until the last days of March 1989 to return with full force, deploying 14,000 combat police in a predawn assault by land, sea, and air against strikers at the Hyundai Heavy Industries shipyard in Ulsan. The pitched battle across the yard and into company dormitories, the rolling clouds of tear gas mixed with the smoke of firebombs, the eventual arrest of 700 strikers—all announced that the government would henceforth, again, be exercising its control over Korea's most valued resource.[8]

THE MORNING AFTER

Assessing the impact of Korea's labor mutiny is impractical at this writing, simply because it has yet to run its course. However placid the surface of events may appear, too many conflicts remain unresolved, too many aspirations unrealized. Yet certain observations can hardly be avoided.

At first glance, one is struck with the conviction that a sea change has occurred in Korea's labor relations. Strikes have run into the thousands, new labor leaders have risen up to challenge the corrupted old guard, common men and women have risked their livelihoods and the sanction of their co-workers to claim their rights. Wages have been increased and a modicum of dignity restored. On reflection, however, the actual gains seem illusory. Broad institutional transformations have yet to be manifest, and those changes that have taken place do not seriously undermine the power of government and the chaebol. Meanwhile, the very real costs of labor's upheaval—in lost wages, services, and economic expansion—have been documented and advertised, to discourage similar action in the future.

The first good reason for skepticism about this supposed sea change is that the raw number of work stoppages is somewhat misleading. Many of these actions were spontaneous, wildcat strikes grounded more in passion than in common goals and resolve. New unions were often formed in the heat of the moment and lacked the strength and experience to hold together against entrenched management and the leadership of existing FKTU-aligned unions. Consequently, many faltered soon after their founding.

In addition, support among workers may not be as broad as the raw numbers seem to indicate. Although 1987 and 1988 brought a phenomenal surge in the frequency of strikes, fully three-quarters of those strikes involved sit-ins. Because the government declined to intervene, companies that did not physically eject workers with kusadae were forced to cease production. As a result, one study claimed, "it was possible for a handful of disgruntled workers to totally disrupt operations. . . . Consequently, several thousands of workers were caught up in Korea's strike activities even though in the vast majority of struck facilities fewer than 6% of the employees were so-called active strikers."[9]

Furthermore, the chaebol bore the brunt of these strikes. Nearly 70 percent of all large companies (more than 1,000 employees) were struck, despite the fact that their wages and working conditions were much superior to those of smaller corporations. In contrast, only 0.58 percent of Korea's small companies (fewer than 50 employees) experienced labor unrest.[10] And the vast majority of small and medium-sized companies still have no unions. In other words, the companies that employ the bulk of the Korean work force (and are expected to employ an even larger percentage in the future) were not directly touched by labor activity.

The overall significance of the strikes may also have been misconstrued. In the West, a massive outpouring of labor discontent would indicate a demand for economic restructuring. In Korea, strikes have frequently indicated demands for *political* restructuring. They tend to occur during periods of political turmoil: in 1960 during Rhee's demise, again in 1979–1980 during the transition from Park to Chun, and then in 1987–1988, during Chun's fall and the mayhem thereafter. And while economic demands were made and often accommodated during all three periods, political demands figured heavily. Speaking in late 1988, Park Fun-Koo, vice president of the government-funded Korea Labor Institute, noted that workers "are concerned about many issues, about half of which aren't under the control of the factory manager. They are upset about the concentration of wealth, about housing and income distribution." They were, in short, generally fed up with their circumstances.

After 1960 and 1980, the return of political stability brought stability in labor relations. This phenomenon can be interpreted variously. Some find it a confirmation that strikes are simply a Korean method for expressing political sentiment—"emotional outbursts," in the words of an experienced observer. One could also argue that a return to political stability means that a new dictator has established a firm grip on the security forces and can use them to *enforce* a calm in labor relations. In any case, something similar has happened since the first, hectic days of liberalization in 1987: strikes have continued and their duration is longer, but there are fewer of them. There have been dramatic incidents (such as labor protests at Hyundai Heavy Industries in 1989 and 1990), but demands have generally been contained to individual work sites. Crackdowns in 1989 and 1990 showed that the government is still willing and able to use its powers—legal and otherwise—to contain labor activism. The upshot is clear: in the absence of genuine reform, the balance of economic power has remained with the government and business groups.

Unfortunately, such reform does not appear to be forthcoming. Although the turmoil of 1987 and 1988 has brought legislative and regulatory changes, these do not seem to have truly recast the Korean labor system. The minimum wage, for example, finally materialized, several years after it was promised. In the words of a Western labor organizer, though, it "is a joke, because at the outset it only covered 10 percent of the work force and it was set at a ridiculously low level." Regular raises and coverage expansions are making the law more meaningful, but it is far from curing poverty among Korea's production workers.

Labor laws were also amended to allow workers more freedom in forming regional unions, in unionizing shops with fewer than thirty workers, and in calling strikes; furthermore, the government's authority was diminished in that it could no longer require binding arbitration or the dissolution of a union. But while these are substantial additions—particularly those that allow the formation of regional trade unions instead of enterprise-based groups—they will not effect a transformation until union leadership is transformed.

An act prohibiting sex discrimination was also passed, but enforcement was expected to be less than vigorous. This is a safe bet, because Korea's most promising, high-tech, relatively nonpolluting, value-adding industries—electronics is the obvious example—rely extensively on the labors of women in the years between school and child rearing. These industries are currently thriving precisely because they pay women a fraction of what their male counterparts make; to pay them equally would erode much of the manufacturers' cost advantage. Consequently, the ban on sex discrimination will be enforced selectively (if at all), with likely targets being flagrant violators in less desirable industries. Present sex inequalities are sure to persist unless, as one observer noted, "the companies can find a way to cut the men's wages in half."

In short, recent changes in Korea's labor laws have been mostly piecemeal or unenforceable. Meanwhile, three years after Roh's famous liberalization speech, some of Korea's most constraining labor laws—like the restriction on third-party intervention in disputes—were still on the books. If there has been an improvement in the lives of Korean workers, it is probably the result of more aggressive enforcement of existing laws. Workers are now guaranteed, for example, that they will be paid for the hours they have worked, and they are relatively sure to be paid overtime rates for overtime hours.

In any case, true reform must go beyond simple lawmaking. "We need institutional changes," Sogang University's Park Young-Ki explained, "especially a reduction of control in the executive branch, coupled with independent judges and legislators." But before improvements can take place in the judiciary, for example, capable individuals will need to be trained—a process that will take years.

What was gained in the mutiny, then, was limited. Between 1986 and 1989, wages have soared by 60 percent in won terms (and 90 percent in dollar terms), but food and housing costs have also sky-rocketed.[11] If the forty-four hour standard workweek is phased in, as scheduled, in 1990 and 1991, it will mean an increase in overtime and therefore income, but employers will be able to adjust bonuses to compensate for this added labor cost. New unions were formed, but they appear to spend as much time fighting against the FKTU as they do against unscrupulous employers. Furthermore, as these unions compete for membership, they pressure each other into increasing and destructive radicalism. Over the long term, these extreme positions will only undermine labor's support and make government intervention more palatable to the larger population.

At the same time, the costs of labor unrest have been severe. According to one study, the 1987 strikes caused a loss of over 8.2 million working days, with an additional 3.4 million in the first ten months of 1988.[12] In 1988, the loss of production was calculated to be $3 billion; lost exports were set at $.7 billion. In the first ten months of 1989, lost production was estimated to be $5.5 billion; lost exports were $1.15 billion.[13] Both the Daewoo and Hyundai motor companies fell far short of their production targets during periods of labor unrest. Hyundai Heavy Industries claimed that it lost $6 million in sales *daily* during its extended strike in 1989.[14] Thousands of other company problems—among chaebol and small and medium-sized enterprises—were also documented in the Korean press. While it is difficult to draw direct parallels between individual strikes and overall economic performance, Korea's citizens were well aware that persistent labor unrest had been costly to their economic well-being and security. The backing of the common man and women, so crucial during the ground-breaking labor actions of 1987 and 1988, wavered in the years that followed.

A CHANGE OF HEART

In the aftermath of profound political and economic disturbances, the inclination is to calculate the shifts in power: one group is stronger, another freer to act, another retreats, bides its time, rebuilds. In

Korea's case, these computations are intricate but revelatory; they help one understand what happened and serve as useful predictors of future activity. But the most significant postmutiny variable has nothing to do with power per se; it has to do with Korean workers' hearts and minds. Have they been changed by what they have seen and done? If so, how? And, most important, will they continue to work as hard, as long, as cheaply, and as well?

Again, it is too soon to look for answers. Nevertheless, certain observations can be made, and these help to define the range of the possible.

First, consider the ideal outcome of Korea's labor unrest. In the best of circumstances, the difficult standoffs between labor and management would breed mutual respect. After months of negotiation and compromise, each side would come to appreciate the other, would—in a startling epiphany—realize that neither can exist without the other, that a true partnership is in the best interest of all. Workers would negotiate in good faith, accept as binding the provisions of their contracts, and strive to improve productivity. Management would recognize that autocratic control cannot be sustained in a modern society; it would acknowledge the value of a work force organized under a leadership that is stable, legitimate, informed, and circumspect in its agenda. Large and small businesses would seek to distribute economic benefits equitably and improve often shameful working conditions. Responsibility and cooperation would reign.

This is a theoretical possibility; so is reincarnation. In both cases, the transformation is thorough and unlikely and, in any case, will take a lifetime to occur. Korea has a long tradition of stern and autocratic management; that tradition will not be softened or replaced by months of name-calling and hand-to-hand combat. After years of locking horns with organized labor, Korea's flagship business group, Samsung, remains at least as intent on keeping independent unions out of its affiliated companies.

This best of all possible outcomes, then, will probably not obtain. What about the worst outcome? Has the mutiny infected Korea's workers with complacency and disrespect for authority, making them lazy, ill-disciplined, unfit to work?

Some labor experts claim to have seen indications that laborers are, at a minimum, less enthralled by their superiors. "Following the recent liberalizations, workers are definitely less disciplined," explained the Korea Labor Institute's Park Fun-Koo. "We know that absenteeism is way up. At one of the big companies, it's becoming a major problem just to get workers to come to work on time and leave on time. Compared to [the years before June 1987], we can all see the difference. It used to be the voice of the supervisor that controlled everything. Now we say that his voice doesn't carry like it used to. People don't respond."

Yet a psychology built on several thousand years of history is unlikely to be overturned by the events of a single season. Korean workers have clearly not "gone soft." They remain interested in working long hours, especially now that they can expect to be paid at overtime rates. As noted in Chapter 2, a 1988 FKTU survey found that women workers' greatest desire was for better treatment, not fewer hours or more pay. The nation clings to a sense of equilibrium, an understanding of how far to press. Order is still valued, authority is still understood and respected. Ironically, the disposition toward regimentation and authoritarianism can be seen, very much intact, in the operations of the radical student organizations and the new unions. While these groups have pressed their demands for democratization, they have operated along very traditional autocratic lines. In part, this simply reflects the culture; in part, it denotes a lack of experience. "In the unions," a Korean labor expert complained, "the democratic processes haven't been learned. Even the idea of majority rule isn't universally understood or observed."

Furthermore, before Korean workers can become truly complacent, they will need to believe deeply that they are secure. That will require an end to the threat from the North and an economy that expands so regularly for so long that growth becomes a given.

None of that will happen soon. North Korea will remain a genuine and unpredictable danger for the foreseeable future. And even if that nation's insanity stays in remission, the South faces fearsome economic perils. Another oil shock or a recession in the United States, to pick two easy examples, could send its economy reeling. Ironically, labor's assertion of power and independence has shown that Korea's sole resource is now unreliable and its economy vulnerable; that, in turn, gives workers cause to worry about their security and more incentive not to disrupt the economy.

And no economy—not even Korea's—is ever guaranteed success. "Nothing is sure," noted Park Fun-Koo. "Things can fall apart. In Korea, we like to say, 'Don't get too loose, keep everything tight, remember Argentina and Chile.' They were very developed countries before World War II. They had the upper hand and now they've lost it."

Assume that the Republic of Korea will somehow co-opt the North, peacefully seducing it with promises of prosperity and VCRs. Assume also that its economy will become less vulnerable to outside resources and markets. Even then, Korean workers would not feel truly secure. They would still need to shake off their hahn, that sense of anger, frustration, and inferiority instilled by millennia of domination and general bad fortune. That too could happen, but not in one lifetime, maybe not in two.

For these reasons, Korea's labor demonstrations can be highly dramatic—because there is the real sense that the natural Korean order is being strained, that a deep-seated sense of authority and discipline is being temporarily abrogated, that anything could happen. When average Koreans discuss these events with an outsider, they do so awkwardly, as if shamed by them: this is a failure, they seem to say, an embarrassment in the family. Please do not look too closely, because this is not our better selves.

So after all the considerations, the surest observation about this workers' mutiny is the most obvious: yes, there have been shifts in the power structure, and, yes, the people have grabbed certain freedoms that they will not lightly surrender. Yes, attitudes have changed. But the changes have been limited, and what remains—a potent military, a sense of foreboding and insecurity, a respect for authority, and a craving for harmony—is probably definitive.

Before this century, the die of history and tradition seemed to be shaping Korea's people to a specific thread, at a specific angle, with a singular purpose in mind: to create an educated, hungry, dedicated, docile work force. The Japanese, with their exploitive designs and autocratic colonial methods, locked onto that potential with startling precision, as though they, too, had been engineered for the job. Together, they started Korea's transformation.

Until recently, Korea's postwar industrialization was a continuation of, not a retreat from, the principles established during the Japanese colonial period. A similar militaristic, state-controlled capitalism operated; a similar combination of forces—economic incentives (for the owners) and physical repression (against the workers)—stood behind the bureaucrats; the same absence of individual liberties and democratic involvement prevailed. With no alternatives open to them, Korea's first industrial workers acquiesced in their fate; if anything, they became even more docile after the profound terror and physical deprivations of the civil war. They felt that their salvation and that of their children and their nation would come from economic success, and they brought to that goal their wartime discipline and willingness to sacrifice. They have demanded, of late, a greater return for their sacrifices, but their dedication and economic patriotism are undiminished.

But cultural and historic factors only partly explain Korea's brilliant triumphs. If the base metals of poverty and war and repression were sufficient to produce economic gold, the world would be rich beyond measure. In addition to those powerful motivations, Korea's work force has been orchestrated by a management style that combines a dissonant mix of ancient patterns and modern methods, of paternalism and brutal indifference.

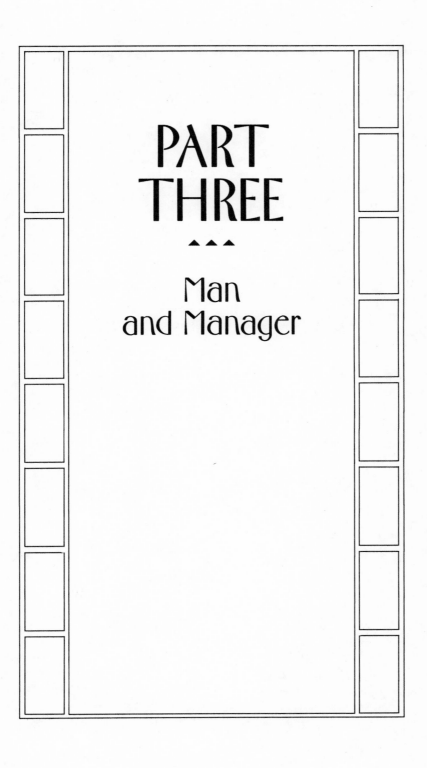

PART
THREE

▲▲▲

Man
and Manager

8
▲ ▲ ▲

The Korean Way of Working: My Boss, My Father

"We have a propaganda," said the guide with unintended accuracy, "of this being the steelworks in the garden."

Pohang Iron and Steel Company (POSCO, for short) built this huge harbor/storage area/blast furnace/steel mill complex from the ground up in the early 1970s, transforming a subsistence-level fishing village into a world-class steel producer in a matter of years. Inside the buildings, there are the inescapable scalding heat and noise and raw power of making steel, but outside, the grounds are landscaped with flowers and trees. Even the slag heaps, steaming in the cold, seem beautiful.

The Pohang steelworks, while less automated than the company's newer works in Kwangyang, is nevertheless a monument to orderly procedure. Ships are unloaded automatically, with ore and coal transported along the complex's miles of conveyor belts. Here, the coal is dropped into a symmetrical mound; there, the scrap metal is stacked in neat piles. Along the roads, singly and in small groups, uniformed workers clean the grounds.

The same sense of crisp organization radiates out to the community—to the bachelor quarters, the rows of worker apartments in the Hyo Ja Housing Complex, the schools, the parks, the shopping center and performing arts center, which are all provided by POSCO. "This is part of the company tradition," a company information officer had explained back in Seoul. "Pohang was a village when this started. It couldn't accommodate a large work force, so the company had to provide facilities. Management also realized that steelmaking is difficult work, and workers would need comfortable housing so they could get their rest. And it would be necessary to provide housing and schools to take care of their families, because good workers would not leave their families behind."

POSCO looks after its 22,000 employees, orchestrating their lives to their benefit and that of Korea. Wages are above average; medical care is provided; and college tuition is awarded to the bright sons and daughters of production and white-collar workers alike. "The paternalism is quite absolute," the information officer had explained. "The company supports, advises, and supervises. Workers are well taken care of."

The small electronics assembler is located south of the Han River in an area called the Kuro industrial district or the Kuro industrial estate. No one ever calls it the Kuro industrial park for obvious reasons: the walls around the factories are high, capped with broken glass, usually guarded. Along the narrow streets, the smell of solvents sometimes throws itself across the sidewalk like a cordon; beside one plant where the smell is particularly noxious, a clear, viscous fluid flows out a cracked drain down a spillway into the sewer.

It is 3:00 P.M. on the day after the shortest day of the year. The sky is cloudy, and, in the murky light, the factory ahead looks like it belongs in Beirut. Strikers have shattered the windows in buildings on both sides of the gate. The gate itself is wrapped top to bottom in a skein of barbed wire. Yellow-and-black barricades wait just inside the compound, 5 feet from a sign that says "showroom" in English.

The main office is long, filled with desks, overly warm from several kerosene space heaters. At the far end, center, where a teacher would sit if this were a classroom, the general manager stands. A short man in his late fifties, he smiles readily and shakes hands; his hair is thick, combed straight back, and very black. He leads the way to a smaller office. Here, bright, empty cartons printed in English, Spanish, Italian, Japanese, and Arabic proclaim that this is an OEM supplier with clients around the globe.

The general manager answers questions quickly and confidently. He explains—inaccurately, as it turns out—that the strike is now over. The problem, clearly, is that young Koreans don't want to work. "Before, they wanted to make a lot of money," he says. "Now they don't care. It's the U.S. and Japanese influence."

Although he does not say so, it is clear that he finds the workers ungrateful. The company has provided them with dormitories, but most of the workers have chosen to live outside the factory in rented rooms. It gives the workers food in a company cafeteria. It has built a company chapel for prayer services. Most of all, it has given them jobs.

Inside the three-story, red-brick assembly building, maroon-jacketed girls and blue-jacketed boys work side by side. The line is well lit and small. (It is, in fact, smaller than usual, running at about half strength because of the supposedly concluded strike.) The room is warm but stuffy; even though the teenagers wiring these car stereos have small ventilation hoods set directly over their work spaces, the acrid smell of lead soldering still creeps up into the room. Earlier, one of the strikers had explained that the fumes had given her headaches, breathing problems, and nausea.

A week later, over the phone, the general manager confirmed an additional detail about the factory's working conditions. The strikers had claimed that he sometimes demanded that they work all day Saturday, through Saturday night—an around-the-clock shift—then go back on the lines Sunday afternoon. Again, his answer was quick and assured. "Yes," he said, "sometimes. Of course. We are a small company. If we need to fill orders for our overseas customers, we will work the hours we must."

The first subway stop south of the Han River, Tangsan station stands elevated in the night, throwing faint illumination over the small restaurants and shops below. In the distance, dark rows of apartment houses rise up, and farther, just across the channel to Yoido Island, lights shine on the National Assembly building. The winter wind is bitter, even behind the station's glass walls.

Directly below, a metal shop is in full production, with three workers fabricating door and window frames out of lengths of anodized steel. A few bare light bulbs burn coldly over their heads; sparks fly in the dark as metal is cut. This is all visible from above because these men are working out-of-doors, their only shelter a tarp thrown over a frame in one corner of the yard. One man stops to warm his hands over a chopped-down oil drum where a wood fire is burning. It is five minutes shy of 10:00 P.M.

A STEW OF MANAGEMENT METHODS

Koreans live in a phenomenally homogeneous society, but they have little trouble mixing heterogeneous elements in their management practices. In the process, they have evolved a style that has mingled Japanese and American influences yet remains thoroughly their own. Before detailing the clearly successful methods of Korean corporations, however, a few caveats are in order.

First, some observers might be inclined to dismiss the following discussion out of hand, claiming that the simple brute force of Korean corporations cannot intelligently be called a management style, any more than the incentives and disincentives employed in the Gulag could be called a management style. This obviously overstates the case, but the point is taken: as noted in chapter 3, the severe repression of labor in past years has made management science largely a theoretical discipline at Korean universities. Nevertheless, the chaebol in particular do have distinctive ways of organizing and motivating their employees.

Second, much of the discussion in the coming chapters will pertain to the chaebol, because they are the most successful Korean businesses and the most likely to have some applicability to Western corporations. But the organization, working conditions, and wages of chaebol workers are hardly representative of the spectrum of Korean companies. The small and medium-sized operations that make up the nonchaebol private sector have their own methods, but reliable information about them is scarce.

Finally, again, nothing about Korean industry is fixed: management style, like labor practices and government strategies, is in tremendous flux. This is perhaps especially true of management technique, because the work force is changing radically. Older Koreans, with their recollections of Japanese rule and the Korean War, are moving out of their productive years; their heirs are more likely to perceive the world through Western, particularly American, values. Motivating them requires new methods.

With that understood, the easiest way to grasp Korean management style is to recall that the country was industrialized by Japan, when that nation was a militaristic colonial power. The Japanese taught their subjects how to work a twelve-hour day under abominable conditions for abominable wages. Thus indoctrinated, Koreans continued to follow—or were forced to follow—similar work patterns. After their ouster, the Japanese remained a potent influence on the young republic. Many of Korea's early industrialists were either educated at Japanese schools or visited Japan regularly, returning to the peninsula with new technologies, product ideas, and management techniques.

A superficial glance at Korean industry reveals innumerable parallels with Japan—the open layout of most offices, the emphasis on exporting, the reliance on joint ventures to acquire foreign technology, the strategy of offering low-end, low-cost products, then gradually moving up in quality and cost. Indeed, it is said that the Japanese have become almost fanatical in their efforts to keep Koreans away from their factories. While Americans or Europeans might pick up hints about new Japanese methods, only rarely will these insights translate into Western plants; if Koreans make similar observations, they can be applied easily and almost overnight.

In part, Korean management has followed the Japanese model because of historic ties between the two countries; in part, Korea (like America) envies and appreciates the success wrought by the techniques used in modern Japan; in part, Korean industry is still too young to have developed its own traditions. But it would be a mistake to characterize Korean managers as Japanese clones or wannabes. In fact, they have an amalgamated approach, based on indigenous values, lessons from Japan, lessons from the American military and business, and lessons garnered while scouring the world for customers, products, and resources. As exporters for almost three decades, they have been exposed to innovations in production, quality control, and management techniques around the world. And it is clear that Koreans, once exposed, have little trouble discerning the advantages and disadvantages—and rapidly assimilating the former.

BUSINESS PHILOSOPHIES

Although it is perhaps not their most significant characteristic, any discussion of Korean management style should begin by mentioning the philosophies that each corporation promotes. With a few exceptions, workers in the West tend to be fairly cynical about corporate philosophies, seeing them as little more than empty slogans manufactured to foster good public relations—the jingle beneath the logo. In Korea, however, the corporate philosophy comes closer to being a genuine guide for managers and workers. The chaebol proclaim their principles over corporate public-address systems, in huge signs around the factories, in full-page newspaper ads; smaller companies, with smaller budgets, settle for plaques over the managers' desks.

This tendency to declare corporate ideals stems from a desire to build and reinforce group consciousness in the work force—and put it to good use. One Korean business consultant offers the following advice to foreign corporations coming to Korea: "Try to develop a culture of belonging where there is sharing of a common value and commitment. For this, a firm leadership is necessary, and a company slogan or motto under which every staff member can unite. It is desirable to have regular and intense training or 'brain-washing' sessions for the whole company."[1]

In general, Korean corporations decline to be overly specific in their philosophies, stressing benign intangibles instead. Lucky-Goldstar, for example, emphasizes *inwha*, which can be translated as "harmony among people," a message so pleasant and vague that it seems designed to incite skepticism. At Korean Air (part of the Hanjin group), the intangible is "a progressive spirit." According to a public-relations manager, "The prevailing atmosphere around the group is that a business, especially a transportation business, becomes obsolete if it fails to move. So we are asked to move ahead and not to look back. That's what our progressive spirit means." Hanjin also stresses "patriotism and servicemanship."[2]

The first page of a Daewoo fact sheet is labeled "Daewoo Spirit," followed by three words: "Creativity, Challenge, Sacrifice." The corporate philosophy is developed at greater length in the "Daewoo Family Song," which includes the following verses:

> Six continents and five oceans where the sun and moon rise over the great cosmos; there are our work places.

> We are in one family, the Daewoo Family. Let's move toward the entire world which is our work place.

> Firm will and honest mind which are the sources of establishing the bright accomplishments; they are our resources.

At Hyundai, a young assistant manager explains, the motto is "diligence, frugality, and harmony among employees," although corporate literature refers to the somewhat broader "Hyundai Spirits," which ignore harmony but add perseverance, "positive thinking," and a "creative and pioneering spirit." Samsung summarizes its group philosophy in three phrases: "Serving the country through business, putting human above material resources, efficient management."[3]

While these explicitly stated philosophies are clearly significant, there are also underlying, unstated corporate principles that are perhaps more definitive. For example, because they tend to suspend caution and leap into new projects or even industries, many Korean business philosophies could accurately place "daring" or "audacity" alongside frugality and diligence. Korean corporations are renowned for taking big, if not excessive, risks, a tendency that can be traced to the nation's quick development and its long-term instability: "We haven't had time to gain the experience," the reasoning goes, "and if we wait for experience, or for planning or market research, we'll lose the opportunity. Anyway, everything will be different next month." In short, damn the torpedoes.

Korea's corporate folklore is rife with stories of successful risk taking. While Daewoo's founder, Kim Woo-Choong, was en route to England to visit his fiancée, he stopped off in an Asian city to collect textile samples; at the next stopover, he met with customers and got orders to produce the textiles at a rock-bottom price. After writing the young woman that he was detained by business, Kim flew back to Seoul and began searching for the manufacturing capability to fill his orders. Hyundai's Chung Ju-Yung has moved with similar panache; he threw the resources of his group into shipbuilding, even to the point of taking orders for ships, without a shipyard or any experience in the industry. Chung was apparently motivated by an opportunity for new growth and his conviction that "the capabilities required to build ships were quite similar to those required to effect construction projects."[4]

More recently, Samsung entered the microwave oven industry with too few engineers, only a little experience in home appliances and none in the technologies needed to make the ovens, after the United States and Japan had already staked out solid market positions. Undeterred, the chaebol sent out a sales force while still working on prototypes, built a crude production line before the salesmen had orders, then took a large order from J. C. Penney without adequate production capacity to fill it—leaving themselves with the daunting prospect of turning "a still primitive assembly room into an efficient factory almost overnight."[5] Of course, this inclination toward action (as opposed to the formation of task forces and study groups) is easier to accommodate in Korea's highly centralized, tightly held corporations, where one man will often have the power to set the course for a massive business group.

Public projects, too, seem to follow this headlong approach. A good case in point is the construction of Seoul's subway system, which was undertaken in a single, grand coup: four lines were simultaneously carved into the city, even though everyone recognized that this approach would reduce the already congested streets to a state of vehicular entropy.

CORPORATE PATERNALISM

Perhaps the most dominant principle guiding Korean management— sometimes stated, sometimes not—in large and small companies alike, has been familism, both literally (because ownership and upper management are frequently passed on from father to son) and figu-

ratively, in that employers oversee and control employees' lives like
attentive parents. This latter quality, also called corporate paternalism
or even corporate welfarism, can blanket every aspect of a worker's
life. Blue-collar workers might receive low-cost dorm rooms (or, if they
are married, apartments), meals, and free medical care. Managers
might also be given meals and homes, as well as cars, various family
allowances, and college scholarships for their children. At the Hyundai Motor Company in Ulsan, 45 percent of the workers live in a
company village that includes a library, public bath, barbershop,
athletic fields, playgrounds—even a billiard hall. The company also
built condominiums, which it sold to the employees at cost, and
maintains dorms at popular beaches, which it rents to employees for a
nominal fee.[6]

But this paternalism can go beyond simple benefits and per-
quisites. At smaller companies some managers will make a special
effort to look after their workers, especially the young women, by
watching their health, diet, family problems, and future plans, especially with respect to education.[7] If a young woman who usually sends
money home decides to take her full wages, management may ask
why.[8] Supervisors will often visit an employee's home when there is
illness or a death in the family or to celebrate a child's "one-hundredth
day" after birth; they will also attend and occasionally officiate at
employees' weddings.

The sense that they are part of a corporate family is important to
workers, for a simple reason. According to a public-relations manager
at Lucky-Goldstar, "Korean workers select a company, first of all, on
the basis of office atmosphere. Money comes second. Because we
spend so much time in the office, we see our fellow workers more than
we see our real families. So the office must be like a family, too."

Koreans have attempted to graft some of this family feeling—if not
outright paternalism—onto their American operations. Managers will
attend office parties, visit sick employees (or even their employees'
family members), and make a sincere effort to know their workers
personally. At Samsung's color television plant in New Jersey, management celebrates Thanksgiving by giving its employees a buffet lunch.[9]

There are three historic bases for this deeply rooted paternalism.
First, Korean Confucianism stresses family values and articulates
relationships in family terms. Employers think of themselves as "fa-

thers" because they head the organization and are therefore responsible to look after their subordinates.

Another basis for Korea's paternalism can be found in Japan. Because of that nation's abrupt transformation from a rural to an industrial economy, there were no large cities filled with workers looking for employment in the factories. This lack forced owners to send recruiters into the villages to find young men and women who could be put to work making textiles and other industrial goods. Parents were naturally reluctant to release their children into the charge of strangers, even though the money was doubtlessly tempting. Employers were pushed to create the kind of environment that would assuage parental concerns, including the provision of living quarters, food, medical care, and even education. (This was especially true for the young women, who needed to know housekeeping skills when the time came for them to marry.)

This tradition—much muted—continues in Korea. Faced with the prospect of sending their sons and daughters to the city (which is well known for its seductions and lack of affordable housing), parents look for an employer who can provide a dormitory and will act in loco parentis, at least until the young woman can get herself established and find a place of her own.[10] This pattern is changing at smaller manufacturers, because most young men and women would prefer to live apart from the supervision of the factory owners, but the dorms still fulfill a function at the large corporations. And even if a new worker desires to move out of company housing, the dorms serve as a way station while he or she explores options in the city. The factory will also provide social and recreational outlets, from sports teams and choirs to guest speakers; some will establish a lending library and arrange classes for workers; managers may help workers put aside some of their salary by arranging for a banker to visit the facility on payday.

And finally, the overarching paternalism (or, more accurately, institutionalism) of the military obviously served as a model for postwar Korean industrial practices. As the nation was mobilized toward specific economic targets, workers were occasionally uprooted and moved to new locations, where they needed to be supported like any modern soldier on campaign. When Korea's famed construction teams go overseas, for example, they must rely on their employers for total support. And similar situations have arisen within Korea. As noted at the beginning of the chapter, Pohang was a sleepy fishing village when Park Chung-Hee picked it to be the site of Korea's steel industry (under the direction of former general Park Tae-Joon). To attract skilled workers and executives—and their families—it was necessary to provide a social infrastructure: accommodations, schools, stores, medical facilities, and other services. More recently, the development of new steel mills in another village, Kwangyang, has again required comprehensive reliance on the corporation; virtually all employees there reside in company housing.

LIMITS TO PATERNALISM

Korean paternalism is genuine, and it clearly offers benefits to employees and employers alike, but it has its sinister side. The caretaking of a responsible superior too easily and too often slides into an all-encompassing authoritarianism, a level of control over private and occupational lives rivaled only by the military. Exercising the power given them by Korean tradition and the urgency of national economic success, employers have made encroachments on personal behavior on a scale that would be intolerable in the West. Laborers throughout Korea are frequently denied firm schedules and expected to work long overtime hours without notice; employees at several chaebol acknowledge that they have been obliged to take part in company-sponsored savings plans. And in status-conscious Korea, hierarchical work relationships invariably spill over into the company-run community, affecting workers' after-hours lives and the lives of their families.

Although much has changed since 1987, this level of company control of workers' lives is still common, particularly in the smaller, nonchaebol companies. In the worst circumstances, encompassing authoritarianism combines with an utter disregard for the well-being of the worker. The results can be merely grim: crowded dorms, repetitious or poorly prepared food, prohibitions on conversation during work, extreme forms of surveillance. But sometimes the results are tragic, especially relative to the economic success that Korea has achieved.

Younger workers, particularly girls, are the most likely to suffer from severe exploitation. An American labor representative in Seoul compared the situation with something from the early days of the industrial revolution in the United States. The dormitories keep the workers "entrapped on the compound," he said. "They have forced overtime, so that they work twelve to fourteen hours a day, six and sometimes seven days a week. They don't leave until their supervisor leaves, and if he decides to stay and stay and stay, then they stay."

The garment industry, with its roots in the earliest days of Korean industrialization, is probably the worst offender. Even today, it is common to find two-tiered sweatshops; in these, a second floor is built in a room with a normal 8- or 9-foot ceiling, so that twice as many women and machines can be crammed into the area. Child labor, which still exists in Korea, is most likely to occur in this industry.

Conditions can sometimes be lethal. For the twenty-eight women who worked at the Green Hill Textile Company in suburban Seoul, the factory was also the dorm. They worked (a minimum of eleven hours a day, more when there were rush orders to fill) and slept (three young women to a windowless room) in a 40-square-yard area; they received a half-hour or less for lunch and got two Sundays off a month. For maintaining this dehumanizing routine, they earned from $270 to $340 a month. The day-to-day stresses of working under such conditions were perhaps known to them, but they were either unaware of—or powerless to change—the other dangers around them. In March 1988, a fire in the shop-cum-dorm took the lives of twenty-two of these women.

The limits of Korea's industrial paternalism are evident in the "corporate fathers'" abominable record for on-the-job safety. The death rate in Korean factories is three times higher than in the United States. Compared with Asia's other rapidly industrializing nations, Korea is by far the most negligent with respect to worker safety, with nearly 3 percent of the work force injured every year. (The rate in Singapore is 0.93, in Taiwan, 0.70, and in Japan, 0.61 percent.) And no relief is in sight: in 1987, over 25,000 workers were permanently disabled, up sharply from 17,000 in 1983. While Korea has laws concerning worker safety, the Ministry of Labor has only one hundred investigators to check compliance. Meanwhile, pitched competition, especially among small subcontractors, keeps revenues low and discourages employers from voluntarily installing safety equipment.[11]

And accidents are perhaps less of a concern than the long-term results of dangerous working conditions. Statistics on occupational diseases (collected by an optimistic government) are unreliable; most observers believe such afflictions to be rampant. One study of twenty-two factories in a single industrial complex, for example, found that nineteen were in violation of industrial safety and health laws.[12] And the long-term effects of working protracted shifts without proper respirators, goggles, or other protective gear will probably not be manifest for several years, when the work force is older.

Pharis J. Harvey, executive director of the North American Coalition for Human Rights in Korea (an organization formed by several Catholic and Protestant agencies), has pointed out that Korean employers' paternalism will evaporate rather quickly when a worker's productivity lapses: "As of a few years ago, most workers in electronics manufacturing were losing their eyesight within four or five years. That is, they lost so much eyesight that they couldn't continue working. And then they lost their jobs." Another group, the Washington, D.C.–based Asia Watch, has detailed additional horror stories: laborers forced to work twenty-four-hour shifts, company stores that charge more than off-site retailers, workers docked three days' wages for a one-day absence, factories so cold that workers suffer frostbite.

No amount of money is sufficient to compensate workers who suffer permanent damage to their health, but it seems an even greater offense that workers are subjected to dangerous circumstances while they are being deprived of a fair wage. Long after Korea had entered the ranks of industrialized nations—indeed, long after the benefits of that development were appearing in upscale boutiques and supermarkets—workers still did not have a guaranteed minimum wage. It had been much discussed and long promised, but debate faltered over decisions regarding eligibility and amount. As noted earlier, this law is now on the books, and eligibility is scheduled to expand annually, but it initially covered only about 10 percent of the work force. Furthermore, the amount was considered by most to be grossly inadequate. As of January 26, 1988, the minimum monthly wage had been set at around $150. According to a study conducted by Seoul National University, that constituted roughly 70 percent of a subsistence wage; the Federation of Korean Trade Unions put a living wage at about double the minimum wage.[13]

▲

In sum, the distinctive management style that has guided Korean development reflects the mélange of influences that have been visited upon the nation over its long history. Its business philosophies and practices are clearly rooted in Confucian values (especially familism), modified by modern Japanese and American management practices. But the Korean way of working is not innocent of Japanese colonial lessons or its own military's devotion to efficiency and economic development.

The result is a frightening but effective approach to motivating and overseeing workers. It has not been bereft of personal touches, nor has it been without its blessings for employees. But, at base, labor and management both recognize that the supposed paternalism of Korean corporations is a hollow promise. Managers condemn workers for being disloyal and complaining sons; workers cite managers for their indifference and exploitive demands. Both are correct in their accusations. In fact, Korea's "paternalistic" management style more closely resembles the all-embracing institutionalism of military life. It seems to be changing now, but this much remains true: in Korea's long-running battle for economic success, its solitary weapon has been its workers, and toward that end they have been inevitably—albeit unwillingly—sacrificed.

9

▲ ▲ ▲

The Life Cycle of
the Korean Employee

At the gates of Samsung's huge electronics manufacturing complex at Suwon, security guards inspect the trunks of all cars entering and leaving. They are looking, one assumes, for the pilfered microwave or television as well as the prototype video camera, the lab report, the business plan: there is much to guard in this warren of offices, research labs, and assembly lines.

Presumably, the thousands of employees who walk on and off the campus each day are subjected to less exacting scrutiny. They would have trouble smuggling out a major household appliance, after all, and only a very few have access to sensitive information and equipment. Perhaps most important, who among these workers would be willing to jeopardize their relatively secure, relatively high-paying jobs with Korea's largest employer? Who would risk losing all that overtime?

As they take an afternoon break in the front lobby of their plant, the young, blue-uniformed men who work the VCR assembly line seem at once exhausted and animated. They drink fruit juices and smoke and talk passionately, releasing the tension of many quiet hours on the line, preparing themselves for another long stint before supper. One of them, Kim Y. K., a twenty-seven-year-old technician, laughs at the idea that his eleven-hour workday is unusual. He is content with his current position, his pay ($300 a month), and his benefits: he expects to move into the company's free dorms soon. He also feels that the company offers opportunities for advancement. Samsung provides on-the-job training that could bring him raises, promotions, and more exciting work, possibly in one of the company's research labs.

"This is a good job," he says emphatically. "You can never be sure, but it's very likely that I'll stay with Samsung forever."

On an upholstered bench in the hallway outside the offices of POSCO's senior executives, three young men sit erectly, their hands in their laps. They wear what appear to be identical dark suits and ties; their white shirts also match, down to the small, tight, rigidly starched collars. Their faces gleam with optimism, their mouths twitch with diffidence. It is the look of the desperate patient facing the miracle cure: a "this operation will either cure you or kill you" kind of look.

"Them?" an executive replies. "They're the interviewees. They are looking for a job." His laugh is a snicker, tinged with sympathy.

JOINING UP

It is said that while all Japanese managers enjoy equal status, the personnel manager is most equal, because he is responsible for attracting and developing the corporation's greatest resource. At some companies in Korea, similar tribute is paid to the importance of recruiting worthy employees. For example, Samsung's corporate lore holds that the group's founder and patriarch, Lee Byung-Chull, devoted 80 percent of his time to hiring and other personnel matters; it is further claimed that he interviewed every final candidate for a managerial position. (It is also whispered that Lee conducted these interviews with a fortune-teller at his side, but company literature is mute on this point.) He also pioneered (in 1957) Korea's first open, competitive system for hiring new employees, which mimicked the traditional

Confucian examination system while undercutting the Confucian tendency toward nepotism.

Today, the recruitment of new white-collar employees at all of Korea's major chaebol is ostensibly open and competitive, based on academic records, detailed tests, and brief interviews. The elaborate system at the Daewoo group is representative. Typically, officials at the Daewoo Corporation (the group's trading arm) begin the process in September, working with the other affiliates to determine the number of new employees that are needed. Shortly thereafter, announcements are placed in various newspapers and at the universities, detailing application procedures and the schedule for submission. Students usually have about three weeks to submit pertinent data on their academic record, experience, and family.

The test usually takes place on a Sunday early in November, just after most university seniors have completed their last classes for the year. All the chaebol offer their examinations at the same hour, on the same day, with the exact date and timing established by the government. This scheduling is clearly designed to force an applicant to declare his corporate loyalties at the outset, because it eliminates the possibility of applying to several major corporations at once. And there is no looking back, no recanting: although one is technically eligible to apply at another chaebol during a subsequent recruitment round, no one at Hyundai is going to hire a Daewoo reject.

Despite this fairly ruthless attempt to winnow the field, the major chaebol can expect to see 10,000 to 20,000 hopeful young men on that November morning, vying for 1,000 to 2,000 jobs. Every applicant takes two hour-long tests, one in his major field of study and one in written English—an implicit acknowledgment of the importance of exports.

Anywhere from two-thirds to four-fifths of them will not be called back for an interview. For those applicants who are asked back, usually two or three weeks after the test, the interviews are brief but terrifying encounters. At Daewoo, each candidate is called before a small group of senior executives (which could include, at least up until a few years ago, group chairman Kim Woo-Choong), where he spends two to ten minutes nervously answering questions on his school activities, home life, and ambitions. Technical or professional knowledge is not the issue here. The executives are assaying and the candidate is striving to make manifest an earnest and respectful personality, a pleasant manner, a passion for work—in short, a good attitude. Throughout the interview, the candidate is aware that there is just one job for every two young men waiting on benches in the lobby.

Minor variations obtain at other chaebol. At Hyundai, for example, applicants must take a second English test, covering listening comprehension, on the morning of their interview. And Samsung has created a routine that wrings even more prickly sweat from the palms of interviewees: in the morning, five or six applicants are brought before a group of about ten senior executives, and each applicant is grilled in front of his potential employers *and* his competitors. In the afternoon, ten to fifteen applicants are forced to take part in a group discussion on, for example, the role of the university in society, while the executives who ring the room score each candidate's opinions and his ability to interact with others.

The chaebol's method of hiring appears to be open, competitive, and generally democratic. In actuality, though, entry to a Korean corporation is frequently determined by something other than strict merit. After the tests and interviews have been scored, the social factors—family status, personal contacts, and educational background—come into play. The candidate's place of birth is also included on the application and, while the major chaebol deny its significance, it is common knowledge among Koreans that some companies will favor candidates from a particular region. A chaebol with an opening in a specific province will often attempt to fill the post with a young man from that area. "Sons shouldn't be separated from their families," explained a personnel manager at Daewoo. "After a few years, when they have their careers under way, then they will be more adaptable and should be able to accept transfers away from the family." (Implicit in this is another, usually unstated criterion, which is gender. Korea's large conglomerates have virtually no female managerial employees.)

Applications also reveal a number of other important personal factors. At Hyundai, for example, preference is given to military service, especially ROTC training, because this implies, in the words of a company spokesman, "that applicants are healthy and have leadership qualities." (A spokesman at a competing chaebol added

that former officers fit well into Hyundai's severely regimented overseas construction teams.)

Family history is also revealed through the application and interview process. American employers, who are obliged to ignore a candidate's marital status, may be shocked to learn that some Korean
chaebol pay close attention to a candidate's *parents'* marital status. In
the words of a Daewoo personnel manager, that chaebol is looking for
"the most normal people. If the office is a family, then those from
ordinary families can easily adapt, but those who have had trouble
growing up will be likely to encounter trouble in the office. For
example, if a man's father died when he was young, he will have had a
hard time developing during his youth." As a result, Daewoo prefers—
and can always get—applicants with two parents who are not di-
vorced, separated, or even remarried after the death of a spouse. Even
the candidate who grew up as an only child is considered tainted,
because "he is likely to be egoistic in his outlook."

At other companies, this hunger for the perfect corporate family is
less pronounced, although actual blood ties to the corporation are
valuable. Samsung officials readily acknowledge that they favor relatives of current employees. (In fact, by one account, it is even useful if
one's name is Lee, even though a huge proportion of the Korean
population has this surname.) Similar family ties are valuable at other
chaebol.

As a Daewoo manager explained, "In the United States, hiring is
too inflexible. In Korea, we will sometimes hire those who are under-
qualified but have a strong connection to the company, either through
their family or through the community. We would be inclined to hire
the sons of important residents, like bankers. This is true for both
blue- or white-collar positions." Indeed, a potential employee's family
and social contacts—and their ability to help him fit in—may be even
more important than test scores and academic records. According to a
personnel manager at the Hyosung group, "However excellent an
applicant's individual ability is, he is not permitted to enter the group
if his ability is incompatible with others."[1]

This emphasis on personal contacts has been a feature of Korean
business for decades. One study conducted in the mid-1960s found
that 70 percent of all employees owed their jobs to some kind of

connection.[2] That pattern has clearly abated at the largest conglomerates, but a recent study of the executive officers at the top twenty chaebol found that 31 percent were still related to the founding family. An additional 40 percent were recruited from outside organizations; in large degree, these were "high-ranking public officials and retired generals . . . [who] were scouted not because of their managerial expertise but because of personal or political influence."[3] And the remaining 29 percent, who were promoted from internal positions, often received their initial placement through personal or family contacts.

Applicants who pass the written test and measure up to other criteria are offered positions with one of the affiliated companies in the business group. In matching new employees with the affiliates, personnel managers consider each affiliate's needs and the preferences of the employees. Applicants typically specify three companies, and the top candidates usually get their first choice. Obviously, not all can be accommodated. Because of their high pay and promising futures, the securities companies are currently among the most highly prized assignments; according to a company spokesman, roughly 30 percent of the liberal arts graduates applying at Hyundai list its securities affiliate as their first choice.

Finally, before they can join the corporate family, applicants must satisfy two requirements. In most cases, they must pass a physical exam. And, more significant, they must recruit two wealthy people (often relatives) to act as their personal guarantors, pledging to repay the corporation for any damages incurred through the new employee's negligence or malfeasance. To verify that they have sufficient resources, guarantors must be willing to show their tax returns to the corporation. In recent years, some chaebol have moved toward insuring themselves against employee damage, with the cost of the premium split between the employee and the company. This less-than-familial arrangement continues throughout the employee's career.

In sum, the process of coming on board a major Korean corporation is designed to select employees who will be bright, composed, and exceedingly grateful. The new hires have been aware, since they arrived at the test site in early November, that their future lies at this group and no other. Although a second round of recruitment takes place in the spring, its targets are midterm university graduates or those who have recently been discharged from the military. Applicants who were rejected during the first round of tests and interviews will sometimes apply again at this time, but they are easily spotted by personnel managers and have a slim chance of success. In any case, the spring round often results in fewer hires and can be a much less involved process; Daewoo, for example, does not even conduct the usual examinations but relies instead on grades, recommendations, interviews, and, of course, personal and family connections.

In addition to being grateful, the new recruits can be counted on to blend in seamlessly with the rest of the corporate work force, because of their similarities in upbringing, education, race, sex, and, sometimes, regional background. The chaebol usually couch these preferences in terms of family building, but in fact the aim is to build a homogeneous institution, wherein all the participants recognize the same values and goals and respond to clearly defined authority.

This attempt at uniformity can have positive results, in that co-workers enjoy an extraordinary level of trust and an intimate understanding of one another's strengths and weaknesses. In the worst cases, though, it creates a stifling "old boy" network that blocks the participation of many of the society's most talented youths. Moreover, the use of social and family contacts will often *create* in-house rifts. New employees come to the group owing their good fortune (and therefore their loyalty) to someone else in the corporation. As a result, Korean businesses are often riddled with cliques and factions that reflect family, personal, school, and geographic rivalries, which can lead to pronounced and sometimes destructive internal competition. Graduates of Seoul National University will join forces against graduates from Yonsei University, or those from the city of Pusan will pit themselves against those from Taegu. According to one Korean business consultant, "Given these conditions, it is easy to see that the addition or removal of a single staff member can create profound changes in the *status quo* of office politics. Such changes are discussed late into the night by members of the groups involved and are evaluated in the light of possible gain or loss of power to the group as well as the individual."[4]

And if the leader of a departmental clique takes a position with a competitor, his loyal subordinates will often follow—with devastating effect on the original employer. "We have a saying in Korean business," said one management consultant, "Hire away the boss, and his staff will follow like a string of beads."

Foreigners conducting business in Korea can be severely handicapped by ignorance of these subterranean loyalties, because they influence developments in both the private sector and government. "When people come here and want to do business with Korean companies," an attaché at the American embassy in Seoul explained, "I advise them to put a person in a hotel for six months and let him fill up notebooks and floppy disks—get a solid data base—on who's related to whom and who went to school with whom."

The reliance on personal and family connections is waning. Executive recruiters—who are presumably unburdened by kin or regional loyalties—are beginning to appear in Korea. But it is evident that the placement of both entry-level employees and executives will continue to be colored by factors that have little to do with an applicant's professional merits.

BLUE-COLLAR RECRUITMENT

The process for bringing on new production workers—whether male or female—is much less competitive and, because each subsidiary typically hires as needed, its procedures are less elaborate. Advertisements are placed in local newspapers, at high schools, or on factory gates. Word also gets out through the employees, who tell their friends and family members when work is available. Often, laborers coming to the city from an outlying village will find employment through a relative or village acquaintance who has preceded them. As a result, an assembly line in a Seoul factory can be operated almost exclusively by young men and women from a town hundreds of miles away.

This, again, is hardly accidental; corporate officials repeatedly note the importance of hiring relatives and friends in developing a sense of family at the workplace. Often, only a brief interview and test of skills is required; occasionally, a well-recommended applicant will be hired without an examination. In any case, many factories demand that an applicant furnish two guarantors, who will vouch for the applicant's identity and promise to pay the costs of any damages incurred by the would-be employee. Some companies prefer that the guarantors be employees at the factory; giving current workers a role in the award of a good job increases their status and the sense of mutual obligation within the labor force.

Some studies suggest that as the Korean economy has matured, geography and social contacts have become less relevant in blue-collar recruitment. For example, before 1978, over half the workers at the Hyundai Motor Company were from the region in which the factory was located, and about 70 percent had some sort of social contact with a worker at the plant. Between 1981 and 1983, though, recruits came from farther afield, and 45 percent came to the factory without prior social contact. An even bigger shift occurred in the means of recruitment, with fewer taking entrance examinations and many more attending a company-run vocational training program—an acknowledgment of the need for more skilled workers.[5]

TILL DEATH DO US PART?

In theory, Korea's white-collar chaebol workers retire not long after they turn fifty-five, although chief executives might continue working into their early sixties. (And, of course, a chaebol's chairman might stay at the helm into his seventies.) In practice, however, many Koreans leave the chaebol much sooner.

There has been some disagreement about whether Korea's labor practices include a guarantee of lifetime employment; typically, these discussions compare Korea with Japan, where approximately 30 percent of the work force—usually civil servants and male employees of large corporations—prosecute their careers with a single employer.[6] In part, the lack of concurrence regarding Korea stems from that country's relatively recent industrialization, the continuing evolution of its industrial practices, and its strikingly youthful work force, all of which make hard-and-fast judgments premature.

The first factor determining lifetime employment, obviously, is the employer's loyalty to his employees, which varies considerably among the major chaebol. Of the top four groups, Lucky-Goldstar is probably most committed to retaining employees over the long haul, while Samsung is generally considered least likely to clutch a worker to the company bosom—a tradition (or at least an image) that it is now striving to change. At Hyundai, the company claims that it keeps workers on the payroll whenever possible and will even find make-work for overseas construction crews when they are back in Korea between assignments.

Many observers are skeptical about chaebol pronouncements on lifetime employment, however, and some chaebol officials will privately admit that the practice is more of a desire than a reality. Workers are rarely fired outright, but an employee who does not continue to advance will usually leave the firm in embarrassment after a few years of stasis. A personnel manager at Daewoo suggested that the country was moving toward the military model of "rank retirement," whereby one either continues to be promoted or is retired. "That way, there are no majors past a certain age and no colonels past another," he explained. "The military is the best-run organization in society. For private corporations to adapt this system now would be premature, but I believe that the private sector will ultimately follow it."

Nonchaebol employees, especially civil servants, are in a better position to secure lifetime employment. White-collar government workers can continue on the job until the hoary (at least by Korean standards) age of sixty-five; even so, some occasionally attempt to circumvent mandatory retirement by falsifying data in their family registers.[7] Influential bureaucrats, on the other hand, will sometimes retire early, to step into lucrative positions in the private sector; those at the Ministry of Trade and Industry can reputedly find jobs with trade organizations at twice their government salary.

For Korea's blue-collar employees, lifetime employment is especially chimeric. In fact, most production workers find that the physical demands of their jobs—and the availability of younger workers—will force them out of the work force long before they are ready to retire. At Hyundai, for example, a spokesman noted that "there is no set retirement age for blue-collar workers. These are hard jobs. No one over fifty can keep doing them." In other words, a man must either angle his way into a foreman's position or work until his body fails him. A woman, in contrast, will usually stay on the job until marriage in her mid-twenties.

While Korean employers are usually indifferent about providing their workers with long-term job security, they do tend to keep their employees on the job for as long as possible during economic downturns. One study has shown that Korean workers, more than Americans or even Japanese, think that their bosses would be willing to keep them on the payroll during hard times.

When they leave a job, blue- and white-collar workers usually receive a lump-sum separation or retirement payment of one month's pay for each year worked. (At some corporations, the figure is considerably higher; POSCO workers receive 1.7 months' salary for each year.) Smartly handled, this money can be the seed for a new small business. In many cases, however, it is poorly invested or squandered pursuing a new job—a faint possibility for an older Korean. Samsung claims that it is now working to place retired managers with subcontractors, in much the same way that Japanese firms will ease their older employees' transition out of big business. (This also reflects Samsung's desire to expand and support its network of subcontractors.) But many still-active Korean men, both white- and blue-collar, cannot find new employment and so must rely on the benevolence of their children. This clearly represents a failure in the system. As the life expectancy of Koreans continues to rise, the retirement age will have to follow.

WORKER MOBILITY: HELLO, I MUST BE GOING

The second factor determining the extent of lifetime employment is the employee's loyalty to the employer. Here, Koreans show the limits of their allegiances. They are, in brief, quick to move.

Research suggests a lack of strong worker loyalty. Even in the mid-1960s, when the nation was getting its first tentative taste of economic success, Korean managers were not content to sit still and reap the benefits; over half said they would quit if a better opportunity presented itself.[8] Another study, comparing Korean workers in 1981 with Americans and Japanese in 1960, found that the Koreans were the most inclined to leave.[9]

More recent statistics indicate that Koreans' willingness to move has not diminished. As noted in chapter 2, overall turnover rates in manufacturing run from 4.3 percent to 5.6 percent, higher than those in the United States and much higher than in Japan. There are exceptions—ironically, the Korea Explosives group reportedly has less turnover, probably because the constant dealing with hazardous materials builds lasting friendships—but pronounced worker mobility seems to be the rule.

This pattern can be variously interpreted. The rosiest explanation is that in an open, booming economy—especially one that has been rapidly metamorphosing from light through heavy industry to high tech—workers *should* move around, because new industries should be outbidding older, stagnant industries for their services. This probably best applies to job switching at the higher levels of a corporation, among executives and technical specialists. A less optimistic interpretation, applicable to blue-collar workers, holds that employee loyalty is likely to be undercut by harsh treatment, lousy wages, and the practice of occasionally withholding pay—conditions that exist because employers do not *care* if their workers leave, since there have always been other workers willing to replace them. In fact, continued employment can lead to costly increases in fringe benefits, so corporations might even encourage unskilled workers to depart after a short time.

In Songnam City, an industrial suburb of Seoul, activists who work with laborers claim that mobility is primarily related to wages and working conditions. "Their situation is so bad," explained a young Korean woman, "some people here leave a workplace every month. They are always hoping that things will be better at the next factory. And the work is there, until they are around thirty. If they haven't learned a skill by then, it is hard to find work. Then they go into day labor, which tends to be seasonal and pays even less."

Like everything else about Korea, the lack of lifetime employment and the high rates of mobility are still evolving. The Japanese "tradition" of guaranteed employment (and subsequent worker loyalty) is relatively modern, a response to workers' demands for long-term job security after World War II. Korean workers are certainly not immune to the attractions of such guarantees, and, as they begin to register their own demands, these may include a pledge of worker loyalty in exchange for security. Employers too seem to be changing their attitude. In some companies, retirement pay is being calculated on an accelerating schedule, so that after ten years, for example, an employee receives a lump sum equal to fifteen months' salary—which constitutes a strong inducement for loyal service. [10]

FIRING

Korean companies are usually very reluctant to terminate an employee, especially a white-collar worker, except under extreme circumstances, such as criminal activity.

Legally, the situations in which an employee can be dismissed are ill defined; Korea's Labor Standards Act prohibits the firing or suspension of any individual without a "justifiable reason" but does not detail what constitutes such a reason. Ministry of Labor (MOL) staff have suggested that employers consider the "relevant rulings of the MOL and the courts, the opinions of legal commentators, the general practices in Korea and the relevant provisions of a collective bargaining agreement or the rules of employment, as well as past practices of the work place" in determining what might be allowable grounds for termination.[11] Some observers claim that this lack of definition is purposeful, designed to provide vulnerable workers with a degree of legal protection; this protection also reinforces the common perception that the private sector has responsibilities for social welfare and, therefore, should fire a worker only under the gravest of circumstances. This supposed protection is belied, however, by the ease with which employers have dismissed workers who are active in opposition politics or labor organization.

Regardless of the legalities, many employers feel that firing an employee—even one who is known to be unproductive or prone to error—would be so disruptive and outside the norm that it would have repercussions throughout the work force. Consequently, a common (if brutal) method of handling such a situation is to keep the worker on the payroll but take away all his duties and responsibilities. Other workers will soon recognize that he has failed in some significant way and will gradually disassociate themselves. Ultimately, the shunned worker will resign out of humiliation. A less drastic approach is to exclude the employee from the expected annual cost-of-living and seniority raises. A single exclusion may bring the worker around or elicit a resignation; a second exclusion will almost always result in a resignation. The employer will pay the required severance pay, and the relationship will be concluded.

10

▲▲▲

Daily Rhythms:
Working Eight to Eight

It is 4:00 P.M. on a Saturday in the Hyundai Motor Company assembly plant in Ulsan, a port town on Korea's southeast coast. Conditions are far from ideal. The plant is unheated despite the crisp Korean winter. The noise in the press shop, where doors and panels are punched out, is deafening, and the men wear no ear protectors. But the plant is efficient. Electronic signboards overhead track production against goals: 347, 348 . . . Today, a new car is being minted every fifty-seven seconds.

Chung Seong-Yul is a troubleshooter, chasing down a bad connection on a red Excel GL destined for export to the United States. When he quits work at 8:00 P.M., Chung—like all his fellow workers on the assembly line—will have logged sixty hours for the week, just as he had the week before and the week before that. He will earn $600 for the month, plus a sizable bonus several times a year.

He is not eager to be interviewed. His job is to chase ghosts out of cars, not make small talk. Only at the urging of a company interpreter does he slide into the open, his screwdriver remaining poised in the air. Asked how he's spending his high salary, he replies that he's saving almost everything. Told that he works long hours by American standards, he shrugs. Would he like more work? He shrugs again, then admits that he gets tired on his current schedule. He has little time to himself. Single and twenty-nine, he'll spend Saturday night in his dorm room—provided by the company, a five-minute walk from the plant. He'll read, then sleep. On Sunday, he'll visit his family, a short bus trip away. Come Monday at 8:00 A.M., he'll be under another Excel. "But if the company needs me to work more hours," he says, "I'll work them."

He nods impatiently toward the car, indicating that he has work to do, and crawls back under the bumper. But as his visitors move on, his head pokes out by the front wheel. "You must remember," he calls after them, "not every worker has the privilege of working overtime."

At Daewoo, the young manager explains, white-collar workers commonly put in more than sixty hours a week. They regularly get Sundays off, and for their annual vacation the company allows a long weekend—four days, including Sunday. Company policy also grants an additional day off each month, but most workers decline this holiday and take an extra cash bonus. The money isn't the point, though. "We all feel very responsible for the company's performance," he says, "so—if we have nothing else to do—most of us prefer to take our holiday at our desk."

NOTHING ELSE TO DO: THE KOREAN WORKDAY (AND NIGHT)

Koreans log the longest workweek in the world, a record they have earned by putting in more days than anyone else and working longer hours on each of those days. Clearly, the statistical averages are weighted by sweatshop laborers, who are sometimes obliged to stay at their machines or assembly lines for inhumanly long shifts. What is less clear—and perhaps more significant—is that production laborers at many of Korea's largest and most technically advanced factories work almost as many hours. One researcher complained that it was impossible to interview Hyundai Motor Company workers in their homes, because they were usually on the job from 8:00 A.M. to 10:00 P.M., six and often seven days a week. Moreover, their hours were not fixed; each day's schedule was based on a production plan announced the afternoon before.[1]

White-collar employees at the chaebol put in as much and sometimes more time than do their blue-collar co-workers. This practice starts at the very top—Daewoo's chairman Kim Woo-Choong regularly works twelve- to fifteen-hour days and reportedly has not taken a holiday in the twenty years since he started the company—and runs through every other stratum of the labor force. "The peer pressure can be very strong in a chaebol," a Korean businessman confided. "I know one man who lied and said he had to take Sunday mornings off so that he could go to church. Actually, he just wanted to spend time with his family, but he didn't feel comfortable saying that."

Normal hours vary from chaebol to chaebol, but the schedule at Hyundai is representative. Monday through Friday, white-collar workers are at their desks from 8:30 A.M. to 6:30 P.M.; on Saturday, they leave early, at about 1:00 P.M.; subtracting an hour for lunch each day, this constitutes a forty-eight-hour workweek, the standard in Korea. Typically, however, workers will stay beyond 6:30 on weekday evenings, putting in approximately fifty-five to sixty hours each week. In contrast, production workers at the chaebol (where labor laws are more likely to be enforced) are eligible to receive overtime pay for anything over forty-eight hours a week, and so are less likely to put in such long hours. There are exceptions, however. At Samsung's Suwon complex, assembly-line workers, their supervisors, and company engineers all clock eleven-hour days, twenty-seven days a month.[2]

Office workers at Hyundai are allowed an additional unpaid holiday each month, but most workers prefer to work and receive an extra payment. In their second year with the company, they become eligible for a four-day vacation; with additional years they will be awarded more vacation days. While this schedule obviously allows for minimal leisure time, the conglomerates do try to accommodate the key events in a worker's family life. In those companies that have labor contracts, an employee might get seven days off for his own wedding; for a grandparent's sixtieth birthday, one day; for the death of a grandparent, five days. At Daewoo, a worker's wedding anniversary brings a paid day off, with vouchers for transportation, lodging, and meals at a group-run resort.

While the grueling fifty-five-hour workweek has become common among Korea's managers, it by no means defines the limits of their endurance. When a crisis or crucial project arises, the hours are extended: cots go up in the back offices or labs and toothbrushes appear in staff washrooms. And Koreans seem to live in a perpetual state of crisis. They will apply to mundane product development—the microwave oven is a pointed example—the fervor that Westerners usually reserve for a startling scientific breakthrough. The engineer who developed Samsung's microwave oven worked a *year* of eighty-hour weeks, only to have his first prototype melt on its trial run. This was followed by more eighty-hour weeks, marital discord, and, finally, success.[3]

(It is worth noting that the private sector is not alone in its eagerness to overwhelm a problem with sheer endeavor; scholars have noted that, in critical situations, Korea's technocrats will often retire to "a suite of hotel rooms in order to avoid interruptions, preserve secrecy, and allow around-the-clock efforts.")[4]

SALARIES AND WAGES

For their efforts, Korea's managers and production workers are far from lavishly rewarded. At the chaebol, both types of employees will make more than their counterparts in smaller companies, and some chaebol pay better than others; officials at Samsung claim that pay at their group is approximately 15 percent higher than at the other chaebol, a strategy at least partially designed to minimize the appeal of organized labor. Still, compared with their Western counterparts, Koreans take home very modest paychecks.

For example, at POSCO, the highly productive and successful steel corporation, entry-level laborers have a base salary of about $675 per month, including bonus; with two days of scheduled overtime, earnings usually approach $750. Salaried workers receive about $850 a month to start. Compensation for top executives is difficult to figure because bonuses and fringe benefits—including homes and chauffeured cars—are substantial and complicated. By one estimate, these senior directors receive a base salary and bonuses of more than $3,000 per month—a tidy sum in Korea, but hardly extraordinary when compared with the bottom of the scale. More significant, the next echelon of senior executives reputedly earn about $2,300 per month, or not much more than three times what the entry-level steel-worker makes. Furthermore, this penultimate bracket is open to production workers who achieve the rank of "technical master," based on their seniority and experience. (As of 1988, only one production worker had ever achieved this status, but this may reflect the company's tender age; its first production facility was dedicated in mid-1973.)

This pay structure influences both company morale and overall labor costs. Comparing Samsung's and General Electric's costs of manufacturing a microwave oven in 1983, one analyst found that assembly labor at GE was $8.00 per oven, versus just $0.63 at Samsung. The differential in supervisory, maintenance, and setup labor was even greater: $30.00 at GE and $0.73 at Samsung. But the contrast was most stark when line and central management were compared: $10.00 per oven at GE, but only $0.02 at Samsung.[5]

Despite being more egalitarian than in the United States, pay differentials in Korea are hardly negligible. White-collar Koreans earn, on average, three times what their blue-collar colleagues make. Education is also highly correlated with income: a university graduate is paid twice as much as a worker who only completed high school, and three times as much as the worker who left school at age sixteen. And princely rewards are sometimes used to seduce anyone with unique abilities; Korean-Americans with business experience and special technical knowledge gleaned from American industry have been lured back to the peninsula with salaries and benefits that allow them to live in luxury.

None of this surprises Korean workers, yet they are discontented with the distribution of riches. "Those who study well should be paid more," explained a manager at Lucky-Goldstar. "It is common sense in Korea. Even blue-collar workers agree. But they also resent rich men, and they are indignant about the lack of opportunity. Many white-collar workers agree that the discrepancy is too great. Perhaps because of Korea's great homogeneity, these discrepancies are more keenly felt. The dispute is over the speed of changing these imbalances, not the desire to change."

THE SHAPE OF MONEY

Korean workers have traditionally had many components to their overall compensation. Salaries often include a myriad of allowances and adjustments; at Daewoo, the white-collar pay stub has boxes for eighteen possible kinds of compensation, from basic wage and overtime to allowances for meals, families, transportation, children's tuition (for the first two children only), overseas residence, and so on. The stub also has a similar number of deductions, including income, residence and defense taxes, medical insurance, an optional savings program, employee association dues, and the repayment of any loans from the employee association. A separate check is used to pay seasonal bonuses.

In 1981, the average Korean worker got 70 percent of his compensation in the form of straight wages and salary; the remaining 30 percent was split evenly between bonuses and overtime. Predictably, production workers got a large percentage of their compensation in overtime, while salaried managers got little overtime pay but larger bonuses. For example, production workers in the largest corporations (more than 500 workers) got almost one-fourth of their income in bonuses and 13 percent in overtime. In other words, their wages constituted just two-thirds of total compensation. By adding in the value of company housing, medical care, food, and—at some chaebol—occasional gifts, the proportion of wages is even less.

In some cases, salary can be an even smaller part of total compensation. As of April 1979, a college graduate starting work at one of the banks in Seoul could plan on receiving only 38 percent of his total compensation in salary; the rest came in overtime, allowances, and bonuses. It is interesting that both private and public employers give bonuses; even university professors receive only about half their wages in a regular salary. They receive additional payment in the form of special grants based on merit or other considerations—a system which not incidentally lets the government apply quick and meaningful pressure on an individual, academic department, or even entire institution.

The history of these compensation schemes is mildly surprising; after having been instituted by the Japanese during the colonial period, bonuses largely died out during the years of U.S. military rule. Later, in the 1950s, they were resurrected. Over the next couple of decades, they became increasingly popular among employers, so that, between 1972 and 1981, white-collar workers saw their bonuses grow in a nearly unbroken line.

For employers, the appeal is simple and straightforward. By holding back compensation for seasonal or annual bonuses, employers can reward workers in the good times and preserve the viability of the corporation (and workers' jobs) during economic downturns. In this way, the bonus system provides at once an employee incentive, a relief from periodic cash-flow problems, and a general corporate contingency fund. By compensating in bonuses instead of base pay, employers also reduce their overall labor costs, because Korean law specifies that certain benefits—retirement pay, for example—are to be computed using basic wages. From the worker's perspective, it would be advantageous to receive compensation as it is earned, in straight wages and salary; this would also provide workers with an explicit statement of their annual salary, useful for household planning and comparisons between employers. Finally, there is the question of basic fairness; by funding a corporate contingency fund, workers are weathering the risk of the business without having any control over how that risk is handled.

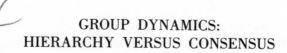

GROUP DYNAMICS: HIERARCHY VERSUS CONSENSUS

Pay and hours may be relatively evenly divided in a Korean corporation, but power is another matter.

Day-to-day relationships in the chaebol and smaller companies are governed by unambiguous relationships between superiors and subordinates. According to a senior executive at Daewoo, "Koreans still don't have the concept of colleagues. Someone is either my boss or my boy."[6] In this sort of environment, individualism is an early casualty: "The orderly manner of Samsung's organization always overwhelms the employees' individual characters, although each member represents the intellectual elites of Korea," a company spokesman explained. "All work done by employees is closely monitored and supervised by senior members."[7]

It is thus not surprising that information moves up and down the chaebol according to the strict, "stovepipe" patterns of communication mentioned earlier; it moves laterally only through informal alumni and hobby groups. While Koreans will make passing references to consensus building (called *pumi* in Korean, but described by the same Chinese character as the Japanese term *ringi*), it tends to be much closer to rubber-stamping a superior's desires: "One stamp, one meal" says an old adage.

Authority is often explicitly proclaimed through the use of uniforms and insignia that indicate rank. At Samsung's electronics complex at Suwon, for example, the young women assembling J. C. Penney and Curtis-Mathes television sets wear tan scarves with their blue jumpers; workers' scarves are trimmed in blue, supervisors' in white. Similar systems are used in plants throughout Korea and on overseas construction teams.

This distinctly top-down style is hardly surprising. For one reason, concentrated authority is traditional in Korea. "As a result of Confucian upbringing," one scholar noted, "the Korean people on one hand developed an authoritarian attitude and, on the other, failed to develop into self-reliant individuals."[8] Here again, even the language reinforces submissiveness and authority; whenever one speaks, the verb endings and vocabularies express precisely the hierarchical relationship with the listener.

This tradition of concentrated authority is hardly diminished by Korea's highly concentrated economic power. At the same time, the educational system breeds workers who are inclined toward rote memorization and received wisdom rather than individual initiative and creativity, thus making centralized authority a matter of necessity as much as preference. Furthermore, in a society where economic success has depended more on contacts with an all-powerful govern-

ment—on intrigues and intangibles rather than on productivity—
lower-level employees can hardly be expected to anticipate what their
superiors or the corporation will require.

As a consequence of this authoritarianism, Korean workers are
known for being highly motivated but not self-starting. "There's very
little delegation of authority in Korean business," said an American
who's worked in Korea for more than two decades. "The most effective
managers have to lay everything out for their employees—the task, the
deadline, and the responsible person. And they have to follow up
constantly." On the one hand, this concentration of power obviously
allows for quicker decisions and the ability to act fast when opportunities or crises arise. It also means that responsibility—and
credit—can be easily fixed. On the other hand, middle managers are
less actively involved in day-to-day decision making.

The relationship between the group chairman and each affiliate's
senior executives is the subject of some debate. Observers claim that
the group chairman is an absolute commander who readily intervenes
in affiliate affairs; at Samsung, for example, the chairman's office "will
actually descend on a poorly performing member company if corrective action submitted by that member company's president doesn't
produce results. The committee is like a paratrooper and will investi-
gate and audit to the point where a better corrective action plan could
be written and executed."[9] Nevertheless, chaebol spokesmen will
frequently insist that an affiliate's top executive is independent and
virtually autonomous—remarks that seem designed to doctor the public impression that too much economic power is concentrated in the
hands of too few chaebol families.

Perhaps the most significant factor affecting executive control is the
sheer magnitude of the larger chaebol; any group with 100,000 employees in thirty affiliates must accept a degree of decentralization. At
the Daewoo group, for example, chairman Kim Woo-Choong prefers a
hands-on approach: "I am not satisfied only with reports," he has said,
". . . I must confirm them." But his schedule means that considerable
responsibility accrues to the group's top executives.[10] This is especially the case since 1987, when Daewoo's affiliates were organized
into nine major divisions, each with its own chief executive. But while
some chaebol delegate authority, others continue to resist the pressures brought about by their mammoth size. At Hyundai, for example,

corporate organization remains very flat, with the twenty-seven affiliate heads all reporting directly to the chairman.

Although subordinates remain, for the most part, in thrall to their bosses, several chaebol have begun to stress the importance of individual initiative. Some new employees at Daewoo, for example, are trained for particular positions, but others become "all-weather employees" without specific assignments. According to one executive, "Nobody teaches a new employee what to do. They are the ones who have to find out what to do and how to do it."[11] Another manager noted that, with time, "good workers will find their niche."

There have been efforts to make the Korean workplace less authoritarian and more open to bottom-up suggestions and complaints. Korean companies with more than 100 workers have been required to form labor-management councils to resolve workers' grievances. In reality, a 1983 study found that only about one-fourth of these employers had formed such councils.[12] And where they existed, their value was suspect. During a 1987 visit to the Hyundai Motor Company, managers could come up with only one issue that the council had resolved: workers on the assembly line had complained about the company policy stipulating military-short hair for men. Too much money and too much of their precious free time was going to haircuts, they said. After deliberating, the committee of management and labor representatives announced a new policy: a company barber would roam the assembly line, providing subsidized trimming. End of controversy.

In some companies, the councils may have actually served the purposes of the employers. According to the North American Coalition for Human Rights in Korea, "Grievance procedures, which exist on paper, are almost never used to satisfy complaints by laborers. Rather, the labor-management councils set up by government and management are used as a means of identifying workers with complaints so they can be weeded out of the work force."[13]

There are exceptions to the purely hierarchical management style practiced by most Korean corporations; for example, Hyosung, a chaebol with roughly twenty affiliated companies, has a reputation for hammering out group decisions. But in the larger economy, such teamwork is usually found only on the factory floor, where a team might be formed around a specific function or operation. Within the team, each worker learns his or her assigned task and generally sticks with it throughout the period of employment. This is especially true of young women, who are expected to leave the factory at some point to be married. Men may learn one or more tasks and move around somewhat, but they are essentially wedded to one function until the technology becomes outdated or a crisis arises.

AMBIVALENT INDIVIDUALISM

Notwithstanding the overarching importance of hierarchy and its depressing effect on personal initiative, a strong streak of individualism thrives within Korean society. With increased modernization and exposure to other cultures, the desire to "go it alone" offers more and more allure.

Within the chaebol, ambivalence reigns. Some corporations are dedicated to preserving the old ways; Samsung's tendency to "overwhelm the employees' individual characters" is a good example. At others, personal ambition is gaining more acceptance as a motivational tool. Indeed, it is said that one of "the most important roles of superiors in Korea is to promote individual aspiration in order to achieve the goals of the company."[14]

This acceptance of individual aspirations may be nothing more than a pact with reality. Korea's young people have been inspired by the rags-to-riches stories of men such as Hyundai's Chung Ju-Yung and Daewoo's Kim Woo-Choong. The most ambitious of the nation's promising managers are impatient with the stifling hierarchy of Confucian corporations; they long instead for the freewheeling, entrepreneurial environment of American and European start-up companies— as well as the rewards that such ventures can bring. Companies that accept such ambition may have a better chance of recruiting and holding on to bright, motivated employees.

In addition to the inspirational exploits of the chaebol founders, Korean individualism can also be traced to historic influences. During the country's many periods of upheaval, survival hinged on one's own abilities and the support of one's family. In sum, then, while Confucian-based obedience to one's superiors is both pervasive and genuine, it is tempered by two complementary realizations: first, in the good times, there is money to be made if one is sufficiently determined and willing to take the (sometimes weighty) risks; and second, in times of crisis—which always seem to loom on the horizon—one will have to fall back on his individual resources.

PROMOTION AND EVALUATION

This same dichotomy, between Confucian traditions and a more Westernized sense of individuality, is reflected in procedures governing evaluation, promotion, and pay increases. New practices are arising, but old traditions die hard.

In the award of promotions, the traditional emphasis in Korea, as in Japan, has been on seniority. "The company is like a home, with the senior men given an advantage," explained a spokesman for Lucky-Goldstar. "Then we consider capability and personality." Similarly, the Confucian web of social relationships—contacts and status, in Western terms—operates in promotion as it does in hiring. "Your advancement," a knowledgeable Westerner maintained, "depends on who you went to kindergarten with." This probably overstates the case, but the assertion that background can virtually program a career remains largely accurate.

As always in Korea, the best bond is blood. The top positions in chaebol affiliates—especially the most significant affiliates—are frequently held by members of the founder's family: Hyundai Motor Company was directed by Chung Ju-Yung's brother before he became chairman of the group; Hyundai Electronics was run by Chung's fifth son; Goldstar Semiconductor was run by a brother to group chairman Koo; Lee Byung-Chull's offspring have worked in various Samsung affiliates, with third son Lee Kun-Hee eventually rising to the chairman's office; and the list could go on and on. There are, however, important exceptions: at several major chaebol—particularly Daewoo and Kia—family status plays little or no role.

After family, other variables—age, status, and social contacts—become important. Western companies in Korea can run afoul of the culture by attempting to promote meritorious workers over their "betters" in age or social standing, because doing so creates a relationship in which two individuals are simultaneously superior *and* inferior to each other. In the worst cases, the company becomes hamstrung: the newly promoted worker will still defer to his social better; the young climber will have trouble directing and reprimanding his older subordinate; communication becomes difficult because the correct form of speech is ambiguous and cannot be resolved. Companies encounter similar problems when women are promoted to supervisory positions. Even though the de facto sexual segregation of most production work guarantees that a woman will not be overseeing male workers, she will still be part of the supervisory force and expected to contribute to decisions that have a broader base of application. In these instances, her input is likely to be ignored by her male colleagues.

Despite this deeply rooted traditionalism, many corporations are adopting distinctly Western methods that reward achievement, punish failure, and stimulate upward mobility. Typically, rewards come as increased pay or bonuses. The award of a new title is another, particularly coveted, reward. "In America," a business consultant noted, "you are Mr. Jones both on and off the job. In Korea, you are Manager Kim, Section Chief Kim, Director Kim both on the job and off. It goes with you everywhere. Even your neighbors will call you Manager Kim." In part, job titles are used in this way to simplify personal identification, a genuine consideration because the majority of the populace is named Lee, Kim, Park, or Choi. But titles are also a badge of status in a country where respect is often considered more important than financial remuneration.

Punishment usually takes the form of a reduced bonus, or being denied an annual cost-of-living/seniority raise—a blow to earnings and a severe loss of face. While this practice is no longer rare in Korea, some Koreans still find it shocking. A company spokesman for Lucky-Goldstar adamantly maintained that his chaebol "would *never* lower a worker's bonus as a means of penalizing performance" on the ground that it "would cause real distress for the employee." Instead, positive incentives are provided for good employees. "After all, if my brother isn't capable, I don't *penalize* him," the spokesman explained.

Other companies—Samsung, most notoriously—treat their employees less tenderly, making performance the primary key to survival. Rewards can be garnered by individuals or they can be awarded to a group's higher-performing affiliates, so that its employees enjoy faster promotions and better benefits. Typically, though, the merit approach is most likely to be found in sales forces, where evaluation can be simply and definitively based on achievement.

For most white-collar workers, evaluation takes place once or twice a year, using a three-grade system adopted from the Japanese. At Daewoo, for example, the annual evaluation awards workers a poor, average, or excellent rating that is directly reflected in salary. An "excellent" rating is worth approximately $15 per month more than a "poor." The money, clearly, is not as important as the symbolism; because each worker's salary is common knowledge in a Korean office, the results of an evaluation are easily calculated. The rating—translated to a numeric score—is also applied in figuring promotions. For example, an assistant manager begins at grade 3.0. To this, annual evaluation scores are added; an excellent is worth 0.3, an average 0.2, a poor 0.1. A grade of 3.9 must be attained before the assistant is eligible for promotion to manager, at which time one's grade goes to 4.0. If no openings are available, or if the assistant manager is passed over, scores are still added, making it possible to achieve a grade of 3.11 or 3.12. People are never demoted, but if a worker is repeatedly passed over, he will almost inevitably resign.

The Daewoo system represents an elegant mix of seniority and merit criteria. A good assistant manager will rise quickly, but it will take a minimum of three years before he is eligible for promotion to manager. If he does not advance over time, he will likely resign, thereby eliminating the disruption that occurs when a young employee is promoted over his elders. In other words, achievement keeps one in the firm, where he will rise with time.

In the relatively mechanistic environment of the assembly line, advancement—at least in terms of pay increases—is less affected by social factors and more often based on performance. But other criteria still operate. A study of the Hyundai Motor Company revealed that education and military service were used to determine a worker's initial hourly wage, but seniority was the primary criterion with respect to subsequent increases. Marital status was another significant variable, with married men earning 5 percent more than single men of similar background and abilities.[15]

TRAINING

The investment that Korean corporations make in developing human capital varies widely from company to company—even within a group—and between blue- and white-collar positions.

A white-collar worker's training begins with orientation, which constitutes a sort of managerial boot camp. Like the Japanese, Koreans spend considerable time and effort molding their new recruits. The emphasis is on attitude—fostered in general orientation and motivational seminars—rather than specific skills, the reasoning being that you can always give a worker skills or information once he has the right frame of mind. The casting of correct corporate mentality that starts with orientation is continued on the job, through periodic refresher courses and individual lecture programs.

New recruits at Daewoo, for example, take part in a sixteen-night, seventeen-day orientation that includes an introduction to "Daewoo-manship" and the corporation's philosophy. The curriculum includes classes and lectures by executives, university professors, and others. Topics can range from abstract issues (economic trends, for instance) to basic office skills, such as sending a telex and preparing a memo. Recently promoted managers are given a four-night, five-day refresher course that covers, among other topics, assertiveness training and team building. Evening hours concentrate on "unity and resolution," according to Daewoo. (Even the wives of senior directors attend three-day courses, where topics include "Daewoo's business philosophy and spirit," "Office and home," "Economic common sense," and "What's a happy home life?")

Daewoo's concern for good corporate-home relations is echoed in the group's practice of pairing green male recruits with more experienced female office workers. This results in a high rate of marriage among employees, which both settles the young men and creates Daewoo wives who are already indoctrinated into the corporate culture and are therefore less likely to complain about their husbands' demanding schedules.

The other chaebol's orientation and on-the-job training offer fewer opportunities for romance. Hyundai's three-week orientation most resembles a military indoctrination. New white-collar employees receive lectures on Korean economics and politics, go on factory tours, engage in mountain climbing and other forms of vigorous exercise, and, during the evenings, join in roundtable discussions on how to be (in the words of a young manager) "good company men." During their first year at the group, new recruits also spend their four-day summer vacation together at a special seaside training-and-bonding session, billeted side by side in a huge tent; activities include wrestling, volleyball, singing contests, and an address from the chairman. Into his seventies, chairman Chung Ju-Yung would also take part in the wrestling matches. Employees being upgraded to a new position receive week-long refresher courses that presumably do not involve grappling with the group's founder.

Orientation at Samsung's huge electronics affiliate revolves around a one-month course at the company training center, filled with eight hours of classes each day and group and individual study in the evening, all designed to create a grasp of the huge group, inculcate a sense of the corporation's philosophy, and familiarize new recruits with basic office behavior, "such as working in a group and general manners." Later on-the-job training can last up to eight months, during which a new employee is tutored for a specific position. Regular employees continue to receive training; the company claims to offer about 300 technical, managerial, and language courses.

Blue-collar training has tended to teach specific job skills—a necessity because most new hires lack vocational education. In part, this can be traced to the country's Confucian–yangban heritage, which disparaged manual or trade work. Young men are still directed toward a general high-school curriculum, in hopes that they will blossom as students or that luck will provide an opportunity for them to enter a good university, while vocational schools are neglected and underused.

If university openings elude them, these young men appear at the factory gates, eager to work but thoroughly unprepared to do so. This places the burden of blue-collar training on the employer. POSCO has responded to the shortfall of qualified applicants by recruiting workers directly out of regular high school and providing them with six months of vocational training, followed by up to three months of on-the-job tutoring; during this time, the new employees are paid, but at a much reduced rate. Hyundai Motor Company also trains unskilled workers. Fully two-thirds of its new recruits from 1981 to 1983 first attended the Hyundai Vocational Training Institute, which provides attendees with textbooks, meals, housing, uniforms, and a small stipend. (Of course, not all chaebol training needs to be so extensive. At Samsung's Suwon complex, assembly workers usually get only a few weeks of training.)

Job rotation—with necessary additional training—occurs in Korea, but it is not pursued with the fervor that is evident in Japan. As noted earlier, Korea's blue-collar workers tend to stay with a single function or group of functions for the duration of their employment. White-collar workers with specific technical training are also likely to remain in one position, but other employees may move around within the corporation. At Hyundai, employees might move every three years; at POSCO, workers are given the opportunity to move from department to department and tend to do so every four or five years.

While some rotation does occur, Korean authoritarianism reduces its value to the corporation. After all, a broad understanding of corporate operations and objectives is unnecessary if orders are limited and explicit. For blue-collar workers, the lack of rotation probably reflects the Korean tendency toward high worker mobility. It is expensive and ineffective for employers to invest heavily in training workers if those trained are likely to take that investment to another employer, perhaps even a competitor.

PRODUCTION METHODS
AND QUALITY CONTROL

The split in Korean industry—between the chaebol and the small and medium-sized industries—is nowhere more apparent than in their production techniques. At the high end of the spectrum, Korean corporations are conducting research in biotechnology, building sophisticated semiconductors, and gaining a foothold in the aerospace industry. Even the country's heavy industries are exceptionally advanced, which explains why POSCO boasts the world's record for steel productivity. On the other end, production methods can be extremely crude and unsophisticated—a mix of sweatshops, home assemblers, and archaic backyard welding and metalworking operations.

Unfortunately, primitive methods are not limited to small producers. In the words of an American who spent several years overseeing a joint venture in Korea: "Throughout Korean industry, the processes usually are not very sophisticated by Western or Japanese standards. They will often have just-in-time delivery, but purely by accident—it's just that the parts didn't get there any sooner. Sometimes, they won't order parts until a few hours before they are needed, instead of two or three weeks in advance. I've seen some of the major manufacturers in this country build the products they have the parts for, rather than what they need to fill inventory or market demands."

Given relatively crude production capabilities, it is hardly surprising that quality has only recently surfaced as a significant issue. Obviously, Korean goods have had sufficient quality to compete on the world market, but the strength of these goods has been their price, not their excellence. Korean factories are known for having large rework areas and, by one account, even operate separate lines dedicated to reworking defects.[16]

The problems with Korean quality can be traced, again, to the lack of respect for manual labor. Koreans find little or no pride in production, be it steel, color televisions, or running shoes. Embarrassed and accepting, a young woman will take a factory job without regard to the type of industry and sometimes even without asking what her salary will be (because wage scales for the unskilled are roughly equivalent). The type of product and the kind of work are secondary to the availability of housing and the possibility of friends or relatives in the same factory. One scholar put it bluntly: the "sense of commitment to plant and product, so apparent in Japan, is lacking in Korea."[17]

Moreover, the exigencies of war and poverty have bred an accepting or even resigned mentality. Author T. W. Kang has written about the Korean expression *koenchanayo*, which he translates as "that's all right" or "that's good enough." "In the business context," Kang writes, "if, for example, someone is requested to get a certain set of data but can only come close, the requester shows tolerance and appreciation through the use of this expression. Being big-hearted and not excessively picky is a key part of *koenchanayo*."[18] In other words, when the

world has been crashing down around your ears for a half-century or
more, perfection is an unaffordable luxury. (At the same time, though,
Korea's exposure to the American military did increase its understanding of modern management, including quality standards. During an
interview at a small factory on the outskirts of Seoul, the general
manager proudly hauled out a faded chart labeled, in English: "Acceptable Quality Level-Mil-Std-105D Level II," a quality-control system he'd learned at Fort Lee, New Jersey, in the late 1950s.)

Korean manufacturers are rehabilitating their reputation for marginal quality for several reasons. First, as producers for high-end
American companies, they have had to satisfy those corporations'
requirements. At times, this effort has been facilitated by technical
guidance from American quality and manufacturing engineers. Second, following the example set by Japan, Koreans are eager to break
into higher-end, higher-tech markets and establish more brand-name
awareness. Hyundai, for example, has introduced its Sonata, a more
costly, midsized successor to its small, inexpensive Excel. And Goldstar is promoting its label with a flashy prime-time advertising campaign, timed to coincide with improvements in its product line and
retail outlets.

The move to upgrade products and product lines has, in part, been
forced on Koreans. Recent wage hikes, the appreciation of the won,
and the growing economic sophistication of countries such as Indonesia, China, and Thailand have caused many labor-intensive industries to go offshore. This is particularly the case with garments,
footwear, and some low-end electronics. If the Korean economy is to
continue growing, it must move up to more sophisticated, more skill-
intensive products, and that means better quality: "close enough" isn't
good enough for semiconductors and aerospace. But even if Korea
wasn't being pushed by lower-wage workers, there would be ample
incentive to leave behind the exceedingly meager returns from low-
value products. According to one report, for example, fierce competition in the inexpensive home electronics market has pushed the return
on exported Korean black-and-white televisions to between ten and
twenty cents per set. [19]

For these reasons, quality has become a government and industry
byword. Authorities claim that there are now more than 100,000
quality-control circles in all industries, involving roughly half Korea's

production employees. This figure is probably inflated, however. In any case, the profoundly hierarchical nature of Korean manufacturing means that workers cannot easily voice suggestions for improving products or processes.[20]

CONCLUSION (AND DISCLAIMER)

Korea's authoritarian management style is changing in the near term and long term, for chaebol workers and small-company employees. For the moment, however, as during the years of Korea's great economic transformation, these corporations reflect a paternalism that is pervasive yet limited in scope. Like the institutionalism of the military, corporate paternalism has provided basic needs while viewing the individual as a resource, to be expended as needed.

Because this management style balances the ancient Confucian past and a modern industrial present, it is particularly effective for Korean businesses. By maintaining certain traditional elements, such as the recognition of social contacts in recruitment, employers enjoy the benefits of strong personal connections and group pressures within the company. Similarly, by providing workers with meals, dorms, medical care, and other services, corporations can exert extraordinary control over their employees and demand that employees reciprocate with traditional respect and obedience.

At the same time, however, more modern and performance-oriented attitudes are invoked by these same corporations to justify exploiting workers during boom periods and edging out older and less productive employees during the hard times. The use of performance reviews also allows the companies to reward bright and aggressive workers without totally abandoning advancement through seniority.

These advantages have proved tempting to the Japanese, who are moving away from lifetime employment and seniority-based compensation—moving, in other words, to create the same balance of traditional and modern influences that has helped Korea to thrive. As newly industrializing countries in Asia and elsewhere develop and refine their management methods, the Korean model offers links to the past and the future and, most significant, the promise of rapid economic success.

With that said, a qualification from the beginning of this section should be repeated: While it is instructive to isolate specific practices regarding payment or hours or training, the Korean management style has been firmly grounded on the control of workers by the government's security forces. Whenever this very tight lid is loosened, it reveals that the mix of old and new methods is not always smooth; indeed, since 1987 it has appeared to be exceedingly volatile. If the government opts to relax its control over labor, the tension between these poles might be more pronounced, and the changes in Korean corporate life could be appreciable.

And another qualification should be added: corporate cultures around the world—like the larger cultures in which they exist—are an amalgam of ancient values, modern historic influences, public policy, and specific practices. But they also echo the minds and hearts of their founders and chairmen, individuals of vision, intelligence, audacity, and will. In Korea, where the power of a mammoth chaebol is often concentrated in the hands of a single man, this is dramatically the case.

11

▲ ▲ ▲

The Industrialists

It had all the elements of a prime-time soap opera, but on a more fabulous scale: the richest man in the nation, billionaire patriarch of a massive empire, expires after a long and questionable life. Despite the manifest grief of his children, they immediately leap into a bitter battle over succession and the disposition of his wealth. The eldest son had been branded an incompetent by the now-departed father; he still holds some control, though, simply because he is the eldest son in this Confucian society. The second son, convicted of black-market dealings, has served his time and gone on to head his own successful corporation; now, it is rumored, he wants to return to the family businesses. A sister, her options pared by her gender, nevertheless has large stock holdings and the clout of her highly placed husband. An illegitimate son, born of a foreign mistress (indeed, a virtual second wife), has recently entered the country and been given a post at a crucial subsidiary; forced by birth to remain on the sidelines of the struggle, he may be nursing a resentment toward the other contenders. He may want to play the spoiler. In any case, his standing in the corporation can be parlayed into new power and other prizes.

The final player is the designated heir—the patriarch's third legitimate son—who strikes quickly: he assumes command within fifteen minutes of his father's passing, but family and public sniping appear to undercut his authority. In a bold move, he consolidates two subsidiaries, forming an electronics and telecommunications giant with international holdings; in the process, it is said, he has diluted the power of his familial adversaries and maximized his personal control. Still, his position is far from solid. Asked to cite his greatest accomplishment to date, he says, "I'm proud that I could survive the last four months." He acknowledges that he does not have complete support in the family or the business and government communities. Rumors begin to swirl.

Welcome to Samsung, the series.

THE WARRIOR INDUSTRIALIST

Korea's blue- and white-collar workers have been the engine of its extraordinary growth. But their endeavors have been shaped by a small group of men, the field officers of that army of workers. They have weathered occupation, wartime devastation, hyperinflation, interventionist dictators, and shortages of material and capital—and still managed to create some of the most powerful corporations on the globe. While the government has generally directed much of Korea's development, these men have made most of the practical decisions. The country's transformation rests on their varied skills, their intelligence, their determination—in short, their entrepreneurial and managerial talents. They have filled every developing nation's greatest need, because, unlike capital or technology, such talent cannot be borrowed, imported, or stolen.

They are distinct personalities, from the square-jawed physicality of Hyundai's Chung Ju-Yung to the silver-haired salesmanship of Daewoo's Kim Woo-Choong, but they have common characteristics. For starters, they have all resisted the Confucian disregard for business as a career. In addition, because their wealth is almost always first generation, they have tended to be exceedingly frugal, indeed ascetic, in their life-styles. And finally, for the most part, they have not been saintly figures. Dedicated to expedience and working against poverty, instability, and sometimes rampant corruption, Korea's industrialists have been accused of much: legal trickery, stock manipulation, gross mismanagement, collusion, collaboration, and out-and-out fraud. Ultimately, they must be held responsible for much of the abuse and exploitation suffered by Korea's workers.

But they are men of homeric proportions, driven to extraordinary achievements by patriotism, a commitment to economic development, and, to be sure, self-interest. And their passing, as illustrated by the death of Samsung's Lee Byung-Chull, leaves a vacuum that their offspring will be hard-pressed to fill. Granted, the self-indulgent heirs who were once branded the "Seven Spoiled Princes" are now largely rehabilitated, but it remains to be seen if they have the abilities to oversee the mammoth conglomerates their fathers created.

The stories of Korea's chaebol founders give insight into the skill, nerve, and staunch resolve behind their corporations and the impressive victories scored by the Korean economy. Each story has its special appeal, but three—those of Samsung's Lee Byung-Chull, Hyundai's Chung Ju-Yung, and Daewoo's Kim Woo-Choong—are particularly revelatory with regard to Korea's past and its future.

LEE BYUNG-CHULL (1910–1987): SAMSUNG'S PATRIARCH

Back in the early 1930s, Lee Byung-Chull was an unlikely candidate to lead one of Korea's largest business groups and spearhead the nation's economic transformation. The second son of wealthy landowners, he enjoyed a privileged upbringing, but he betrayed neither drive nor personal ambition. After a spotty academic career—he never completed middle school and left Tokyo's Waseda University after several semesters, supposedly because of poor health—he returned to Seoul, where he spent the next few years "doing nothing in particular." Even when he began his entrepreneurial endeavors, he seemed lackadaisical and undirected. With money inherited from his parents, he established a rice mill in 1936; later on, he admitted "that his decision was rather hasty, and he [was] not really sure why he chose this career."[1]

But by 1938, when he was twenty-eight years old, something had clicked in the young man. That year, in the southern city of Taegu, he founded the "Samsung Store," which flourished during the later years of the Japanese occupation (a potentially awkward issue that is rarely discussed). Activities included trading, brewing, noodle making, transport, and the export of fruit and dried fish to Manchuria and Peking.

In the void left by the Japanese retreat in 1945, Lee found plenty of new opportunities. He moved his headquarters to Seoul and thrived over the next five years, but the company—indeed, the entire economy—was dealt a near-lethal blow when the North Korean army invaded in 1950. Unable to get out of the city, Lee watched as Communist security personnel tramped through his house, investigated his affairs, and confiscated his new Chevrolet. By the time MacArthur recaptured the city, one of Lee's warehouses had been looted by the invaders and the other, Lee claimed, by a powerful South Korean politician. Lee fled before the reinvasion of Seoul with one business, a brewery, still functioning in the south. Drawing on funds from this operation, he started over again in the southern city of Pusan. By reaping windfall profits in imports, compounded by soaring wartime inflation rates, the reborn company grew by 1,700 percent in its first year.[2]

Around this time, Lee later claimed, he experienced an epiphany of sorts, which is best described in his own words: "After the Liberation and the independence of Korea, having spent time in leisure, I encountered a great transformation. I began to form the conviction that I had to do something not only for my own development but also for my country. Along with it, my views of the state, business and life—all changed in a rush." He set about creating enterprises that he considered "indispensable pioneers for national development."[3] The first of these, in 1953, was a sugar refinery, which was soon augmented by a hugely successful woolen mill. He was later accused of profiteering, but Samsung now maintains that mass production actually cut the price of sugar to one-third and cloth to one-fifth their previous levels.

With the end of the war, Lee expanded his chaebol by acquiring smaller firms. At one point during the late 1950s, he reputedly owned one-half of all commercial bank shares in the nation. But Samsung also took some knocks in peacetime. With the rise of each military regime, a new assault was mounted on Lee's assets. Soon after Park

Chung-Hee took control of the country, he cited Lee—along with Korea's other prominent industrialists—for accumulating illicit wealth during the reign of Syngman Rhee. The resolution of these charges cost Lee a considerable sum, but in its aftermath his position seemed enhanced. He helped form and became the first head of the powerful Federation of Korean Industries. Perhaps more important, as Park began to pursue both national development and political legitimacy, he knew he would have to rely on the talents and financial resources of Lee and other wealthy Koreans. Preferences and benefits began to accumulate, and Samsung continued to expand.

Lee's troubles were far from over, though. In 1964, he borrowed $44 million from Japan to build "the world's biggest single fertilizer factory" and one of Korea's most significant industrial efforts to date. As the project neared completion, however, Samsung became embroiled in a serious and well-publicized scandal. Several company officials, including Lee's second son, were accused of dealing on the black market, smuggling saccharin among other, legally imported materials from Japan. Lee protested that the incident grew out of nothing more than carelessness, that a fine had already been paid, and that its reemergence was part of a "hidden conspiracy of a few politicians." Moreover, Lee later wrote, he had rebuffed the demand for a "donation" of 30 percent of the fertilizer company's stock made by "a person within the ruling power structure" shortly before the scandal erupted. All his protests, however, went for naught: his son was convicted and, to assuage public opinion and political demands, Lee was obliged to hand over his majority share in the fertilizer company to the government. In recollecting the affair, Lee called it the "bitterest event of my life."

When Chun Doo-Hwan seized control of the government in 1980, he also made a point of jerking the leash on Korea's most powerful businessmen. To this end, several conglomerates were forced to divest their real-estate holdings and subsidiaries, and credit limits were imposed. Lee's radio and television stations were seized and absorbed into the Korea Broadcasting System—an act, he later wrote, that "shattered my heart into millions of pieces." On balance, though, Lee got more from the government in access to credit and other preferences than he gave in stocks, property, or developed businesses. Samsung's fortunes got their greatest boost with the promotion of exports in the mid-1970s; in the dozen years from 1977 to 1989, its revenues jumped from $1.3 billion to $35.2 billion.

Certainly, there was more to Lee's corporate strategy than supplicating the government for special treatment. More than most Korean industrialists, he followed a management style modeled closely on Japanese methods. He would visit Japan for months every year, learning about new products and technologies, and he maintained a second family there. The Japanese influence is observable in the group's twenty-four-day orientation program, which Lee fashioned after a similar program at Matsushita; as in Japan, Samsung's new recruits start the day early, sing national and corporate anthems, and then take part in physical exercise—in Samsung's case, a brisk, one-kilometer jog. Efforts to automate production lines are likewise modeled on Japanese successes, and Samsung's attempts to upgrade its technologies and quality, with an eye toward eventually marketing more advanced products under its own mark, mimic Japanese tactics.

Like his Japanese counterparts, Lee put enormous weight on personnel management. In 1957, he initiated Korea's first open-recruitment process. As mentioned in chapter 9, Lee claimed that he spent 80 percent of his time on personnel functions and sat in on the final interview of every managerial candidate. But while he was intimately involved in certain aspects of his businesses, he avoided most of the minutiae of management. "I have consistently employed the system of total delegation of power in my business management of all my ventures, big and small," he wrote. "I have never done any actual tasks such as handling paperwork or issuing checks in my entire business career. . . . I have never tried to learn small details of the routine business and know nothing about them." (Despite Lee's professed belief in the delegation of authority, it should be noted that he did not like to see it drift too far down the organization. His group's management was and remains highly centralized under an executive staff, directly beneath the chairman's office, that oversees financial controls and coordinates investments and other operations.)

Over the years, Lee provided workers with above-average wages and working conditions. In part, this was a reflection of his attention to personnel and worker relations. It was also an acknowledged tactic in Lee's strategy to keep Samsung union free, which was one of the founder's "most important management principles," according to a company spokesman. Lee once said that he would rather go out of business than deal with unions, and that sentiment still guides the group. Among Samsung's affiliates and subaffiliates, there are only a handful of unions, and those were inherited in acquisitions.

A final aspect of Lee's style was his conservative approach to new endeavors. While he certainly did not lack boldness—his investments in semiconductors, to be discussed, are a good example—he tended to be deliberate and cautious. This inclination prompted him to pursue "markets where demand was assured, comparative advantage clear and the risks small," in sharp contrast to his daring archrival, Chung Ju-Yung at Hyundai.[4]

Lee's legacy—the result of hard work, political maneuvering, and a lifetime of "accusations, praises, and the crisscrossing of glory and ignominy"—is an empire of staggering dimensions. Samsung is in a seesaw battle with Hyundai to be the largest chaebol in Korea; according to *Fortune*, the group is the world's twentieth-largest corporation. The company's annual report describes a core group of more than twenty companies, but cross-holdings, personal contacts, and sub-affiliate relationships with the group's general trading company mean that actual control extends over almost fifty companies. Operations include genetic engineering, semiconductors, robots, aerospace, and a grab bag of other activities around the world. Samsung makes color TVs in Malaysia, microwave ovens in England, and men's suits (500,000 annually) in Costa Rica. Other operations include paper, shipbuilding, construction, watches, department stores, insurance, food processing, hotels, a newspaper (which Lee created to counter "senseless and silly opinions"), medical systems, a hospital, a credit card company, a cultural foundation, institutes for economic and technological research, and more. Company literature notes that with 159 branch offices in forty-six countries, "the sun never sets" on Samsung.

The chaebol's 1989 revenues of $35.2 billion were equal to 17.25 percent of the nation's GNP. Net profits were reported to be $515 million, but that, as they say in Korea, is the public number. Employment in 1989 was around 177,000—including, by one report, "the biggest company engineering pool in any developing country."[5]

Although the sun may never set on Samsung, the conglomerate is certainly facing one of its darker hours; the passing of founder Lee

Byung-Chull has put the future of his monumental legacy in question. More than fifteen years before his death in 1987, Lee named his third son, Lee Kun-Hee, as his successor. The choice ran distinctly counter to Confucian practice, and there were murmurs about the young man's abilities—hardly surprising given that he was just twenty-nine years old when he was designated to be the next chairman. To his credit, Lee Kun-Hee has put aside all the doubts and second guessing and begun to make his own imprint on the group. He announced the construction of a new petrochemical plant and, perhaps more significant in the long run, he initiated the transfer of low-value, low-margin product lines (small color TVs, fans, speakers, motors, telephones, and other goods) to small and medium-sized enterprises. The move seemed designed to blunt antichaebol criticism, remove potential problems in the most labor-intensive (and, hence, most troublesome) industries, and focus the group's efforts on products with more value-added. Despite these advantages, the plan had to overcome considerable internal resistance from affiliate executives because the value of those lines ($2 billion over three years) would severely undercut their long-term sales projections.[6]

But Lee Kun-Hee's most impressive move was to unify the group's consumer electronics affiliate with its semiconductor and telecommunications operation, forming a globally active corporation with more than $5 billion in annual sales and 38,000 employees. The move was interpreted as a power play by the new chairman—in that it diluted the power of family stockholders—but it also made economic sense by eliminating overlapping product areas and increasing coordination among designers. It also reduced management redundancies at a time when qualified middle managers are scarce in Korea. Finally, the merger promised to reduce substantially the semiconductor operation's high debt-to-equity ratio.

That semiconductor operation represents Lee Byung-Chull's last obsession and an important component of Samsung's future. The elder Lee moved with astonishing speed into this sophisticated technology, with Samsung Semiconductor and Telecommunications (as it was then called) leaping from 64K DRAMs to 256K DRAMs to 1-megabit chips to prototype 4-megabit chips in under five years. This rapid progress did not come cheaply; between 1984 and his death, he spent an estimated $875 million on the Samsung plant in Kihung, about forty miles outside Seoul. Profits were meager at first, but chip shortages and better world prices have since boosted revenues and improved the long-term outlook.

Certainly, there are tarnished memories of Lee Byung-Chull: of his milking the government during the 1950s and his cozy relationships with Korea's repressive military rulers (a connection that was reinforced in late 1988, when security forces used a Samsung advertising blimp to monitor student demonstrations). But Lee also gave Korea a beachhead in the modern global marketplace and, along the way, created an array of potent industrial and commercial resources and a massive payroll—all of which remain as a tribute to his vision, intelligence, and curious, late-blooming ambition.

HYUNDAI'S CHUNG JU-YUNG:
BIG RISKS, BIG PROFITS

The image was powerful: new Hyundai employees, as part of their orientation, were engaged in contests of Korean-style wrestling. At their center, stripped down to athletic shirt and shorts, arms locked around a new recruit, muscular legs planted in the sand, was Chung Ju-Yung, then seventy years old, the chaebol's founder and chairman. Here, the picture said, is a man of spirit, physical strength, and aggressiveness—at once the indisputable commander and the ideal symbol of this immense group. Several years later, even though he had passed the operating chairmanship of Hyundai to his younger brother, Chung remained its ultimate authority, and his values and example continue to influence its operation.

The hard-won success of Chung and Hyundai, familiar to U.S. consumers as a maker of inexpensive cars and personal computers, parallels Korea's own spectacular transformation. Born in 1915, the eldest son in a large family, Chung grew to manhood on a small rice farm during the economically depressed years of the Japanese occupation; in 1989, he was among the richest men in the world, and his business group was vying with Samsung to be the largest in Korea. In the 1930s, he worked as a bricklayer at Korea University; fifty years later, he was serving on that institution's board.

Unlike Samsung's Lee Byung-Chull, Chung seemed to have been

born with an implacable drive for economic success. After he had
finished primary school—the end of his formal education—his parents pleaded with him to join his father in farming, but the small
village was too confining for the ambitious fifteen-year-old. Chung ran
away from home and soon found employment as a roadworker. In short
order, he was retrieved by his father and spent the next two years on the
family farm. But at age seventeen, Chung again packed his bags, this
time for good.

He landed first in Inchon, where he labored as a dockworker.
Soon, though, the young entrepreneur was learning the rice trade,
starting as an errand boy at a mill in Seoul and later becoming the
company bookkeeper. After several years, he branched out on his
own, initially opening a retail shop, then expanding into wholesale.
Unfortunately, like so many other Korean entrepreneurs of his generation, Chung had to stand aside as external events swallowed up his
earliest endeavors: as a result of its military expansion, the Japanese
government tightened control over the rice trade, and Chung was
forced to shut his doors. Undaunted, he jumped into new businesses,
opening a small auto repair shop in 1940, expanding into transportation services shortly thereafter, then forming a construction company
in 1947.

Chung numbered the U.S. Army among his customers, and those
contacts were to prove invaluable when the Korean War broke out. He
moved his enterprises to the southern city of Pusan, where his younger
brother, a former translator for the U.S. military government, helped
him to corner a near-monopoly on construction contracts from the
Americans. In addition to being profitable, these projects also provided the entrée to later construction activities in Thailand and
Vietnam.

Work with the U.S. Army also meant that Chung was established as
a reliable contractor when postwar reconstruction began. These were
dicey years for men like Chung: work was abundant and alluring, but
treacherous inflation made every contract a potential trap. As noted in
chapter 3, Chung was soon caught in a disastrous commitment to
rebuild a bridge over the Naktong River. Skyrocketing costs threatened to bankrupt him, but Chung remained tenaciously dedicated to
finishing the job, drawing on personal loans from his friends and
family to do so. President Rhee was impressed with and appreciative of

his resolve and made sure that later—and more rewarding—contracts went to Chung.

It was the support of President Park, though, that put Hyundai on the road to becoming a world-class corporation. Chung captured a high percentage of the projects as Park undertook to transform Korea's infrastructure, including the contract to build the Seoul-Pusan Expressway. During these same years, Chung began to export Korea's strongest resources—its workers—to build roads in Thailand, housing in Guam, military installations in Vietnam. Many of these contracts were money losers, but they brought Hyundai international experience and reputation, which proved invaluable when the early-1970s oil boom helped create a host of lucrative contracts in the Middle East. Of these, the most important was for the $931 million Jubail Industrial Harbor Complex in Saudi Arabia, which Hyundai won in 1976.

Chung was by no means content to pursue growth in just one industry, however. In the late 1960s, he decided to create a world-quality shipbuilding industry in Korea, even though Hyundai had no dry dock and no experience in shipbuilding, even though no corporation in the entire country had built large ships, even though there was no historic precedent for a nation at Korea's level of development successfully tackling such a project. All that notwithstanding, Chung—with nothing to show but a photo of undeveloped beach property and the considerable support of President Park—set out to find his first customers. To the surprise of almost everyone, he found a venturesome Greek shipping magnate, who agreed in 1972 to accept delivery of two substantial vessels (both around a quarter million tons) within thirty months. True to form, Chung built the dry dock, trained the work force, and completed the order on time.

Chung's accomplishment was monumental—among "the most impressive entrepreneurial feats in Korea, and indeed, the world," by one analysis; a transcending of the "fixed idea of space and time," according to the company. [7] But it could not have been accomplished without the fervent encouragement of President Park, who made sure that bureaucratic approvals came promptly and assured the industrialist that he would not suffer overly for his efforts in behalf of the Korean economy. And Park eventually had to make good on those assurances; in 1975, soon after the shipyard was completed, world shipbuilding fell into a slump. Cancellations left Hyundai with three completed tankers, which would have constituted a devastating loss had Park not pressured Korea's oil refineries to begin leasing the ships from the struggling chaebol.

Chung's entrance into the auto industry was perhaps less astonishing, but his success has made the project as dramatic as anything he has undertaken. Although Hyundai's automobile affiliate was founded in 1967, its main function was to assemble passenger cars for other manufacturers; Chung did not produce his first proprietary model until 1975. In 1979–1980, during a slump in the domestic market, he announced his intention to invest almost $500 million to produce a subcompact auto to be marketed overseas, despite the government's conservative suggestion that Korean firms concentrate on exporting auto parts. Like most of Chung's ventures, this risky gambit has paid off handsomely. The Hyundai Excel, which was first shipped to the U.S. market in 1986, sold more than 168,000 units that year, giving it the best first-year sales for an import in the history of the industry. (In a footnote to the enduring Korean-Japanese rivalry, Hyundai literature specifically notes that the Excel bested Honda's first U.S. entry by over 16,000 units.) In less than eighteen months, with only partial distribution, the Excel had topped long-standing foreign favorites such as Volkswagen and Mazda to become America's fourth-best-selling import. In 1988, it was the best-selling subcompact import in America, and Hyundai added the upscale Sonata to its line.

Much has been made of Chung's flair for making calculated risks pay off. At times, his exploits have seemed almost whimsical, as when he cut corners by landscaping a U.N. military cemetery with barley shoots. At other times, his actions have seemed dangerously flaky, as when he opted to save money on the Jubail port project by forming pylons and other large structures in Korea, then shipping them by barge to Saudi Arabia—without insurance. More recently, Hyundai's quick decision making, based more on the chairman's gut feeling than on market research, has been cited in reference to its $270 million automobile assembly facility in Canada. "They've been designing and engineering it as they've been letting contracts," a project consultant told the *Wall Street Journal* in 1988. "They didn't even know if they'd be building one car here or two when they were clearing the land."[8]

Were he not so successful, it would be easy to condemn Chung for his impulsiveness. But Chung has been improbably successful: President Eisenhower personally complimented the cemetery's barley lawn, the Jubail structures reached their destination on time and undamaged, and in all likelihood the Canadian facility will eventually be configured into a productive and profitable operation. Furthermore, there is much more to Chung's style than simple "luck-and-pluck." Although he has certainly played fast and loose at times, his efforts have been buttressed by a tight, even rigid control over his operations and a personal and corporate austerity.

An account of Chung's daily morning meetings with executives, drawn from his days as group chairman, provides a glimpse of his office demeanor: "The meeting is no place for collegial debate as the chairman's personality dominates the proceedings. Without a word of dissent, he'll check on assignments, issue instructions and do some browbeating. An order by Chung to survey a possible business project means the immediate formation of a team of engineers and project managers, and sometimes an all-night session to quickly prepare documents for possible bidding."[9] His tendency toward control is also reflected in the group's organization, which calls for all the affiliate heads, even the heads of Hyundai's overseas branch offices, to report directly to his office; it is further exemplified in the group's emphatically militaristic corporate culture.

Given this dictatorial manner, it is hardly surprising that Chung has vehemently resisted the encroachments on his authority mounted by the government and labor. Despite official pressure to offer stock in his affiliates, only ten of Hyundai's twenty-seven companies are publicly traded, and two of those are troubled companies forced on the group by the government. Chung's argument against selling shares has been that they would profit only those rich enough to play the stock market; instead, since 1977, he has used group resources to endow the Asan Foundation, which funds scholarships and medical care. He has also chafed at the demands of workers. Labor organizers almost universally point to Hyundai as the most virulently antiunion chaebol, and recent events—from the kidnapping of activists to the request for the massive assault by 14,000 security forces on strikers at Hyundai Heavy Industries—give credence to such charges.

Chung has also viewed most partnerships as a threat to his absolute control. While his group has entered into some alliances—with Mit-

subishi, Westinghouse, and General Electric among others—Chung
has tended to build his affiliates from scratch, avoiding acquisitions
(except in two cases, Inchon Steel and Aluminum of Korea, when the
government strongly requested that Hyundai step in) and joint ventures. This was precisely his strategy in forming Hyundai's electronics
affiliate and, as a result, that corporation spent years trying to catch up
with Korea's other electronics giants. But Chung's fierce independence
and broad diversification now seem to be paying benefits. Hyundai's
IBM-compatible personal computer sells for appreciably less than its
Korean competitors, because the group controls more of the manufacturing process and because it "built the factory that makes its computers, built the trucks that carry them to the dock, built the
containers and ships that carry the computers to market and even
insures the cargo through its own insurance company."[10] That price
advantage made Hyundai's PC the sixth best-seller in the U.S. market
in mid-1988.[11]

At other times, however, Chung's intransigence over matters of
control has cost him dearly. In 1980, for example, the Chun regime
pressured Hyundai and Daewoo to reduce their competing investments
in automobiles and power-generating equipment. Instead of duplicat-
ing each other's efforts, the bureaucrats strongly suggested, each
should take one of the industries and buy out the other's affiliate,
creating two virtual monopolies. Daewoo's chairman, Kim Woo-
Choong, deferred to the wishes of the elder Chung, who chose the auto
industry. But this opportunity to eliminate his only serious domestic
competitor ran aground when Chung refused to become a minority
partner with General Motors, which held a major share of Daewoo's
auto operation.

Chung's fixation on going it alone—which has led some observers
to brand Hyundai the corporate incarnation of Korea's Hermit
Kingdom—has had other negative repercussions. At times, his refusal
to work with other companies, even as suppliers, has bordered on the
ridiculous. Even more important, his avoidance of joint ventures has
meant that Hyundai must try to keep abreast of advances in the most
sophisticated technologies by itself, while many other global companies have found the pace too fast and too costly for an independent
effort. Finally, Chung's insistence on centralizing authority in himself
reputedly created a stifling environment at the highest levels of the

group, promoting a cadre of yes-men and inhibiting talented young managers—so much so that a Seoul-based stock analyst compared Chung to a "banyan tree under which nothing can grow."[12]

But Chung has been nothing if not confounding. True to form, he startled his critics in 1987 when he ceded operational control of the Hyundai group to his younger brother, retaining for himself only the title of honorary chairman. According to Hyundai employees, Chung still arrives at his office early every morning and retains the final say-so on the major issues facing the group. Nevertheless, he seems to recognize, however reluctantly, that he can best preserve his achievements by gradually prying them out of his own grasp, rather than waiting for nature to do the job for him.

Another puzzle in Chung's style is that while he may exercise near-monarchic authority, he lives modestly and does not encourage others to indulge themselves. The common explanation for this plain-and-simple mentality is that Chung's early poverty taught him frugality along with the virtues of hard work. The now-honorary chairman himself lives in a sparsely furnished home in Seoul. He long ago "foreswore smoking and religion," and most of the trappings expected of a world-class business tycoon. In the past, he attempted to transplant that same tightfistedness to his workers by instituting a mandatory company savings policy that appropriated 30 to 40 percent of their paychecks. And while it probably has little to do with his management style, it is at least indicative of the man that he has never bought his wife a birthday present in fifty years of marriage. It would be grossly inaccurate, however, to depict Chung as a latter-day Scrooge. To the contrary, he has given his country a twofold legacy: a business group that borders on being a national institution and the promise of an extraordinary gift of hard cash.

The size and scope of the Hyundai group is difficult to comprehend. In magnitude, it compares well with Samsung, with 1989 revenues of around $32 billion, 166,800 employees, and an astonishingly diversified product list that includes pianos, dry docks, microchips, oil-drilling platforms, kitchen tables, petrochemical factories, golf balls, industrial turbines, toys, and nuclear-power plants. Its affiliates operate department stores and hotels, reclaim land, sell insurance and securities, and pursue resource development around the world, from copper in Peru to oil in Yemen to coal in Alaska. While Hyundai has its consumer-oriented affiliates and a general trading company, the chaebol's main thrust has been in construction, shipbuilding, and other heavy industries. For this reason, Chung's efforts were much appreciated by the development-obsessed regimes of Park and Chun; at the same time, because of the high risk and high investment required for heavy industry promotion, Chung has been particularly reliant on government support, especially in the Park years.

Through Chung, Korea has gained a modern industrial infrastructure, and the nation's goods and workers have earned international credibility. More than just a risk taker, he has been a risk absorber, conquering new territory and new technology. These, alone, are impressive contributions and would have been enough to assure him a place in Korea's economic history. But there is another, more quantifiable aspect to his legacy: in 1985, on his seventieth birthday, Chung announced that he would eventually bequeath only 10 percent of his wealth to his offspring; the remainder would be donated, in ten years, to his Asan Foundation. This action can be interpreted as another move to deflect governmental pressure to offer his companies on the equity markets. But donating 90 percent of one's wealth—even *promising* to donate it at a later date—can hardly be called a tactic. Chung's act seems to be one of genuine philanthropy and a corroboration that, while he has worked for his own aggrandizement, he has never forgotten his humble origins or the country that made him wealthy.

As Chung removes himself from Hyundai's day-to-day operations, his interest in national issues is becoming more apparent. At times, he seems to be sounding an alarm. "The next ten years will be very critical for Korea," he told one interviewer. "If we can't bring our country up to the level of advanced countries, we may not get another chance."[13] At other times, he takes an active role in affairs of state, promoting delicate trade with the Soviet Union and, more emotionally important for Koreans, developing personal and commercial links with North Korea. There seems to be a poetic logic to that effort; when years of bloodshed and futile negotiations have failed to unite the two halves of the peninsula, why not turn to a man who has made a career of, literally, moving mountains? If he should succeed at such a complicated task, no Korean would be surprised. Despite Chung's hand-to-mouth upbringing and rough-hewn image—the wrestler, the gambler, the bullheaded autocrat—there is nothing simple about him; among the extraordinarily talented group of chaebol founders, he seems the most complex and the most in tune with the ancient heart and hahn of his country.

DAEWOO'S KIM WOO-CHOONG:
THE PURITY OF WORK

Love and money are sometimes complementary, often not. For the twenty-six-year-old Kim Woo-Choong, the heart's gentle urgings were drowned out by the siren call of the international textile market.

In 1963, on a trip to London to visit his fiancée, the young trading company employee took advantage of free stopovers in Hong Kong and Saigon to collect samples of popular textiles. He soon realized that the cloth could be made at significantly less cost at Korean mills, so at his next stopover, in Singapore, he deplaned in search of customers. Presenting the Saigon and Hong Kong samples as his own, he wrote up $300,000 in orders and got back on a plane—but this time he was headed home to Seoul. The lover was abandoned—she and Kim never did marry—and Korea was launched on one of its first forays into textile exports, a key event in the nation's economic development.

At the time, Kim's actions were probably seen as a comment on the jilted fiancée; later experience suggests that few women could have distracted the young entrepreneur from such an appealing commercial adventure. Like his counterparts at other chaebol, the founder and chairman of the Daewoo business group possesses a profound—in Kim's case, almost knightly—dedication to the economic development of his nation and people, as well as a huge appetite for work. But Kim is perhaps most notable for the distinctions between him and the other chaebol founders, in age, experience, and entrepreneurial style. Born in 1937, he is too young to be grouped with Lee Byung-Chull and Chung Ju-Yung, yet he is appreciably older than their sons and successors. For this reason, Kim is said to be part of the "1.5 generation" of Korean entrepreneurs, a breed that has grown up in an independent, export-oriented, economically thriving nation—a blessing that translates into high expectations among his countrymen. "We are the first generation of college-educated Koreans to come into business," Kim once said. "People are pushing us very hard—their expectations are very great. We have no choice but to work hard."[14]

That is not to say that Kim has been spared the privations and instability that have long marked Korea's history. He was just thirteen when invading North Korean troops killed his father and older brother; with his mother and remaining siblings, he fled Seoul on top of a boxcar and relocated in the south. There, among the other destitute Koreans who had escaped from the war, he had to scramble to provide food for his family. He guided other refugees and sold newspapers, eventually expanding his delivery territory and hiring other young boys to carry the papers. "It was during this period that the idea of becoming a businessman took hold of me," Kim later said. "I had a dream that the best way to be of service to my country would be to build a great company—a company that would create jobs for our youth and contribute to the prosperity of Korea. I did not see business primarily as a way to make money."[15]

Neither poverty nor the chaos of the war was sufficient to disrupt Kim's grand ambitions. After passing a rigorous entrance exam, he was admitted to one of Seoul's most exclusive high schools, which became a springboard for acceptance into prestigious Yonsei University. There he distinguished himself as a leader and was elected president of the student body. His climb continued when he was hired, shortly after graduation, by a medium-sized trading company, where he began his exploits in the world marketplace.

Those experiences—and the acquaintances he made—were Kim Woo-Choong's primary resources when he and several friends struck out on their own in 1967. With a $5,000 loan and additional capital from a textile manufacturer, To Dae-Hwan, Kim began his own trading company, creating its name from his and To's first names. (The result, Daewoo, means "big cosmos.") Building on foreign contacts made at his previous job, Kim rapidly expanded his customer base. Unlike the older chaebol founders, Kim had the distinct advantage of starting his business group during the supercharged, export-oriented, high-growth 1960s rather than the hardscrabble days of the Japanese occupation or the corrupt and war-torn Rhee years. Daewoo's explosive expansion (over its first nine years, exports grew at an *annual* average of 122 percent) reflects this accident of timing as well as Kim's special talents in salesmanship and corporate strategy.[16]

From the group's inception, Kim directed his operations toward exports, first as a trader and then, in 1968, as a textile and garment manufacturer. After a bold investment in equipment and many cold calls in executive offices in the United States, he eventually convinced large American retailers such as Sears and J. C. Penney that Korea could provide the quality and volume they needed. His success was built equally on hard work and smart tactical moves: speculating that the United States would soon impose a ceiling on imports, Kim set aside profits and began to flood the country with garments. As a result, when limits were introduced—based on existing levels—Daewoo had rights to over 30 percent of Korea's total quota.

This partial corner on the American market brought huge revenues to Kim, which he in turn invested in a variety of ailing Korean companies; unlike Hyundai's Chung, Kim has always expanded more by acquisition than by building affiliates from scratch. Like that of many of the other highly successful conglomerates, though, Daewoo's diversification followed the contours of Korea's economic development (which, not incidentally, largely followed the government's forceful guidance). In the early 1970s, Kim added finance, construction, and electronics affiliates; in the last half of the decade, he expanded into heavy and chemical industries (steel, automobiles, shipbuilding, and heavy machinery, among others). Since the 1980s, the group has concentrated on high technology: aerospace, consumer electronics, semiconductors. Kim has constantly refocused the group's activities, trying to bias it toward these high-tech growth industries, but the group has been hampered by a shortage of scientific and engineering manpower.

The trajectory of Kim's fast-rising career has its base in Korea's traditional culture. Like the older chaebol founders, he has manifested an astonishing capacity for hard work, a willingness to take risks, a cozy relationship with Korea's military dictators, and an emotional commitment to develop the country as well as his corporate domain. At the same time, though, he has shown distinctly modern qualities. Whereas his counterparts have been autocratic and imperious, Kim has delegated decision making to subordinates and been less egotistic about the group's triumphs. Compared with Chung Ju-Yung, Kim seems especially open to power sharing, both within the corporation and with foreign partners.

Because of Kim's dedication, selflessness, and, not least of all, success, something of a personality cult has risen around him. Workers refer to him—half in jest, half in earnest—as *Tosa*, a title usually reserved for an inspirational kung fu master; company personnel, from uniformed guards to young executives, salute the chairman as he passes; even a young union firebrand, a veteran of strike violence and police interrogation, restrains his criticism of Kim: "When I was in college, my friends and I had a special feeling for Chairman Kim. We held him up as a model of what a modern businessman should be. Even today, most Koreans respect him more than the other chaebol founders."

But Kim's success has derived not from his charm or patriotism or any mystical powers. It has come, by and large, from long hours and hard work: the chairman invariably puts in twelve- to fifteen-hour days. He sleeps only five hours a night, which turns out to be something of a necessity because he travels, often internationally, more than 200 days each year. And Kim's time is rarely squandered on leisure pursuits; he reportedly has never taken a holiday in the more than twenty years since he founded the company. Christmas is frequently spent in the Mideast, where the holiday will not interrupt business. Such behavior might be branded obsessive in the United States, but Kim casts it in a more heroic light. Picasso was great, according to the chairman, "because he put all his life into his art. That's what is called for: concentration, hard work, endless striving."[17]

Walking by Daewoo headquarters in central Seoul, one can be assured that the late-burning lights are not just those of the chairman. Kim expects—and gets—similar commitment from his employees, who are allowed a single annual vacation of just one long weekend. White-collar workers commonly log over sixty hours a week, and sometimes the company demands even more of them: in September 1984, employees at the group's trading and construction arm, Daewoo Corporation, resolved to give up all holidays and days off in order to help the company reach its export targets. Participation, while not required, served as a powerful indication of an employee's dedication to the Daewoo family.[18] Kim has also offered advice to his employees about how to spend the scant free time that remains to them, arguing that in a poor country, people should not indulge in expensive and time-consuming recreation. Accordingly, he has enjoined his executives from playing golf. [19]

Americans and Europeans might suspect that this sacrifice to the corporate family would work a vengeance on one's blood family, but here, too, Kim offers an alternative interpretation: "Daewoo people, including myself, believe that working diligently does not harm the family. . . . Indeed, I feel that the destruction of family life occurs due to immoral conduct, when there is too much free time."[20] (As noted in chapter 10, Daewoo takes pains to inculcate these values in the families of Daewoo employees.) Kim does make one concession to his family; he will accept no business calls after he gets home.

Kim's workers are paid well by Korean standards, although they have been periodically pressured to return part of their paychecks to the company. In one instance, workers were strongly encouraged to invest in Daewoo stock—a good investment, as it turned out. In another, all bonuses from 1983 to 1985 were frozen and placed into compulsory savings accounts, albeit at above-market rates.[21] Like his workers, Kim makes a salary that is high by Korean standards but nothing that a Westerner of comparable stature would envy; the chairman takes home only about $100,000 a year after taxes, with no incentives or other bonuses. He lives modestly with his wife and four children in a smallish brick house in Seoul and has said that he would like to leave Daewoo more or less as he started it—with very modest personal resources. Toward that end, he has donated all his holdings in Daewoo (worth an estimated $50 million) to the Daewoo Foundation, which provides scholarships and funds medical projects. (Cynics point out, though, that Kim may have been partially motivated by external events: the government was trying to palm another failing company onto Daewoo and, by some accounts, Kim simply decided that he would prefer to fund social rather than industrial charity.)

Kim has further distinguished himself from the other chaebol founders by passing up the opportunity to make the Daewoo group a family dynasty. Like himself, his family has no equity position in any of the group's companies. Excepting his wife, who heads the development company that owns the Seoul Hilton, none of the senior managers is related to him. His children have grown up knowing that there are no directorships waiting for them when they leave the university. That means, of course, that the chaebol has been run from the beginning by professional managers. It also means that the group will never have to contend with the palace intrigues that have plagued Lee Byung-Chull's succession at Samsung.

Kim has been willing to share his authority with his managers, so that individual affiliate heads—or the chiefs of the group's major divisions—are more likely to make decisions than are managers at some of the other chaebol. But this professional and (marginally) more bureaucratic organization has by no means made Daewoo more conservative. From its early days, the group has equaled if not exceeded the legendary exploits of Hyundai: its projects at any time read like a U.S. State Department warning on hazardous travel zones. When Chung Ju-Yung sent his construction workers into stable Saudi Arabia, Kim sent his to the shiftier sands of Libya, Sudan, Iran, and Angola, as well as Swaziland, Ivory Coast, and Nigeria. "I like to work in the jungles and the deserts," he has said, "because of the possibilities of high profits. If we're successful half the time, we make money."[22] But while he may be daring, Kim is not foolhardy: just to be on the safe side, he arranged to be paid in advance for Daewoo's endeavors in Libya.

An additional element of vulnerability is Daewoo's pursuit of joint ventures, OEM arrangements, and other alliances, in stark contrast to go-it-alone Hyundai. In textile goods, Daewoo has supplied brand lines such as Calvin Klein, London Fog, and Christian Dior; in electronics and heavy industry, Kim has established partnerships with, among others, Caterpillar, General Dynamics, Boeing, Northern Telecom, General Electric, and British Aerospace. Daewoo's largest joint venture is a fifty-fifty enterprise with General Motors called Daewoo Motor Company, which produces, among other vehicles, the Pontiac Le Mans. These relationships are a good hedge against what Kim sees as the inexorable growth of protectionism, and they provide his group with much-needed capital and technology. They have also proved disadvantageous on occasion, though. Ties with GM have been cited as one reason for Daewoo Auto's slow response to changing consumer tastes. More important, GM's refusal to allow Kim to sell in Eastern Europe (because doing so would interfere with GM's overseas sales plans) cost the chairman dearly in a market that he had spent years developing. (Daewoo has subsequently shipped cars to Eastern Europe, however.)[23]

Daewoo's wide-open style (or recklessness, depending on where one stands) is also evident in its astronomical debt-to-equity ratio: a staggering 13:1 in 1982, it remained high, around 8:1, in 1988. Kim, however, seems unfazed. He maintains that the numbers are unexceptional by Korean standards and that the country's relatively immature credit system requires manufacturers to accept more consumer debt. (As a Daewoo spokesman said, "When car sales are good, debt is high.")

All these risks were once softened by Kim's intimate relationship with the Park and Chun regimes. But while it was advantageous in the extreme to have government support, this was not an embrace that Kim could have rejected; the attentions of Korea's technocrats have been insistent.

Two incidents, both belonging to Daewoo's heavy industry developments, are illustrative. The first took place in 1976, when President Park made Kim an offer he could not refuse. Kim was urged—indeed, directed—to assume control of a failing, state-run heavy machinery plant. "Failing," in this case, is an understatement: the plant had been operating in the red for thirty-seven years, and its debt was twice Daewoo's equity. Undaunted, Kim virtually lived at the plant for nine months, overseeing every detail and lending his inestimable presence; soon after, the plant began to show its first profits.

That success, unfortunately, only encouraged President Park to dump another lame enterprise into Kim's lap. This time, the loser was a huge, uncompleted, and heavily indebted shipyard. Kim demurred, but Park was deaf to all objections; he announced Daewoo's takeover of the Okpo shipyard in 1978 while Kim was out of the country on business. It eventually cost Daewoo $500 million (much of it acquired through low-interest, government-backed loans) to complete the massive 1.2 million–ton yard. While its ultramodern facilities showed great promise and even profits, these were soon scuttled by the triple-whammy of rising wages, steel prices, and currency, all compounded by a glut in world capacity. (In fact, during 1987, all of the country's four shipbuilders were either losing money or just breaking even.) Ultimately, losses in shipbuilding threatened to overwhelm the group, and, in 1988, Kim turned to the government for help. But the less interventionist regime of Roh Tae-Woo was short on sympathy: Kim was told he had to seek other kinds of financing (including the sell-off of Daewoo's more profitable affiliates) before the government would chip in.

On the record, Kim has been stoic about the burden his conglomerate has shouldered for the nation. "The government tells you it's your duty and you have to do it even if there's no profit," he has said. "Maybe after the year 2000, Korean businessmen will be able to put their companies' interests ahead of those of society or government."[24] At the same time, he is not averse to sharing that burden with his workers—whether they like it or not. While Kim may be less autocratic among his managers, he retains a strong sense of authority over production workers, and his insensitivity led to some of Korea's most troublesome labor confrontations, both before and after 1987.

Despite Kim Woo-Choong's youth in comparison to the other major chaebol founders, it is worthwhile to begin considering his legacy. First of all, he has announced his intention to leave the chaebol and start a new business. In fact, he has reportedly begun planning his departure, training three possible successors for his position as well as three successors to follow that chairman. No date has been announced, though, and skeptics recall Kim's stated intention to step down in 1985. But even if he stays on for decades, Kim's contribution to Korea is sufficient to be tallied at this point.

In 1989, Daewoo had sales of $20.0 billion (reported net income, true to Korean form and the group's high debt service, was just $114.5 million) with a payroll of 91,000. In addition to over seventy foreign branch offices, the group operates sixteen overseas subsidiaries, ranging the globe from Antwerp to Panama City, Khartoum to Silicon Valley. It builds roads and dams and railways around the world; it trades commodities and explores for oil; it operates hotels. Among its manufactured goods are the IBM-compatible Leading Edge Model D personal computer, ships, industrial robots, shirts (at the astounding rate of 100,000 per day at its 6,000-employee plant in Pusan, reputed to be the world's largest), forklifts, pianos, lasers, cars, fighter-jet components (for the F-16 and the Royal Air Force's Hawk trainer), and thousands of other products; it also owns schools, Korea's foremost securities firm, and the world's largest single dry dock.

The most significant aspect of Kim Woo-Choong's legacy may be yet to come. He is still young, and his success does not appear to have bred ennui or world-weariness in him. To the contrary: he seems as passionate about development—Daewoo's and Korea's—now as he did when he left his bride-to-be waiting at the terminal. He has been active in pursuing new technologies and, especially, creating new markets. Kim was one of the earliest proponents of trading with Eastern Europe, the Soviet Union, and China and was generally far ahead of the government in establishing relations with the communist world. While Roh Tae-Woo's regime was tentatively lowering legal and administrative barriers to trade with communist nations in 1988, Daewoo's Hong Kong subsidiary cut the ribbon on a new refrigerator plant in China. Kim first acknowledged trading with East Bloc nations as early as 1984; since then he has been active in Hungary, Czechoslovakia, East Germany, and elsewhere. More recently, Daewoo has been cited as a likely participant in Korean efforts to work on Soviet development projects in Siberia.

Kim's age, his style, and his agility in handling all manner of markets, with all manner of services and products, make him a symbol of the future of Korea's economic transformation. It is a promising future; there is no shortage of potential calamities for either the man or the nation, but both possess a powerful combination of experience and youthful drive. At the same time, though, both Kim Woo-Choong and Korea approach their futures heavily mortgaged. Daewoo's extraordinary corporate debt still threatens to crush the group, and Korea has piled up debts of another nature.

The Korean brand of risk-taking entrepreneurship, as embodied by the men profiled here, is a paradoxical blend of fatalism and exuberant optimism. Why not go for broke, the logic runs; win and you win big. And if you lose, well, you probably would have lost it all eventually anyway. This balancing of opposites has never seemed more appropriate than today. The nation is entering a golden age of prosperity and freedom at the same time that domestic demands and foreign competition threaten it from all sides.

Domestic problems are the most immediate. Korea's success has been predicated on two kinds of repression: organized labor has been sternly restricted, and other freedoms and social improvements have been delayed or denied, according to the "construction first, consumption later" strategy first spelled out by Park Chung-Hee. But repres-

sion, obviously, is not elimination. Korea's leaders have been able to
stall and cut corners and intimidate, but they have let slide basic
societal problems. By ignoring these issues—environmental degradation, housing, political freedoms—they have made them more bur-
densome and unwieldy; now they are being dunned and dunned hard.
Handling these debts will require delicacy and a willingness to compromise, talents that have been very much subordinated in Korea's
hard-driven campaigns for economic success.

Even if Korea were to resolve its internal problems, it would face
growing challenges from outside its borders. It is being chased hard by
the developing nations in its backyard. It is running into stiff resistance from the trading partners it so desperately needs. And it
remains seconds away from a fiery confrontation with its neighbor to
the north.

A less tenacious, less disciplined, less hungry nation might falter
under such imposing circumstances. Korea, in contrast, has seen a
reduction in growth to 6.5 percent in 1989—low by Korean standards
but impressive by any other. And its workers and managers continue to
challenge the United States in at least two ways.

First, Korea's management style—that exceedingly effective pseu-
dopaternalistic, quasi-military mix of traditional and modern influences—has been responsible for a loss of employment and commerce
in the United States. When General Motors manufactures cars in
Korea, American jobs are lost. When General Electric obtains its
microwaves from the suburbs of Seoul, the balance of payments grows
more lopsided. When malls from Bangor to San Diego stock their
shelves with Korean shirts and sweaters and shoes, American production workers, the executives who oversee them, and all manner of
service providers from janitors to short-order cooks suffer.

The second face of the Korean challenge is longer-term, somewhat
hypothetical, and, if it comes to pass, much more important. In short,
there is a strong likelihood that Korea's management style will prove to
be a workable model for businesses in other developing countries. If
these nations are even half as successful as Korea, American workers
will find their standard of living, and the terms and conditions of their
employment, in serious jeopardy.

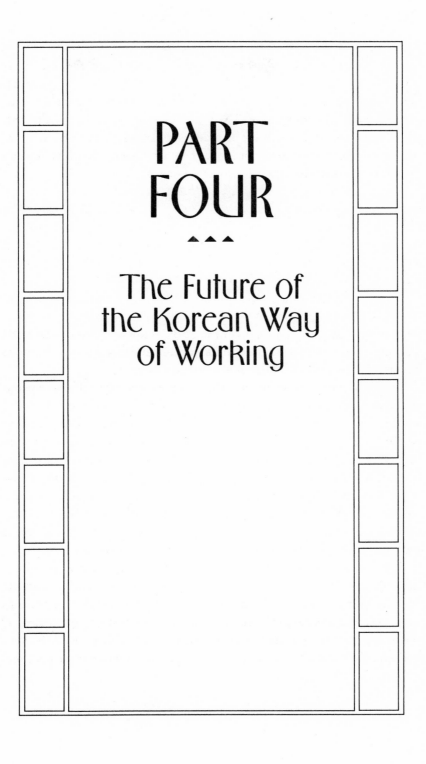

PART FOUR

▲▲▲

The Future of the Korean Way of Working

12

▲▲▲

Bringing the War Home

"I don't think you have that quite right," the young labor activist interrupts. Korean by descent, Australian by citizenship, slight of build, and exceedingly soft-spoken, she argues through her eyes and the sharp angle of chopsticks, poised over a dish of bi bim bap. "Korean workers are not truly militant," she quietly insists. "The style of the strike, the headbands and raised arms, are more form than content. Unions in Australia are much looser in their demonstrations, but they are in fact much more militant."

Perhaps, but labor disputes since 1987 suggest that the regimentation of Korean workers can work for their employers or against them, that workers have embraced the fight for higher wages and better conditions with the same tenacity that they once brought to production quotas and export targets.

The style is clearly militant, from the lockstep marching and the drum-driven chants to the stark orderliness of the proceedings. "I've been in Korean union meetings," an American labor expert confided, "where the blackboard diagrams looked like something you'd find in a military briefing room. Some of their demonstrations are almost cho-

reographed." And there is also evidence of true substance—in the
young worker pushing her face into the screened visor of a soldier, the
better to condemn him, and the outnumbered and unarmed strikers
battling thousands of crack assault troops across the broad Hyundai
shipyard.

These are new and meaningful images in Korea, and, with variations, they have been replayed with startling frequency. They reflect
a deep discontent among many Korean workers, as well as a willingness to act on that discontent. They also underline that the Korea of
Park Chung-Hee and Chun Doo-Hwan is fading. The values and desires that shaped that time are being shed, replaced by a new ethic
and new expectations about work, politics, and the quality of life.

Korea's workers are not likely to lose their focus on the world
marketplace, but long-suppressed domestic issues must now be given
their due. Four of these "home fronts" are of critical importance; their
resolution will determine the direction and competitiveness of the
Korean economy in the coming decade.

THE FIRST HOME FRONT:
A SOCIETY IN FLUX

Korea's economic transformation, crystallized in statistics, appears as
a series of quick but graduated advances: each year more jobs are
created, more income earned, more debts repaid, more cars and TVs
acquired per thousand population. But this metamorphosis has not
always been a smooth progression; it has, at moments, been wrench-
ing. Over the decades, industrialization has severely altered the nation's social framework, dislocating old values and raising new
expectations. Korean society is by no means on the verge of collapse,
but it is being forced to accommodate a barrage of new influences. And
even though Koreans are an adaptable people, there is no guarantee
that their adaptations will be unfailingly wise.

In gauging the effects of modernization on Korea, the standard
Western indexes falter. Statistics on divorce, for example, are not very
revealing, simply because Koreans avoid the practice. (An alien-
ated Korean wife is well advised to separate but remain married,

because divorce will almost never result in remarriage and will surely cause her to lose custody of her children and any financial support.) Crime statistics are similarly inconclusive, indicating level or even declining rates (although the newspapers are filled with lurid reports of rape, forced prostitution, robbery, and street-fighting gangs).[1] But the effects of modernization can be seen in Korea's accelerated urbanization and structural changes in the all-important Korean family.

Urbanization is hardly a modern phenomenon in Korea. For centuries, the largest cities have captivated the nation. "As Paris was for France," noted one scholar, "Seoul was not simply Korea's largest town; it was Korea."[2] But although Seoul had long been a powerful magnet for the nation's brightest and most ambitious citizens, the promise of industrial jobs and a lack of effective farm policies made the pull nearly irresistible in the early 1960s. According to some estimates, over 500 people a day were moving to Seoul in that decade and the 1970s. The urban share of Korea's total population jumped from 28 percent in 1960 to 57 percent in 1980 and was expected to hit *82 percent* in 2000.[3] Such an abrupt demographic shift obviously stresses a city's environment: sewers and the water supply are overburdened, the housing supply dries up, the air thickens with car exhaust and industrial smoke, the cries for better basic services grow more strident.

Modernization has also transformed family structure. Traditionally, the emphasis in Korea has been on large families, which support the parents when the father retires around age sixty; indeed, the single strongest value in the society is probably *hyodo*, or filial piety. Today, however, families are smaller and life expectancy is longer. Compared with the generation that preceded them, Korean men born during the early 1940s have a life expectancy that is six years longer (67.3 versus 61.0 years), and their families are only half as big, with just three offspring instead of six.[4]

With parents living longer and being provided for by fewer offspring, filial piety has been tested. For the first time, nursing homes are being proposed as an alternative to family care for the aged. The government is awarding priority for housing loans to Koreans who are caring for their aged parents; the state, in short, has been forced to offer special incentives for fulfilling what was once an unavoidable duty.[5] While Korea's families remain exceptionally tight-knit by Western standards, young Koreans are growing impatient with Confucianism's restrictive obligations.

Koreans without families often find themselves lacking any support. To pick the most notorious instance, unwed mothers and their offspring fall well outside the safety net of Confucian relationships and obligations. Similarly tragic examples are plentiful, and Koreans are clearly embarrassed by them.

Fortunately, unlike during the grim years of the past, society now has the resources to improve social conditions; the rapid industrialization that has created many of these problems has also broadened society's capacity for resolving them. Unfortunately, for the moment, Korea lacks the public institutions to administer that support. The creation of a welfare and public assistance framework is perhaps the most necessary and most daunting of the tasks now confronting Korea's more democratic leadership.

Clearly, Korea's technocrats have looked at Western systems—with their stratospheric costs and frequently counterproductive outcomes—and shuddered. They are formulating new strategies based, in theory, on Korean culture and attitudes. The Confucian emphasis on paternalism, though, does not figure largely in this initial Korean thinking on social policy. "First," says one report, "the principal aim of a social welfare policy should be to foster people's ability to work and to provide them with opportunities to work. . . . Attempts should be made to establish the kind of social atmosphere that encourages a spirit of self-help and self-reliance and inspires business firms to improve the welfare of their workers." Such a system would revolve around vocational training, scholarship programs (to prevent the "hereditary transmission of poverty"), and public assistance for the handicapped and "helpless" elderly.[6] Other observers have cautioned against the negative side effects of excessive generosity.[7]

In addition to establishing a welfare system, Korea must tackle an acute housing shortage, a brutalized environment, and other social shortcomings. The need for such improvements was an early and often repeated theme of Roh Tae-Woo's administration, but his ability to deliver on these promises has been demonstrated only sparely.

THE SECOND HOME FRONT:
INDUSTRIAL RESTRUCTURING

Korea's quarter century of skyrocketing economic gains has been predicated on cheap labor, an undervalued currency, and easy access to world markets. But now, with wage increases, an appreciating won, and growing protectionism, the nation is losing its competitiveness against lower-wage countries such as Indonesia, China, and Thailand. So, like the Japanese before them, Koreans are surrendering the most labor-intensive and least value-adding industries, concentrating their efforts and investments instead on high-technology and capital-intensive industries. "Indeed," the Korean Development Institute has stated, "the level of technology developing during the next decade and a half will largely determine whether Korea can successfully join the ranks of advanced industrial countries. It is for this obvious reason that the primary emphasis of Korea's economic policy must be placed on the development of new technology, the introduction of advanced foreign technology, and the development of highly trained man-power."[8]

This is a tall order. Of course, Korea is no stranger to economic restructuring, and some would argue that its previous transformation, from a rural, nonindustrialized country to its current status, was more strenuous than the task it now faces. But there is a significant difference: in the past, Korea could anticipate that foreign investors or customers would supply new technology as a way of guaranteeing quality or keeping costs down. In other instances, technological know-how could be acquired through the purchase of turnkey plants and licensing, as was the case in shipbuilding and steel. Today, in contrast, foreign countries have become stingy with their technology, which puts the burden of future development on the shoulders of Korean researchers and technicians.

The origination of new technology within Korea will require large investments in research and development. Such investment has been growing, by an average of 20 percent annually between 1983 and 1987. In 1980, R & D expenditures added up to a paltry 0.58 percent of the

GNP; by 1988, the figure had climbed to 2.00 percent, and expectations are that it will hit 3.00 percent by 1991.[9] According to one report, the Ministry of Science and Technology has a "master plan" that would push R & D spending to 5.00 percent of GNP by 2001.[10]

While expenditures of 2 percent of GNP are well above those of most industrializing countries and respectable in comparison with more advanced nations, the key to technological development is not always a simple percentage; more important is the absolute size of investment. It takes billions of dollars to square the capacity of an integrated circuit, whether one is in Japan or Haiti. The government has tried to help by conducting basic research at its own institutes, but most R & D investment (81 percent in 1986) is made by the private sector, and it is from there that most advances will have to come.[11]

One way to increase the clout of Korea's R & D investment would be for its companies to join forces, along the lines of the research consortia and other alliances that operate in Europe, the United States, and Japan. This has been attempted, most notably in a government-sponsored consortium that unites Samsung, Hyundai, and Lucky-Goldstar in the development of a sixteen-megabit dynamic random access memory chip. But such a strategy runs counter to the clannish mentality prevalent in many of the largest chaebol.

THE THIRD HOME FRONT:
THE LABOR POOL

Even if Korea's close-to-the-vest conglomerates were to join forces, they would encounter a still greater barrier—the worrisome shortage of qualified managers, scientists, and engineers. The same resource that transformed Korea, its people, now threatens to keep it from advancing any further.

The first area of concern is management personnel. As of the end of 1987, only about a third of all companies were being run by professional managers or employees who had risen to leadership positions. The rest were being run by founders or their families. In part, this reflects the Korean tendency to keep corporate control within the sanctuary of the family. And, in part, it highlights the shortage of personnel qualified for senior management positions.

A more pronounced deficiency occurs at the middle-management level, which is hardly surprising given the lightning speed at which Korea's development has occurred. "In an ideal situation," says an American consultant to Korean businesses,

> you have a number of production workers on the floor, and they'll have varying levels of experience. Above them, you'll have foremen with maybe fifteen or twenty years experience. And above them, managers who know the industry from the inside out. Korea has plenty of good production people, but the foremen and managers have roughly the same experience as those floor workers. That's certainly understandable, but when the managers don't have the experience to lead effectively, they become a problem. To preserve their dignity, they rely on traditional respect for authority rather than asking questions and finding out the right answers.

Korea's work force must also become more technically sophisticated. Advances are being made: the nation annually turns out 32,000 graduates in the applied sciences—proportionally more than the United States and almost as much as Japan. Lucky-Goldstar claims to have more than 3,000 researchers with postgraduate degrees.[12] And the number of researchers across the nation soared from 7.2 per 10,000 population in 1982 to 11.3 in 1986.[13]

Nevertheless, the pool of engineers is woefully insufficient to guide Korea's further development. Japan has 240 engineers per 10,000 population, while the United States has 160; South Korea, in contrast, has 32. Furthermore, when Japan was at roughly Korea's current level of development, its ratio was roughly the same as it is today.[14] More important, a cultural bias works against the creation of more engineers in Korea. Confucian tradition lauds the scholar and the official; "hands-on" people, whether in an engineering firm or a welding shop, are less highly regarded. So too few engineers are produced, and many of those who do earn engineering degrees use them to acquire management positions. (It should be noted, though, that Koreans are capable of turning their cultural predispositions on end. The near-total elimination of a similar prejudice against entrepreneurs is a good case in point.)

Software specialists constitute another particularly acute shortage, especially in the factory automation industries that will allow Korean productivity to rise in the face of higher wages. Domestic demand is growing at dramatic rates (from 1983 to 1987, the demand for numerically controlled machine tools and robots grew at an average annual rate of 65 percent). Yet factory automation has found only a marginal foothold in Korean industry, and, without its own developers, the nation remains heavily dependent on imported technologies, mostly from Japan.[15]

Efforts have been mounted to acquire additional technical and scientific help from overseas. There have been numerous reports of Japanese researchers and technical personnel taking the short flight from Tokyo to Seoul for brief—and highly lucrative—holidays. At least one Japanese employer has seized its employees' passports to prevent such wildcat transfers of technology. A longer-term approach has been to recruit Koreans living abroad or other nationals of Korean descent, particularly Americans. Some have worked at Korean-owned facilities in the United States; others are lured with promises of Korean-style authority and U.S.-style compensation. The success of this radical strategy, bringing in outsiders and giving them potentially disruptive salaries, underscores just how resilient a Korean corporate family can be.

But for the most part, Korea will need to develop its own technical and management people. And that presents the educational system with an extraordinary challenge: to create a work force that is at once regimented and creative; at once responsive to direction and open to new ideas; at once traditional and ultramodern. In short, it will be trying to forge that most illogical organism—a thinking man's army.

In pursuing this improbable goal, Korea's educational system has one source of help in the country's changing demographics; the school-age population has already dropped from a high of 38.0 percent of the overall population in 1980 and is predicted to be just 27.7 in 2000.[16] The demand for education is certain to remain high, but this reduction in the student population is expected to mean less intense competition, reduced financial burdens on families and government, and a much-needed improvement in the quality of textbooks and teachers, many of whom are hired through personal connections or outright bribery. (At one point in 1988, the Ministry of Education announced that it had uncovered more than 300 cases in which teachers had paid an average of $5,700 to receive their positions.)[17]

But the most significant—and most difficult—changes will need to be made in the orientation of Korea's educational institutions. If Korea is to keep pace with technological development, more emphasis will have to be placed on vocational and technical training. At the same time, schools must encourage new ideas, experimentation, trial and error. Both these changes fly in the face of the conservatism and classroom autocracy of Confucian scholarship. For Koreans to stake their position in the modern world, they will have to place less emphasis on received wisdom and more on their ancient and long-suppressed talent for innovation.

THE FOURTH HOME FRONT:
LIBERALIZATION

As Koreans confront these social, industrial, and labor changes, they must also tackle the need to restructure the role of government in economic affairs. Politicians and bureaucrats alike recognize that they can no longer maintain their white-knuckled grip on every aspect of the economy, that the days when Syngman Rhee could personally initial foreign exchange transactions are long over.

The first force driving the relaxation of government controls is the sheer size of the economy, which has grown beyond the bureaucracy's ability to track and respond to events and trends. In consequence, central planning has threatened to become more brake than engine. The government has been candid about its shortcomings, acknowledging that past interventions have caused overcapacity, waste, and a general reduction in competitiveness.

The business community has also been actively lobbying for greater autonomy. The powerful Federation of Korean Industries has been pushing for an end to government control (and, therefore, the depoliticization) of commercial banks as well as a more rational tax system, which would rely on fixed rates rather than the current mix of taxes and "voluntary" contributions. The latter, also called quasi-taxes, have been used to pay for public works (the Peace Dam), the Olympics and Asian Games, social foundations (which, in the past, were often headed by relatives of Chun Doo-Hwan), and political campaigns. While the exact size of these levies is hard to pin down, some reports suggest that they exceed expenditures for research and development. [18] In any case, they are doubtless a substantial drag on corporate performance, and they perpetuate a business style that encourages corruption and coercion over efficiency.

Third, the world's more developed nations are pressuring Korea to reduce its protection of some industries and open its markets to imports. Roh has noted that it is "inevitable for Korea to open its market wider to foreign goods," and his government has made strides in that direction. Capital markets are being freed up, and there are promises of more liberalizations. Nevertheless, Korean trade negotiators have proved themselves tenacious and often frustrating opponents. ("It seems impossible to discuss U.S. trade representatives in Korea without using the word *beleaguered*," advised an American who has had close contact with those negotiations.)

Finally, government decontrol is being promoted by Korea's citizens. Granted, they are sending an ambivalent message: on the one hand, they demand protection against Western and Japanese imports that compete directly with Korean products, including beef, wine, and movies. (These protests have been fierce; tactics have ranged from massive demonstrations to the release of poisonous vipers in a theater showing an American film.) On the other hand, workers insist on an end to ham-handed intervention in labor relations, although they recognize that the government has many roles to play: the legislature must enact a more comprehensive and coordinated legal framework, the judiciary must interpret those laws uniformly, and the executive branch must act as a mediator in disputes and, if need be, the enforcer of statutes.

With so many powerful forces pressuring the government to tailor its role in the economy, it would seem impossible for Korea's bureaucrats and politicians to maintain their powerful grip. But additional—and powerful—forces are pushing for renewed intervention.

For starters, there is inertia. "The people of Korea have, unfortunately, become very accustomed to government control," explained Park Fun-Koo, vice president of the Korea Labor Institute. "We are like slaves after the American Civil War. We don't know what to do or how to begin functioning in a free society. This constant reliance on the

government, like any long-term habit, will take some time to break."
And the government, while convinced of the need to reduce its control,
remains hesitant to reject the very methods that brought Korea to its
present economic peak. Finally, the dismantling and reconfiguration
of existing power structures promises to be a clumsy, if not dangerous,
undertaking. As centrally planned economies in Eastern Europe and
China have discovered, the relinquishing of power is no easier than its
consolidation.

Beyond simple inertia and timidity, there are compelling economic
reasons for maintaining government controls. First, certain industries—shipping and construction, for example—would falter without
government help. Second, past interference in the economy has created the now monstrous chaebol, which, if left unregulated, would
overwhelm their small and medium-sized competitors. Even with current controls, it is difficult for the government to supply these much-
needed small and medium-sized enterprises with enough support and
protection. Third, the government has a clear role to play in organizing
and guiding high-cost investments in technology. According to the
director of the industrial policy division at the Ministry of Trade and
Industry, "Korea can't enter all kinds of high-tech industries owing to
limited budget and sources, so we should designate certain sectors and
concentrate our energy on the ones where investment effects are
maximum." Overseeing this designation and concentration, of course,
would be the government, which would also "prevent a private company from monopolizing an original technology or material."[19]

In sum, the Korean spirit seems willing to embrace political and
economic liberalization, and substantive steps in that direction have
been taken; questions remain, however, about how quickly the next
steps will come and how long a stride can be expected. The feverish
optimism of 1987 has been dampened by a strong current of skepticism. Militant workers have seen that Roh, like Park and Chun before
him, is willing to use assault troops as strike breakers. And businessmen have heard free market rhetoric before. Recalling past regimes,
Hyundai's founder and honorary chairman, Chung Ju-Yung, said,
"They propagated slogans for 'private initiative,' but they actually
tightened control over private businesses. Their behavior was impru-
dent and reckless."[20]

13
▲▲▲

World of Warriors

American auto workers, candidate Richard Gephardt told the camera in a presidential campaign commercial,

> work their hearts out every day, trying to turn out a good product at a decent price. Then the Korean government slaps on nine separate taxes and tariffs. And when that government's done, a $10,000 Chrysler K Car costs $48,000 in Korea. It's not their fault we can't sell our cars in a market like that—and I'm tired of hearing American workers blamed for it.
>
> I've been criticized for my trade policy—for saying it's time to open up markets, and push down trade barriers like those Korean taxes and tariffs. The Gephardt amendment calls for six months of negotiation. And if that doesn't work, and I'm president, and we have to walk away from that table, the Koreans will know two things.
>
> They'll know that we'll still honor our treaties to defend them—because that's the kind of country we are. But they'll

also be left asking themselves: How many Americans are going to pay $48,000 for one of their Hyundais?

If Koreans feel like an embattled people, they have good reason. After generations of seemingly endless warfare, they have entered a period of relative calm—only to find themselves beset by conflicts among themselves and with their staunchest allies and trading partners.

Korea's internal troubles would seem most likely to compromise its economic strength and impede further progress. But Korea has repeatedly shown an ability to bend its major resource, its people, to the tasks at hand. So while these battles are loud and chaotic and occasionally bloody, they are probably less ominous than the threats that come from without. Of these, contentions with Japan and the West are the most pressing. The United States has already negotiated an abrupt appreciation of the won and an equally sharp reduction in the U.S. trade deficit with Korea, factors that have contributed heavily to Korea's anemic (by recent standards) growth in 1989.

Other threats lie closer to Korea's borders. The barbaric and totalitarian regime to the immediate north constitutes an economic threat, because it is so prone to the rampant destruction of life and property and because it has the potential for demoting Korea's warrior workers to being, once again, warriors. Koreans also face less violent confrontations, with workers in other countries who will accept even lower wages and who are now maneuvering in some of Korea's most important markets. Korea's response to this challenge will test the agility of its political and industrial leaders because, for the first time in Korea's modern history, they will have to bring about changes in the work force without resorting to simple brute force.

BAD BLOOD:
THE NORTH KOREAN THREAT

As the soldiers say, there ain't no *D* in the DMZ.

Korea's demilitarized zone is, contrary to its label, intensely militarized. With a few exceptions, the residents of this moribund strip of

land are military personnel, all heavily armed. Even with the busloads
of tourists muddling from site to site, there is no confusion about what
is going on here: this is a war zone, inactive for the moment. The
Panmunjom tour is probably the only one in the world where visitors
are required to sign declarations that absolve their hosts of liability in
case of attack by hostile forces.

There is no sense of immediate danger: the Joint Security Area,
where North and South square off, resembles a neatly tended garden,
with flowers and a small pool. Boyish North Korean soldiers peer into
the spare, wood-frame buildings and smile. Across the border, trucks
rumble between rice paddies while rare cranes and other exotic birds
fly overhead. But the calm only accentuates the sense of latent violence. This—as the guides have already detailed in words, photos,
and maps—is where two American GIs were ax-murdered in 1976 by
North Korean troops, where an American officer was beaten in another
brief but savage episode, where the defection of a Soviet visitor started
a bloody firefight that left several North Koreans dead.

It is anxious territory. The edginess seeps closer to the bone as one
descends 250 feet into an infiltration tunnel, discovered in 1978 after
the North Koreans had already burrowed through their half of the DMZ
and into the South Korean side. Visitors run their hands along the
blasted walls and look past the metal doors into the section that still
leads into the North. They are told that this is one of four *known*
tunnels (one of the others is twice as deep and twice as long) and that
American and South Korean experts think there could be as many as
thirty additional tunnels, still undiscovered, designed to infuse shock
troops into the countryside or Seoul's outskirts or, perhaps, the city
proper.

The nettling point, of course, is just that: no one knows how many
tunnels there are, or where they are, or how far they have come. Or
when, if ever, they might be used.

One cannot stay in Korea for very long without being reminded that
it is a country of prosperity but not peace. The North and South remain
technically at war, and the hostilities—in word and action—are constant. The Democratic People's Republic of Korea, under the bizarre
and self-adoring leadership of Kim Il-Sung, has pursued its foreign
policy through kidnappings, senseless commando raids, assassinations, bombings of civilian airliners, and threats of additional vio-

lence; Kim has also created one of the world's least open societies, where the radios and televisions are permanently tuned to North Korean broadcasts, where government loudspeakers feed propaganda into citizens' apartments, where cars and fishing boats and even bicycles are all owned by the state.

As enemy and brother, North Korea has an understandable capacity for provoking fear, outrage, and—after decades of separation—deep longing in the South. There have been periodic overtures from Pyongyang, and they are received in the South with the pathetic enthusiasm of a jilted lover; after addressing the United Nations in October 1988, Roh Tae-Woo noted with optimism that the attending North Koreans listened to his entire speech and passed up the opportunity to excoriate him in their remarks. But these halting moves toward a diplomatic thaw are inevitably followed by recriminations, intransigent demands, and breakdowns in relations. Still, most South Koreans hold passionately to the hope that the peninsula will eventually be reunified, for reasons that are at once familial, cultural, and economic.

First of all, brothers and sisters, parents and children have been separated for more than four decades. An estimated one-fourth of the South Korean population have close family ties with people in the North. Culturally, the South and the North share 5,000 years of history and were part of the same political entity for over 1,000 years. Even today, South Korea's national anthem refers to Mount Paektu, which is located across the DMZ. Economically, each half of the peninsula has something to offer the other. The North has minerals and other natural resources and potential hydroelectric energy. Like the South, it has seen extraordinary growth since the devastation of the Korean War. For what it is worth, North Korea is generally thought to be among the most economically developed of Asia's communist nations.

In any lowering of barriers, though, it is clearly the South that has the most to offer. It has twice as many people as the North, a GNP that is more than six times greater, and a per capita GNP that is three times higher. It produces more food and has a better transportation and communications infrastructure. And the gap is clearly widening: while the South's GNP grew by 12.8 percent in 1987, estimates suggest that the North's was stuck at 3.3 percent. By the year 2000, the South's per capita income will be four times higher than the North's, and its GNP will be seven times larger.[1]

The chasm between North and South is widening in other respects as well. Kim Il-Sung (and his son and presumed successor, Kim Jong-Il) continue to tighten their control while the South moves toward greater personal and economic freedom. As Seoul opens its markets to foreigners and reduces limits on travel for its citizens, Pyongyang withdraws and reaffirms its commitment to *juche*, rigid self-reliance. As Seoul strives to present itself as a responsible member of the world community, Pyongyang thumbs its nose at the West and defaults on its loans. If anything, the two countries are rushing further apart, in political sophistication and material well-being.

That fact alone is destabilizing: South Korea could become too great an indictment of the policies of the impoverished but militarily strong North. South Koreans are also well aware that the North has the capacity to launch a lightning strike on Seoul and quickly mobilize a huge portion of its population for a protracted war. They know that the North spends an astronomical 20 to 25 percent of its GNP on defense, thereby sacrificing industrial growth in nonmilitary industries and even basic infrastructure. (It has been said that the North is so short of basic equipment and machinery that it must use tanks to compact roads.) In addition to being militarily strong but economically poor, the North is volatile, and the potential for instability rises as the only leader it has ever known nears retirement.

In contrast to the North's military investment, the South spends just 6 percent of its GNP on defense. Given its larger GNP, that translates into roughly 50 percent more funds than the North. But despite these higher actual expenditures, the South runs a smaller military: its army has only 630,000 men (including many three-year conscripts) versus the North's 830,000 troops. South Korea also has fewer tanks and less artillery. But the South comes closer to matching the North's resources every year and should reach parity sometime in the 1990s. In the meantime, it can count on help from 40,000 American troops and annual military exercises with the United States that involve some 200,000 additional soldiers.

In the end, South Korea's strongest defense is its thriving economy, which allows for a continued upgrading and expansion of its military and, more important, is linking Seoul with Pyongyang's principal backers in the East Bloc. Despite its aberrant tendencies, the North seems to realize that it might be too absolutely self-defeating to continue its isolation from the South, especially when its communist and past communist allies are opening *their* doors. For its part, South Korea has pursued efforts to open trade with the North; in the months after his election, Roh Tae-Woo pushed for more links, and the major conglomerates responded, usually through Hong Kong and other third countries. In 1990, trade between the two countries was expected to reach $100 million. The North, while it has appeared less than enthusiastic over these overtures, does seem to recognize that it can either play along or find itself increasingly impoverished and paralyzed.

There is a final way in which North Korea imperils the South's continued prosperity. Ironically, unification has become one of the South's most divisive issues, engendering bitter debates, rock and firebomb attacks, and general animosity between the government and those advocating a less cautious rapprochement. To the extent that this emotional issue destabilizes South Korea, it threatens continued growth.

In sum, while South Koreans express an almost relentless optimism regarding reunification, there is a clear wariness and even paranoia about the regime of Kim Il-Sung. And with reason: despite the periodic communications and conciliations, the North is still the most likely source of irretrievable disaster facing the Republic of Korea.

THE EVEN NEWER KIDS
ON THE BLOCK

For several decades following 1961, Korea and the other "little dragons" of East Asia (Singapore, Hong Kong, and Taiwan) had an almost unbeatable advantage over Western manufacturers: they had well-educated, submissive employees who would work for a pittance. Westerners could invest in these countries or face them in the marketplace.

More recently, however, the little dragons are being challenged by other, even less-developed countries, such as China, Malaysia, Indonesia, and Thailand. Like Korea, these nations have low-cost and docile work forces. Like Korea, some of them have a culture that supports authoritarianism in the workplace. Like Korea, some have a history of deprivation that encourages hard work. Some also have government and management strategies that have been modeled on

Korea's, learning from its successes as Korea learned from Japan (see chapter 14 for more discussion of the Korean model).

Unlike Korea, some of them have additional resources—oil, coal, minerals—that can make rapid economic development even more possible. And, unlike Korea, most of these nations have yet to feel the pressure of rising labor costs or an accelerating currency.

The upshot is obvious. In the basic, labor-intensive industries that were Korea's industrial beachhead (textiles, garments, footwear, and consumer electronics), these nations enjoy nearly overwhelming advantages. For example, in 1986, when the hourly wage for Korean production workers was $1.46, Sri Lankans were making $0.29.[2] As Korean wages have risen, the differentials have grown. Korean corporations have been among the first to appreciate these new realities and have responded by moving their production facilities offshore—to Bangladesh, Sri Lanka, China, the Caribbean, Latin America, and elsewhere. Korean textiles, clothing, footwear, and toys lost 24,000 jobs in 1988 alone.

But more than just primitive sweatshop industries are being transplanted: Goldstar produces sophisticated goods such as color TVs, telephones, microwave ovens, and computer monitors in Turkey, Thailand, Indonesia, and the Philippines. Samsung has similar operations in Mexico and Thailand.[3] Obviously, Korean corporations are not alone. Japanese, American, and European manufacturers are also locating in these nations instead of Korea, where they might have gone only a few years ago. Malaysians and Thais are now making disk drives and microchips for foreign investors, and their sophistication is certain to grow at a rapid pace.

Thailand is an excellent example of how such a nation can poach on what was once the exclusive territory of Korea and the other little dragons. Its economy—with a 1988 GNP growth rate of 11.1 percent and manufacturing growth of 12.4 percent—is clearly undergoing a transformation.[4] Exports are expanding by nearly 40 percent annually, and fully 60 percent of those exports are manufactured goods, including shoes, textiles, and sophisticated electronics.

The appeal of the Thai work force to American and Japanese corporations is its youth (the average age is about twenty), education (the literacy rate is 85 percent), and cost: the average wage in Bangkok runs around $3.00 per day; some of the country's 27 million laborers

earn less. The government has supported these advantages by devalu-
ing its currency and keeping a lid on taxes and import duties.[5]
Consequently, Toyota can make dies and jigs for auto panels there at a
cost that is reported to be 40 percent less than that of similar operations in Japan.[6]

Obviously, manufacturing in any less-developed country brings its
share of problems, from an unreliable infrastructure to the economic-
life-sucking imprecations of corrupt officials, ethnic strife, political
instability, and much more. Thailand also suffers from having some of
the world's most radically insecure borders. Its neighbors include
Cambodian soldiers, refugees, and guerrillas of various stripe and
faction; and insurgent tribes, opium druglords, and occasional government troops in Myanmar (Burma). But, like Korea, Thailand has been
able to satisfy the concerns of domestic and international investors.

Thai workers and their counterparts elsewhere are propelling their
countries into the ranks of the little dragons. By undercutting Korea's
advantage as a low-cost manufacturer, they constitute a serious challenge to that country's workers in the chaebol and, especially, the
small and medium-sized industries. But while the pressure from this
quarter is building slowly, Koreans are finding that the power being
exerted by more advanced nations is immediate and impossible to
ignore.

WITH FRIENDS LIKE THESE:
KOREA AND THE DEVELOPED WORLD

In the early months of 1988, Representative Richard A. Gephardt
jolted his presidential campaign into life with a single television ad
that did not attack pollution, or drugs, or crime, or the gargantuan
budget deficit racked up by the incumbent Republican administration,
or any of a litany of horrifying phenomena that lurked in the voters' own
backyards. Instead, he targeted the trade policies of a small Asian
nation that many American students couldn't find on a map, a fact that
was itself one of those horrifying phenomena.

The ad was flawed in its calculations—the actual cost of a K Car
would have been closer to $38,000. It erroneously implied that Chrys-
ler was exporting to Korea. And it missed two salient facts: first, most

of the consumption-discouraging taxes applied to an American car would also be applied to Korean-made vehicles, and, second, not long before the ads ran, the Korean market had been totally closed to imported autos. But despite its shortcomings and the apparent remoteness and obscurity of its focus, the ad touched a nerve with the electorate. Gephardt won the Iowa primary election and placed second in New Hampshire. Meanwhile, his campaign broadside was playing to extremely attentive audiences in Korea. "Representative Gephardt made these people very, very nervous," a Seoul-based American diplomat said later.

In the West, Gephardt's success was interpreted as a sign that Americans were fed up with what they perceived to be shoddy treatment by Asian nations, especially the Japanese. Korea received the brunt of Gephardt's criticism (according to reports) because its tariffs and taxes were easier to understand than Japan's complex and systemic barriers to trade. And Korea was an emerging economic force. Its 1987 trade surplus with the United States was $9.6 billion, up sharply from $7.3 billion in 1986 (although it was already easing back to $8.6 billion in 1988). It had had astonishing success with the Hyundai subcompact automobile, and its microwaves and televisions were showing up in discount stores around the country. All that made Korea a threat in itself and a symbol of how unfair trade practices could spread to other Asian nations. Already, it was noted, the U.S. deficit with the little dragons constituted roughly 20 percent of the overall U.S. trade shortfall.

Koreans viewed Gephardt's pitch—and the retaliation-mandating trade amendment he had sponsored in 1987—as part of an inexorable trend toward protectionism, prompted by the worsening American trade deficit; that imbalance, depending on which Korean one talked to, was the result of an inability to "make industrial structural adjustments after the two oil shocks" or a political inability to say no to special interest groups or an undisciplined work force or any of a number of other factors.[7] The precise driving force behind the trend mattered little; what counted was a strategy that would halt the shrinking of the gateways to America's free-spending masses.

Worries about protectionism had started in the mid-1980s, when the trade balance shifted heavily in favor of Korea. In 1987, the Gephardt amendment was passed by the House. The primary target was assumed to be Japan, and the amendment was ultimately dropped from the trade legislation, but Korea's America watchers could plot the direction and magnitude of the legislative vectors.

Early 1988 produced a double-whammy: Gephardt's Korea-bashing ads appeared just a few weeks after the Reagan administration had announced that Korea and the three other little dragons would be dropped from the Generalized System of Preferences (GSP) program, under which developing nations are allowed to bring certain goods into the United States duty free. Much was made of the positive significance of this event, which was that these previously underdeveloped nations were now deemed sufficiently developed to compete without special treatment. ("Happy Graduation, Tigers!" read one upbeat American headline.)[8] And most accounts noted that the actual cost of losing GSP exemption would be around $500 million for the four countries combined—not a negligible amount but hardly enough to trip up these thriving economies.[9] But the trend, again, was clear.

Korea's foreboding about American protectionism was fulfilled later in 1988, when the U.S. Congress passed the Omnibus Trade and Competitiveness Act. This act included the "Super 301" process, which was appropriately dubbed "Son of Gephardt" by several editorialists. Under Super 301, the U.S. trade representative is required to list those nations with pervasive unfair trade practices that harm U.S. businesses. If negotiations do not lead to a change in the offending practices, the president is obligated to retaliate against practices that breach existing trade agreements; he is authorized but not required to retaliate against practices that are deemed "unreasonable or discriminatory." The actual punishment could come in the form of hefty new duties levied on some imports or outright bans.

Super 301 was directed, as explicitly as possible, against Japan. But Korea—with its "buy Korean" policies, high tariffs, import quotas, licensing restrictions, limits on foreign investment, and poor patent and copyright protection—clearly fit the act's definition of "systematic anticompetitive activities." Indeed, shortly after the trade bill was passed, a former deputy U.S. trade representative told a Seoul periodical that "we got more mail about the trade practices of the Koreans than we did about any other country in the world, including Japan."[10]

The U.S. Chamber of Commerce joined the fray, demanding that

Korea (along with Japan, Brazil, and India) be placed on the Super 301 list. This, of course, marked an unparalleled economic turnaround: in roughly twelve months, Korea moved from being a developing nation with favored import status to a threat to the American economy.

Super 301 is only one component of U.S. trade law, which also incorporates intellectual property protections and antidumping provisions (under which Daewoo, in August 1989, was fined $34 million—the largest such penalty in the 200-year history of the customs service—for selling underpriced steel). It is marked by huge loopholes: the trade representative's decisions can be superseded by the president, and he can cancel the act's supposedly automatic retaliation if he thinks it might jeopardize U.S. security or economic interests. That power, of course, makes the sanctions only quasi-automatic.

All that notwithstanding, the threat of being listed as a Super 301 offender brought a quick response from Korea. It had *already* let its currency appreciate (by almost 20 percent in thirty months) in response to American pressure; had knuckled under to demands that it open its markets to American beef, wine, and cigarettes; had announced plans to cut its average tariff rates, from 16.9 percent in 1988 to 6.2 percent in 1993.[11] Now it accelerated its efforts to placate American demands. Negotiating and goodwill teams (including two groups of national assemblymen) swept into the United States; one trade delegation promptly spent $2.4 billion on airplanes and electronics equipment in a surplus-deflating spree.[12] Negotiating sessions—which reportedly ran into the early morning hours—eventually led to a deal that included liberalized limits on foreign investment and an open door for foreign advertising and travel agencies.[13] Korea also promised to stop closing its borders to protect local producers.

The process reinforced the Korean reputation for ardent bargaining. ("They'll negotiate with you all the way to the airplane," a former U.S. trade official had said earlier.)[14] It also showed that the Koreans knew exactly how much they had to give; of the Chamber of Commerce's top four trade offenders, they alone escaped the Super 301 list.

Although they could score a temporary triumph, Koreans had good reason to worry about what was coming next in the long progression from Gephardt to GSP graduation to the cocked hammer of Super 301.

Ultimately, they feared the closing of American markets, which are already protected by an array of tariffs, quotas, "buy America" laws, "voluntary restraints," "user fees," and outright import restrictions.

Koreans were also worried about markets elsewhere around the world, for similar reasons. The European Community has come down hard on Korea for its alleged dumping (everything from cargo ships to polyester fiber), protection of its growing domestic market, and, ironically for Americans, supposed discrimination in favor of the United States. Unlike other developing countries, which sometimes have ex-colonial ties and therefore defenders in the EC, Korea has had no such support. The chaebol have also had problems in Canada, which once welcomed Hyundai with open arms. Even Japan has taken issue with Korea, charging that it has dumped goods on the Japanese market. The newspaper *Yomiuri Shimbun* put the matter in crisp, if somewhat self-serving, terms: "Offensive-minded South Korean versus defensive-minded Japanese are facing each other in several industries and Japan–South Korean trade friction seems likely to increase."[15]

What Korea has not needed to worry about, curiously, is pressure to reform its labor practices, despite the clear importance of such practices to its competitiveness and provisions in the 1988 U.S. trade bill that allow the trade representative to cite countries for unfair labor practices, such as the denial of the right to organize and bargain collectively and the failure to provide occupational safety standards. These are sensible provisions because a country that allows its workers to be exploited has an unfair advantage over countries that protect their workers. But the trade bill also supplies sundry escape clauses. The president is allowed (but not mandated) to respond to such practices, and a country can avoid citation if the trade representative decides that its labor practices are moving in the right direction or that its practices are consistent with its "level of economic development."

With all this wiggle room, the trade representative's 1989 review could have cited Korea—or any of a number of emerging economies—without committing the United States to meaningful action. It could have made the simple point that labor abuses in Korea harm organized workers in the United States and elsewhere. It did not. And, apparently, no one expected it to do so. Not one labor organization or human rights group submitted testimony to suggest such a citation. The upshot is that the 1988 trade bill—as it is currently enforced—

focuses more on demand than on supply; markets are opened, but the production of goods is left more or less to the devices of each country.

Although this inattention to labor practices ignores a (if not *the*) central force behind Korea's trade imbalance with the United States, the trade representative's office was probably wise to focus where it did. Tariffs and currency rates can be (and were) changed swiftly, by administrative fiat, but finger pointing by the U.S. government would do little to change a work style based in part on values that are centuries old.

At the same time, many Koreans are wondering what else must be done to mollify American concerns. The won has appreciated, the trade balance with the United States has been slashed, markets have been opened. It has hurt the Korean people and has put pressure on elected officials to show that they are not American pawns. While they are eager to maintain good trade relations with the United States, they know that too much conciliation would be politically unwise and heighten anti-Americanism, which has been on the upswing in their country: a 1988 survey of college students found that 95 percent held the United States responsible for the military repression at Kwangju in 1980; 51 percent thought the United States was neither an ally nor an enemy; and none (repeat, none) of the respondents named the United States as a country that liberated Korea from the Japanese.[16]

At first glance, Korea's problems seem staggering.

It remains, at base, a small country with few natural resources. It has yet to see long-term political stability. It faces an extensive, costly, and urgent domestic agenda. It is entering a perilous new phase of development, in which personal expectations are rising at the same time that the nation's economy is less capable of satisfying them. It is beset by old blood feuds and new competitors. And its strongest ally and trading partner has been exerting its considerable power for trade concessions and currency adjustments.

These woes have had a cumulative effect on the nation's competitiveness. Korea's economy faltered in 1989: wages jumped again, exports lagged, and growth slowed. Continued labor unrest has prompted yet another government crackdown in 1990.

But dire prospects and temporary setbacks do not mean failure;

they do not mean that Korea can again be relegated to the rank of docile Asian ally. In Korea, all obstacles—real and potential—seem to translate into stronger motivation, deeper resolve. The ancient and modern history of this nation has prepared the people for plugging through harder times than these. Korea remains a vibrant competitor and a model for developing nations around the world. As such, it will continue to threaten American jobs and American businesses for the foreseeable future.

14

▲▲▲

The Continuing Challenge

To concentrate on Korea's problems—even though they are genuine
and dramatic and worthy of analysis—is misleading. Certainly, drags
on its economic growth exist, and the potential for chaos and destruction is real. But Korea remains a force in global economics, and, as it
moves into products and technologies that were once the exclusive
preserve of more advanced nations, it becomes an even more potent
adversary.

Some perspective is required. Although Korean power and influence are growing throughout Asia and around the world, Korea is
decidedly not another Japan. It is smaller, less confident, more need-
ful of foreign support and technology. But the Korean way of working—
that mix of paternalism, exploitation, and militaristic discipline—has
been hugely successful. More important, that success challenges the
United States and Europe in ways that the Japanese do not.

This is why: many of the methods that underlie Japan's economic
triumphs (especially those that stress worker participation, quality
control, and inventory management) can be applied in the United
States. In contrast, the methods behind Korea's success are often

anathema to American values and could never be duplicated in the American workplace. Put another way, when American workers compete against the Japanese, they use many of the same weapons; when they compete against the Koreans, they face strategies and methods that violate some of their most fundamental beliefs. But while Korean methods mesh poorly with Western values, they may find application among the many authoritarian and oligarchic societies in the developing world.

THE KOREAN MODEL

Any consideration of Korean management style must eventually grapple with the issue of portability: can Korea's methods be applied in other nations, acting independently or with Korean participation? One side of the debate claims that Korea's rise is singular, built on a unique constellation of cultural traits and historic events. [1] Whereas certain economic *policies* may be adapted in other countries, proponents of this view say, the social and cultural traits—which are by far the more important in defining a work ethic—are much less likely to take root in foreign soil.

The other side maintains that behind the Korean facade one finds a simple and brutal exploitation of workers that is by no means unique to Korea, that can be applied to other impoverished nations across the Third World. Moreover, laborers in many developing nations seem to duplicate the human qualities that underlie Korea's success: some put in nearly as many hours as their Korean counterparts (for even less pay), some exhibit nearly as profound a commitment to shake off generations of dire poverty, some manifest similarly close family ties and respect for (or fear of) authority. There is little surprise, then, that Korean corporations find it profitable to build new production facilities in such culturally diverse locations as Turkey, Sri Lanka, and Mexico. Obviously, these facilities cannot be run along strictly Korean lines, but efforts are made to imbue the work force with Korean discipline and a sense of management paternalism; this is true even when the chaebol build production facilities in the United States.

Even where Korean corporations are not operating factories, their example is certainly attractive to leaders of government and industry.

The appeal of the Korean model lies first in its short-term rewards. It provides the elite in government and industry with ample justification for using the police and the army to stabilize labor, increase productivity, and—not incidentally—preserve their power. Even the most beneficent, least self-serving leader might be seduced by the long-range promise of the Korean model: by exploiting your workers now, you will be able to provide them with material wealth, dignity, and, as they succeed, limited democratic freedoms.

Suppose the leaders of a developing nation were still not convinced and decided to shop around for other models. The advanced nations of the West have been too developed for too long to offer pertinent lessons in worker organization and motivation. Japan might provide more, but its rapid economic expansion was based on an industrialization that had begun long before the devastation of World War II. But Korea's experience shows one set of methods for making the economic leap from oxcarts to aerospace in a generation. That is why China, among other countries, has been an avid student of the Korean miracle and, where possible, has entered into alliances with Korean corporations. In fact, say Western diplomats, the appeal is so strong that the Chinese have been "salivating" to get into Korea: "We get so many signs of this. The Chinese are fascinated with the South Korean model."[2]

The Chinese connection is natural. For thousands of years, China and Korea have been inextricably linked—by geography, culture, and history. The two nations share a Confucian heritage and a similar modern experience of war and physical deprivation. There are also living ties between the two: Manchuria has a huge population of Koreans, the remnant of Japanese policies of forced labor and other migrations.

While reform-minded Chinese have been drawn to South Korea as a model for rapid economic development, many Koreans have been drawn to China for their own purposes, trade primary among them. Despite ponderous legal barriers, Korean-Chinese trade in 1987 was estimated to be $2 to $3 billion—larger than South Korea's trade with many countries in Western Europe.[3] Estimates for 1988 jumped to roughly $4 billion.[4] China has been embraced as a supplier of inexpensive agricultural commodities as well as the natural resources that South Korea desperately lacks. Already, some reports claim that South Korea is China's second-largest coal customer (after Japan).[5]

But Koreans have also been eager to give China's low-wage laborers a firsthand look at the Korean way of working. Daewoo was among the first Korean companies to pursue China's cheap labor (an urban Chinese worker's average annual income in 1987 was less than $400) and is already producing refrigerators in a joint venture in Fuzhou. But Daewoo is hardly alone; Samsung is pursuing joint ventures in China that will produce refrigerators, color TVs, and VCRs, with around 30 percent of the output destined for export. In a similar move, the Lucky-Goldstar group is planning an electronics factory in China that would export 80 percent of one product line.[6] Chinese companies are also being used as low-cost OEM suppliers. In late 1988, for example, the Lucky-Goldstar group was reportedly selecting a Chinese manufacturer to supply the chaebol with black-and-white TVs, to be resold under the Goldstar mark.[7] Although such an operation would remain independent from the chaebol, it would clearly be exposed to Korean methods.

Obviously, a Chinese factory cannot be made to mimic a Korean operation. The differences—in discipline, incentives, training, and education—are vast. Government policy also runs counter to many Korean practices; for example, while layoffs are now technically legal in China, they are highly uncommon.

But, as in the Korea of some years ago, Chinese laborers are comfortable with paternalistic oversight and conditioned to respond to authority. Strikes remain illegal, and union activity is under the absolute control of the state. Indeed, labor organization has been pointedly repressed: in late May 1989, the first actions taken against the demonstrators in Tiananmen Square were not against students or sympathetic government officials but against trade unionists. While students were still free to erect the "Goddess of Democracy," the leader of a new labor organization, the Beijing Independent Workers' Union, was arrested, and two of his colleagues were missing and assumed to be under arrest.

All of this has created ambivalence among Koreans. While they are eager to take advantage of China as a trading partner and a source of commodities and cheap labor, they are reluctant to give too much support, in investment or technology, to a nation of hungry and ambitious workers. And not just any nation: the ancient depiction of Korea as "a shrimp among whales" is never more accurate than when its economy or labor force is compared with China's. In 1984, the *growth* of China's gross national product was greater than the *total* GNP in South Korea.[8] The 500 million Chinese work force is twice the total combined populations of the United States and Canada.[9] China's manufacturing work force alone is 50 percent larger than Korea's entire population.

The June 1989 massacre in Tiananmen Square and subsequent retrenchment from liberalization have made China seem less likely to pursue Korean methods and less threatening as a competitor. But China—like other countries in Asia, Africa, and Latin America—remains hungry for economic development. Regardless of the course that those nations follow, their leaders will continue to scrutinize Korea as one of the few models of successful Third World development. And, at least in the foreseeable future, Korea will be sufficiently rich and flexible to participate in the economic advancement of other nations, whenever it suits its self-interest.

STAYING POWER:
THE RESILIENCE OF THE WARRIOR WORKER

As worrisome as the Korean model may be for the West and Japan, the immediate challenge remains Korea itself, as a producer of goods that compete directly with products made by workers in the more developed countries. Despite persistent problems, the values and cultural traits that have supported Korea in the past will continue to make it a force to be reckoned with.

Those problems cannot be lightly dismissed. The pressure for industrial restructuring and the need to upgrade its labor pool obviously affect Korea's ability to compete; over the long term, they also promise to recast the nation's working style. More immediately, the nation's changing social values and its political and economic liberalizations are already altering working style and competitiveness. The dedication to home and community, the traditional respect for authority, the shared sense of suffering, the fire that comes from poverty and rivalry with Japan—all these were less potent influences in 1990 than in 1960. Some of the outward signs of diligence are fading; absenteeism is reportedly up, and workers are less responsive to the autocratic demands of their managers. As already noted, labor unrest and staggering wage hikes have helped push some low-margin manufacturing offshore. Even Korea's overseas construction workers, once the symbol of the nation's ability to compete internationally, are now so expensive that Korean corporations have had to hire more and more foreign workers: the percentage of non-Koreans working for Korean construction firms overseas more than doubled from 1982 to 1988.[10]

As significant as these trends are, too much can be made of them. Koreans are still hungry to improve the conditions of their lives. Korean workers remain eager to put in long hours. Much of the ingrained cultural bias toward regimentation, authoritarianism, and social harmony is intact. And these values continue to be buttressed by the insecurities inherent in Korea's geopolitical and economic condition: this is, again, a country at war, without resources.

Between 1986 and 1989, wages in Korea were among the world's fastest rising, but labor is still a relatively small part of the nation's total manufacturing cost. By one estimate, even a 30 percent increase in 1988 wages would have raised factory costs by just 3 to 5 percent.[11] And Roh has shown that strong-arm tactics still work against militant unionists; after three years of extravagant pay hikes, unions settled for very modest, single-digit raises during the spring negotiations in 1990.

In sum, liberalization and changing social values are having undeniable effects on Korea's ability to compete and its way of working. But compared with the rapid and dramatic shifts in Korean life over recent decades, these effects are distinguished by their circumscription. And some Korean values will become even more pronounced. If an agricultural Korea could sustain an abiding respect for education, for example, surely a modern and industrial Korea will embrace it with even greater ardor.

Indeed, the Korean way of working may not change *soon enough* to accommodate shifts in the industrial base and the desire to create an upgraded labor pool. As the nation moves toward more high-technology and higher value-added products, it will require a new breed of worker—one who is capable of managing and working in an environment that requires more knowledge and more individual initiative, who is more attentive to quality and more likely to return investments in training. For that to happen, the Korean management style will have to become less autocratic. Management's partnership with workers will need to be more evenhanded.

That need not translate into diminished competitiveness. As a Hyundai manager pointed out, "Reductions of corporate authority don't have to threaten our productivity. If better working conditions meant lower profits, then American companies would all be bankrupt. If American workers can do it, so can we."

A true management-labor partnership seems a long way off, though, and the transition will be as difficult as anything now facing Korea. Still, it is not without precedent in East Asia. As one labor expert explained, "The managers come to us and ask how they can restore discipline. We tell them that the old authoritarianism won't work, that they must find ways to restore discipline using democratic methods. We tell them that their homework is to find new methods of motivation. We tell them to look at how Japan motivated its people after similar labor problems. Look at Japan, we say."

In labor, as in any other aspect of economic growth, Korea will look at Japan but develop its own response to its own problems. Korean managers can be expected to bend to the desires of the emerging work force, but they will also be making new demands on those laborers. They will be pushing them (and themselves) to find new products and new markets.

The opportunities now appearing in Eastern Europe provide an interesting case in point. Even before the fall of communist hard-liners, Korean corporations had judged these markets highly promising—so much so that the chaebol were busily pursuing indirect trade (via branch offices in Hong Kong and Japan, for the most part) with these regimes even when it was sternly prohibited by South Korean law. In his 1987 campaign, Roh Tae-Woo acknowledged this obvious reality and openly advocated direct trade with East Bloc nations, who responded by opening trade offices in Seoul and discussing extensive joint efforts. One of the big plums was the prospect of trade with the Soviet Union. Hyundai, among other Korean business groups, announced that it was considering a plan to send Korean workers to help develop Siberia's enormous natural resources, in exchange for Soviet lumber.

LESSONS FROM THE KOREAN WAY OF WORKING

While Koreans are hungrily pursuing business in Eastern Europe, they are also active in other realms of opportunity, in other regions, in new technologies, in novel strategies for manufacturing goods and organizing workers. This fervent endeavor—this capacity for rising above current dilemmas, for seeking new methods and markets without regard for cultural, ideological, or other differences—lies at the center of Korea's economic miracle. And that drive represents a fundamental difference between Korean workers and managers and their counterparts in America. Put simply, work is valued differently in different cultures, and developing economies such as Korea often value it more.

Laborers in the United States and Europe are hardly lazy; as candidate Gephardt pointed out, many of them do "work their hearts out every day." By some accounts, they are working more hours than they did a few decades ago, and their productivity continues to increase. Leisure time has dropped, and the vast majority of workers (92 percent by one study) would not be willing to work shorter hours for less money. [12]

But the rewards of their labor—usually measured in more and better material goods—are clearly less visceral than those experienced by workers in the developing world. In Korea, after centuries of chaos and famine, industrial work is bringing security and food; it has dramatically improved most workers' standard of living and the educational opportunities for their children; it has instilled a new and invigorating sense of personal and national pride. More important, Koreans are far from sated: too many of them are still hungry, too few of them have adequate housing, almost none of them feels genuinely secure about the economic or political future.

The upshot is that Korea—and much of the rest of the developing world—remains more competitive in spirit than the West. Daewoo's chairman, Kim Woo-Choong, who has never taken a day off and regularly logs fifteen-hour days, is a national hero in Korea; in the United States he would be condemned as a workaholic. Because of their advantages in technology, infrastructure, and experience, Western economies could once hold their own despite this deficiency of want. Today, those leads are less significant and under constant assault, and, when all other things are equal, hungrier hearts prevail.

For the near term, it is apparent that Koreans are not going to make substantial changes in their way of working; that means that Korean-American competition must be addressed within the United States. While public policy can play a role in providing a "level playing field," the government is a minor participant. Inevitably, the rough burden must be placed on the backs of American workers and managers.

They will bear it well enough; the United States and other advanced economies will continue to dominate for the coming decades. But they will find no shortcuts. The days of relying on a mystical American ingenuity and initiative ended some time ago. If the advanced economies are to hold their own, they will do so by tiring, often grubby, in-the-trenches labor. Few of the men and women in the trenches like it that way—to paraphrase Mark Twain, unless you'd rather be doing something else, you can't call it work—but, as in any battle, the alternatives are even worse.

Notes

CHAPTER 1 (Pages 3–16)

1. "Economy Grows 12.2 Percent in '88, Boosting GNP to $169.2 Billion," *Korea Herald*, March 26, 1989. (Bank of Korea figures.)
2. *Korea Year 2000, Prospects and Issues for Long-Term Development, Summary Report* (Seoul: Korea Development Institute Press, 1986), p. 21.
3. Ibid., p. 49.
4. *1989 World Almanac.*
5. Louis Kraar, "Asia's Rising Export Powers," Pacific Rim 1989 special issue, p. 50.
6. Federation of Korean Industries, *Korea's Economic Policies (1945–1985)* (Seoul, 1987), p. 184.
7. Fred Hiatt, "Discipline and Death in South Korea: Brutal Military Practices Drive Many to Suicide," *Washington Post*, March 12, 1989.
8. Larry E. Westphal, Yung W. Rhee, and Garry Pursell, "Korean Industrial Competence: Where It Came From," World Bank Staff Working Paper no. 469 (1981), p. 10.
9. Bae Kyuhan, *Automobile Workers in Korea* (Seoul: Seoul National University Press, 1987), p. 37.

10. Christian Institute for the Study of Justice and Development, *Social Justice Indicators in Korea*, 2nd ed. (April 1988), p. 122.

11. Alexander Kim Youngman, "Korean Kundrehwa: The Military as Modernizer," *Journal of Comparative Administration* (November 1970), p. 355, as quoted in Edward S. Mason et al., *The Economic and Social Modernization of the Republic of Korea* (Cambridge: Council on East Asian Studies, Harvard University, 1980), p. 49.

12. "Putting Rumors to Rest?" *Business Korea*, November 1988, p. 35.

13. *Korea Year 2000*, p. 11.

CHAPTER 2 (Pages 17–35)

1. David L. Lindauer, "Labor Market Behavior in the Republic of Korea," World Bank Staff Working Paper no. 641 (1984), p. 2.

2. *International Labor Organization Yearbook, 1987*, pp. 27, 32.

3. This figure should be used with some caution, especially in making international comparisons, because Koreans who work as little as one hour per workweek are considered employed for statistical purposes; U.S. Department of Commerce, International Trade Administration, *Foreign Economic Trends and Their Implications for the United States, Korea*, FET 90–43 (April 1990), p. 2.

4. "Job Marts vs. Manpower," *Korea Herald*, October 29, 1988.

5. *ILO Yearbook, 1987*, p. 74.

6. These data were drawn from the following sources: Economic Planning Board, *Major Statistics of the Korean Economy, 1988*, p. 24; Bank of Korea, *Economic Statistics Yearbook, 1988*, pp. 248–49; Ministry of Labor, *Report on Monthly Labour Survey*, May 1988, pp. 28–42, 88.

7. Economic Planning Board, *Major Statistics*, pp. 23–25.

8. Ministry of Labor Survey, May 1988, pp. 28–42.

9. *An Overview of Small and Medium Industry in Korea* (Seoul: Small and Medium Industry Promotion Corporation, July 1988), pp. 8–9, 61.

10. *ILO Yearbook, 1987*, table 12A, pp. 675, 676. The differences between the United States and Asian countries are actually more pronounced than these numbers indicate, because the Korean, Japanese, and Hong Kong averages cover only hours actually worked, whereas the U.S. average covers all hours paid for, including vacations and public holidays.

11. Ministry of Labor Survey, May 1988, p. 42.

12. "Working Women Prefer Humanitarian Treatment to Higher Pay: FKTU," *Korea Herald*, October 13, 1988.

13. U.S. Department of Labor, Bureau of Labor Statistics, *International Comparisons of Hourly Compensation Costs for Production Workers in Manufacturing, 1987*, Report 750 (February 1988), pp. 5, 7. (Calculated separately, manufacturing wages rose by 11.6 percent in 1987, while the

won, under steady pressure from the U.S. government, underwent a robust 7.2 percent appreciation against the dollar, although it fell against many other major currencies. See also Economic Planning Board, *Major Statistics*, p. 260.)

14. These data are from Economic Planning Board, *Major Statistics*, pp. 259, 261.
15. Ministry of Labor, *Yearbook of Labor Statistics, 1976–1985*; quoted in Park Fun-Koo and Tarsicio Castaneda, "Structural Adjustment and the Role of the Labor Force," Korea Development Institute Working Paper no. 8705 (May 1987).
16. Ministry of Labor Survey, May 1988, p. 89.
17. U.S. Department of Labor, Bureau of International Labor Affairs, *Foreign Labor Trends, Korea*, FLT 89–54 (1988), p. 8.
18. Lindauer, "Labor Market Behavior," p. 22.
19. Ibid., p. 40.
20. *Foreign Labor Trends, Korea*, p. 3.
21. Korea's distribution of income is discussed in Edward S. Mason et al., *The Economic and Social Modernization of the Republic of Korea* (Cambridge: Council on East Asian Studies, Harvard University, 1980), pp. 26–27, 408–44, 481–84. Even Asia Watch, the tenacious human rights organization, has conceded that Korea has a remarkably level distribution of income. See its *Human Rights in Korea*, January 1986, pp. 172, 173.
22. Mark Clifford, "A Productive Approach," *Far Eastern Economic Review*, February 11, 1988, p. 58.
23. Comparisons are based on data supplied by POSCO officials and on a story that appeared in the *Minneapolis Star Tribune*, August 7, 1988, based on Sam Jameson's "Forging an Economic Miracle: South Korean Steel Firm Grows Into Giant in 20 Years," in the *Los Angeles Times*, May 23, 1988.
24. Korea Productivity Center, *Quarterly Productivity Statistics*, July 1988, p. 33. Of course, such comparisons are troublesome; as David Lindauer notes, "Whether Korean productivity data are less reliable than similar data for other nations is open to debate, although some of the Korean computation techniques do stand out as particularly weak." See his "Labor Market Behavior," p. 69.
25. Park Fun-Koo and Tarsicio Castaneda, "Structural Adjustment," Korea Development Institute Working Paper no. 8705, p. 40.
26. *Korea Year 2000, Prospects and Issues for Long-Term Development, Summary Report* (Seoul: Korea Development Institute Press, 1986), p. 33.
27. For 1987 figures, see Mario F. Bognanno, "Korea's Industrial Relations at the Turning Point," Korea Development Institute Working Paper no. 8816 (December 1988), p. 46. For 1986, see *ILO Yearbook, 1987*, p. 971.
28. For a discussion of this phenomenon, see Bognanno, "Korea's Industrial Relations."

29. Ibid., p. 45.
30. Park Young-Ki, "Economic Democratization and Industrial Relations in Korea with Special Reference to the Role of Unions" (Paper presented at the International Symposium on Economic Democracy and Industrial Relations, Soongsil University, Seoul, Korea, June 16–17, 1988), p. 9. Two-thirds of the strikes were aimed at employers with more than 100 employees. Put another way, 70.00 percent of the nation's 374 largest companies (more than 1,000 employees) were struck, while just 0.58 percent of the 92,685 smallest establishments (fewer than 50 employees) experienced a labor dispute.
31. Interview with Park Young-Ki.
32. Ministry of Labor Survey, May 1988, p. 40.
33. Kim Sookon, "Is the Japanese System of Lifetime Employment Applicable to a Developing Country such as Korea?" (Paper presented at the International Industrial Relations Association Sixth World Congress, Kyoto, Japan, March 28–31, 1983). Although Kim's observations are valuable, it should be noted that his comparisons were based on different years: 1960 for the United States and Japan, and 1981 for Korea.
34. Lindauer, "Labor Market Behavior," p. 60.
35. *ILO Yearbook, 1987*, p. 32.
36. Robert F. Spencer, *Yogong: Factory Girl* (Seoul: Royal Asiatic Society, Korea Branch, 1988), p. 14.
37. Ibid., pp. 60–61.
38. Lindauer, "Labor Market Behavior," p. 21.
39. Norman Jacobs, *The Korean Road to Modernization and Development* (Urbana: University of Illinois Press, 1985), p. 153.
40. Ibid., p. 196.
41. Ibid., p. 214.
42. "Han Y.S. Builds Fortune on Tears of a Nation," *Korea Herald*, October 13, 1988.
43. *Korea Year 2000*, pp. 23–24.
44. "Dangerous Levels of Mercury Found in Restaurant Food," *Korea Herald*, November 10, 1988.
45. U.S. Department of Labor, Bureau of International Labor Affairs, *Foreign Labor Trends, Korea*, FLT 87-31 (1986), p. 13.
46. Organization for Economic Cooperation and Development, *World Development Report, 1988* (New York: World Bank, Oxford University Press, 1988), pp. 266–67; Shim Jae Hoon, "What to Teach to Whom," *Far Eastern Economic Review*, June 28, 1990, pp. 45–46.
47. "Multiple Choice Questions," *Korea Herald*, December 17, 1988.
48. "College Entrance Craze," *Korea Herald*, November 17, 1988.
49. "Mother's Devotion Pays off as Son Attains Top Honor," *Korea Times*, December 29, 1988.
50. Jacobs, *The Korean Road*, p. 198.

51. "Korean Teen-agers Excel in Math, Science Performance: International Survey," *Korea Herald*, February 2, 1989.
52. OECD, *World Development Report, 1988*, p. 281.
53. *ILO Yearbook, 1987*, pp. 951–54.
54. Karl Schoenberger, "Korea Shaken by Job Accident Rate," *Los Angeles Times*, July 25, 1988.

CHAPTER 3 (Pages 36–58)

1. Economic Planning Board, *Statistics on Fair Trade*, July 1988, p. 18.
2. Norman Jacobs, *The Korean Road to Modernization and Development* (Urbana: University of Illinois Press, 1985), p. 125.
3. Company figures are from the July 30, 1990, *Fortune* Global 500.
4. These figures were reported in "Hyundai Posts Largest Turnover in '87," in the *Korea Herald*, October 13, 1988, following a Bank of Korea report to a parliamentary audit session.
5. Christian Institute for the Study of Justice and Development, *Social Justice Indicators in Korea*, 2nd ed. (April 1988), p. 24. Figures are drawn from Economic Planning Board data from 1984.
6. Kim Cae-One, "Exports and Business Conglomerates," *Korea Journal*, October 1986, p. 15.
7. "One Fourth of Bank Loans Goes to Top 30 Companies," *Korea Herald*, November 27, 1988.
8. "Putting Rumors to Rest?" *Business Korea*, November 1988, p. 34.
9. Jacobs, *The Korean Road*, p. 115.
10. "Mixed Blessings of Party Ties," *Business Korea*, October 1988, p. 40.
11. "Only Two Firms Allowed to Branch out Into Petrochemical Industry," *Korea Times*, November 23, 1988.
12. Economic Planning Board, *Major Statistics of the Korean Economy, 1988*, pp. 203, 205–8, 225.
13. "Korea's General Trading Companies," *Monthly Review* (Korea Exchange Bank), July 1987, p. 3.
14. Ibid., pp. 3–7.
15. "43 Business Groups Designated 'Giant' Conglomerates of 1988," *Korea Herald*, April 2, 1989.
16. From interviews with Samsung personnel. Of the 5,000 significant subcontractors, 1,500 are directly engaged in manufacturing. Among the remaining are construction and other companies, including apparel manufacturers producing for export. Consequently, the actual number of manufacturing subcontractors is between 1,500 and 5,000.
17. "GTCs Moving to Set up Production Facilities Abroad to Cut Costs," *Korea Herald*, November 13, 1988.
18. Interview with Park Young-Ki.

19. Jacobs, *The Korean Road*, pp. 33–34.
20. Alan Freeman, "Koreans Press Ahead with Canadian Plant," *Wall Street Journal*, July 29, 1988.
21. "Hyundai Posts Largest," *Korea Herald*, October 13, 1988.
22. Mark Clifford, "Playing the Game," *Far Eastern Economic Review*, April 21, 1988, p. 58.
23. "Hyundai Posts Largest," *Korea Herald*, October 13, 1988.
24. Simon Caulkin, "Why Daewoo Works Harder," *Management Today*, July 1986, p. 64.
25. Jacobs, *The Korean Road*, p. 143.
26. *An Overview of Small and Medium Industry in Korea* (Seoul: Small and Medium Industry Promotion Corporation, July 1988), pp. 8–9, 38, 61.
27. *Korea Year 2000, Prospects and Issues for Long-Term Development, Summary Report* (Seoul: Korea Development Institute Press, 1986), p. 56.
28. Shim Jae Hoon, "Time Runs out for the Conglomerates," *Far Eastern Economic Review*, December 12, 1985, p. 71.
29. *Korea Year 2000*, p. 113.
30. Ibid., p. 76.

CHAPTER 4 (Pages 61–79)

1. Lee Ki-baik, *A New History of Korea* (Cambridge: Harvard University Press, 1984), p. 170.
2. Ibid., p. 171.
3. Gregory Henderson, *Korea, the Politics of the Vortex* (Cambridge: Harvard University Press, 1968), p. 16.
4. Lee, *New History*, p. 99.
5. Henderson, *Vortex*, p. 17.
6. Lee, *New History*, pp. 184–188.
7. Henderson, *Vortex*, p. 37.
8. Ibid., p. 41.
9. Lee, *New History*, p. 209.
10. Henderson, *Vortex*, p. 17.
11. Ibid., p. 15.
12. Park Chung-Hee, *Our Nation's Path* (Seoul: Hollym Corporation, 1970), p. 100.
13. For a discussion of the Taewon'gun's efforts at nationalism, see Thomas Hosuck Kang, "The Changing Nature of Korean Confucian Personality Under Japanese Rule," *Korea Journal*, March 1977, pp. 23–24.
14. I have drawn on several sources in this discussion, but special reference should be made to the work of Professor Kim Kyong-Dong of Seoul National University.

15. See Lucian W. Pye, *Asian Power and Politics* (Cambridge: Belknap Press, Harvard University Press, 1985).
16. Kang, "Changing Nature," pp. 22–36.
17. Paul S. Crane, *Korean Patterns* (Seoul: Royal Asiatic Society, Korea Branch, 1967), p. 29.
18. Pye, *Asian Power*, p. 83.
19. Leroy P. Jones and Il Sakong, *Government, Business, and Entrepreneurship in Economic Development: The Korean Case* (Cambridge: Council on East Asian Studies, Harvard University, 1980), p. 211.
20. See Kim Kyong-Dong, *Man and Society in Korea's Economic Growth: Sociological Studies* (Seoul: Seoul National University Press, 1979), p. 142.
21. Lee Ki-baik, "Korea—The Military Tradition," in *The Traditional Culture and Society of Korea: Thought and Institutions*, Occasional Papers of the Center for Korean Studies, no. 5 (Honolulu: University of Hawaii, 1975), pp. 1–42.
22. Kim Kyong-Dong, "The Distinctive Features of South Korea's Development," in *In Search of an East Asian Development Model*, ed. Peter L. Berger and Hsin-Huang Michael Hsiao (New Brunswick: Transaction Books, 1988), p. 211.
23. Kim, *Man and Society*, p. 137.
24. Crane, *Korean Patterns*, p. 46.
25. Henderson, *Vortex*, p. 5.
26. Pye, *Asian Power*, p. 85.
27. Park, *Our Nation's Path*, p. 74.
28. Kim Kyong-Dong, "Social Change and Societal Development in Korea Since 1945," *Korea and World Affairs*, 9, no. 4 (Winter 1985), p. 779.
29. Pye, *Asian Power*, p. 27.
30. Kim, *Man and Society*, p. 19.
31. Ibid., p. 57.
32. Kim, "Social Change," p. 780.
33. Pye, *Asian Power*, p. 58.

CHAPTER 5 (Pages 80–93)

1. Park Chung-Hee, *Our Nation's Path* (Seoul: Hollym Corporation, 1970), p. 118.
2. Ibid., p. 133.
3. Lee Ki-Baik, *A New History of Korea* (Cambridge: Harvard University Press, 1984), p. 282.
4. Chang Dal-Joong, *Economic Control and Political Authoritarianism* (Seoul: Sogang University Press, 1985), p. 27.
5. Ibid., p. 23.

6. Norman Jacobs, *The Korean Road to Modernization and Development* (Urbana: University of Illinois Press, 1985), p. 147.
7. Gregory Henderson, *Korea, the Politics of the Vortex* (Cambridge: Harvard University Press, 1968), p. 51.
8. Ibid., pp. 52–53.
9. Ibid., p. 106.
10. Ibid., p. 17.
11. Ibid., p. 70.
12. Leroy P. Jones and Il Sakong, *Government, Business, and Entrepreneurship in Economic Development: The Korean Case* (Cambridge: Council on East Asian Studies, Harvard University, 1980), p. 19.
13. Park, *Our Nation's Path*, p. 113.
14. Lee, *New History*, p. 318; Chang, *Economic Control*, p. 28.
15. Harold Hakwon Sunoo, *America's Dilemma in Asia: The Case of South Korea* (Chicago: Nelson-Hall, 1979), pp. 14–18.
16. Henderson, *Vortex*, p. 73.
17. Edward S. Mason et al., *The Economic and Social Modernization of the Republic of Korea* (Cambridge: Council on East Asian Studies, Harvard University, 1980), p. 76.
18. Jones and Sakong, *Government, Business, and Entrepreneurship*, p. 21.
19. Chang, *Economic Control*, p. 33.
20. Ibid., pp. 30–31.
21. Suh Sang-Chul, *Growth and Structural Changes in the Korean Economy, 1910–1940* (Cambridge: Council on East Asian Studies, Harvard University, 1978), p. 106, as quoted in Jones and Sakong, *Government, Business, and Entrepreneurship*, p. 24.
22. Chang, *Economic Control*, p. 33.
23. Thomas Hosuck Kang, "The Changing Nature of Korean Confucian Personality Under Japanese Rule," *Korea Journal*, March 1977, p. 32.
24. Lee, *New History*, pp. 352–54.
25. Ibid., p. 357.
26. Mason et al., *Economic and Social Modernization*, p. 10.
27. Sunoo, *America's Dilemma*, p. 39.
28. Lee, *New History*, p. 359.
29. Larry E. Westphal, Yung W. Rhee, and Garry Pursell, "Korean Industrial Competence: Where It Came From," World Bank Staff Working Paper no. 469 (1981), p. 7.
30. Mason et al., *Economic and Social Modernization*, p. 75.
31. Jones and Sakong, *Government, Business, and Entrepreneurship*, pp. 29–30.
32. Henderson, *Vortex*, p. 75.
33. "Roh Willing to Visit Tokyo Early '89: Sankei," *Korea Herald*, December 30, 1988.
34. Gregory Henderson, "Japan's Chosen: Immigrants, Ruthlessness and

Developmental Shock," in *Korea Under Japanese Colonial Rule*, Andrew C. Nahm, ed. (Kalamazoo: Western Michigan University, 1973), pp. 268–269, quoted in Jones and Sakong, *Government, Business, and Entrepreneurship*, p. 29.

CHAPTER 6 (Pages 94–118)

1. Larry E. Westphal, Yung W. Rhee, and Garry Pursell, "Korean Industrial Competence: Where It Came From," World Bank Staff Working Paper no. 469 (1981), p. 8.
2. Leroy P. Jones and Il Sakong, *Government, Business, and Entrepreneurship in Economic Development: The Korean Case* (Cambridge: Council on East Asian Studies, Harvard University, 1980), p. 30.
3. Figures on the postwar repatriation of Koreans vary; the Federation of Korean Industries cites 3.2 million in *Korea's Economic Policies (1945–1985)* (Seoul: 1987), p. 198.
4. *Chosen Ilbo*, August 31, 1946, cited in Gregory Henderson, *Korea, the Politics of the Vortex* (Cambridge: Harvard University Press, 1968), p. 139.
5. Henderson, *Vortex*, p. 123.
6. Harold Hakwon Sunoo, *America's Dilemma in Asia: The Case of South Korea* (Chicago: Nelson-Hall, 1979), pp. 51–52.
7. U.S. Armed Forces in Korea, *South Korea Interim Government Activities*, no. 28 (January 1948), p. 10, quoted in Jones and Sakong, *Government, Business, and Entrepreneurship*, p. 31.
8. Kwang Suk Kim and Michael Roemer, "Macroeconomic Growth and Structural Change in Korea," Korea Development Institute Working Paper no. 7705 (April 1977), p. 40, quoted in Jones and Sakong, *Government, Business, and Entrepreneurship*, p. 31.
9. Director of Review and Analysis, Office of the Comptroller of the Army, *Official Army Pocket Data Book Supplement* (Washington, D.C.: 1963), p. 59.
10. Roy W. Shin, "The Politics of Foreign Aid: A Study of the Impact of United States Aid in Korea from 1945 to 1966" (Ph.D. dissertation, University of Minnesota, 1969), p. 51, quoted in Jones and Sakong, *Government, Business, and Entrepreneurship*, p. 35.
11. Lee Ki-baik, *A New History of Korea* (Cambridge: Harvard Univeristy Press, 1984), pp. 380–381.
12. Edward S. Mason et al., *The Economic and Social Modernization of the Republic of Korea* (Cambridge: Council on East Asian Studies, Harvard University, 1980), p. 40.
13. Lee, *New History*, p. 383.
14. See Kim Kyong-Dong, *Man and Society in Korea's Economic Growth:*

Sociological Studies (Seoul: Seoul National University Press, 1979), pp. 67–70, and Jung Ku-Hyun, "Business-Government Relations in the Growth of Korean Business Groups," *Korean Social Science Journal*, 14 (1988), pp. 67–82.

15. Kim Se-Jin, *Politics of Military Revolution in Korea* (Chapel Hill: University of North Carolina Press, 1971), pp. 65–66.
16. Westphal et al., "Korean Industrial Competence," p. 10.
17. Jones and Sakong, *Government, Business, and Entrepreneurship*, p. 48.
18. Park Chung-Hee, *The Country, the Revolution and I* (Seoul: Hollym, 1970), p. 47.
19. Park Chung-Hee, *Our Nation's Path* (Seoul: Hollym Corporation, 1970), pp. 195–96.
20. Jones and Sakong, *Government, Business, and Entrepreneurship*, p. 43.
21. Mason et al., *Economic and Social Modernization*, p. 51.
22. Ibid., p. 47.
23. Kim Cae-One, "Exports and Business Conglomerates," *Korea Journal*, October 1986, pp. 8–9.
24. Jung, "Business-Government Relations," p. 76.
25. Mason et al., *Economic and Social Modernization*, p. 14.
26. Westphal et al., "Korean Industrial Competence," pp. 18–19.
27. Chang Dal-Joong, *Economic Control and Political Authoritarianism* (Seoul: Sogang University Press, 1985), p. 51.
28. Ibid., pp. 60–62.
29. Jones and Sakong, *Government, Business, and Entrepreneurship*, p. 148.
30. Lee Jeong-Taik, "Export-oriented Industrialization, Labor Control and the Labor Movement in South Korea," *Korean Social Science Journal*, 14 (1988), pp. 108–110.
31. Park Young-Ki, "Economic Democratization and Industrial Relations in Korea with Special Reference to the Role of Unions" (paper prepared for the International Symposium on Economic Democracy and Industrial Relations, Soongsil University, Seoul, Korea, June 16–17, 1988). The data actually pertain to two regimes, from 1975 through 1986.
32. Mason et al., *Economic and Social Modernization*, p. 487.
33. Jones and Sakong, *Government, Business, and Entrepreneurship*, p. xxxv.
34. Economic Planning Board, *Major Statistics of the Korean Economy, 1977* (Seoul, 1977), p. 7, as quoted in Jones and Sakong, *Government, Business, and Entrepreneurship*, p. 86.
35. Jones and Sakong, *Government, Business, and Entrepreneurship*, p. 68.
36. Ibid., p. xxxiii.
37. Ibid., p. 305.
38. Kim Kyong-Dong, *Man and Society*, p. 71.
39. Kim Cae-One, "Exports and Business Conglomerates," pp. 13–16.
40. Jung, "Business-Government Relations," p. 74.

41. Jones and Sakong, *Government, Business, and Entrepreneurship*, p. 68.
42. Kim Kyong-Dong, "Socio-cultural Aspects of Political Democratization in Korea" (revised paper presented at the Conference on Development and Democracy in East Asia: Taiwan, South Korea, and the Philippines, American Institute for Public Policy Research, Washington, DC, May 18–19, 1988), p. 10.
43. Mario F. Bognanno, "Korea's Industrial Relations at the Turning Point," Korea Development Institute Working Paper no. 8816 (December 1988), p. 20.
44. The government continues to maintain that fewer than 200 people died during the Kwangju uprising, but other accounts put the figure much higher. For a terrifying synopsis of events, read the Asia Watch report, *Human Rights in Korea* (Washington, DC, 1986), pp. 36–44.
45. Bognanno, "Korea's Industrial Relations," p. 27.
46. *Korea, Managing the Industrial Transition*, a World Bank country study (Washington, D.C.: 1987), p. 1.
47. Ibid., p. xi.
48. Ibid., p. 31.
49. Ibid., p. 5.
50. Paul S. Crane, *Korean Patterns* (Seoul: Royal Asiatic Society, Korea Branch, 1967), p. 140.

CHAPTER 7 (Pages 119–135)

1. Mario F. Bognanno, "Korea's Industrial Relations at the Turning Point," Korea Development Institute Working Paper no. 8816 (December 1988), pp. 28–29.
2. "South Korea Survey: Plures ex Uno," *The Economist*, May 21, 1988, p. 10.
3. "Labor Trends in the Republic of Korea," American Embassy, Seoul, Korea, July 1988, based on documents from the Bank of Korea, the Economic Planning Board, and the Ministry of Labor, p. 8.
4. Korea Productivity Center, Industrial Relations Department, *Labor Relations Environment and the Labor Disputes*, May 1988.
5. "Labor Disputes up 54.8% Over '88; 71 Cases Unsolved," *Korea Herald*, March 3, 1989.
6. North American Coalition for Human Rights in Korea, *Bi-weekly Report*, August 1, 1988, p. 3.
7. Bognanno, "Korea's Industrial Relations," p. 31.
8. "Police Break Strike at S. Korea Shipyard; 700 Held," *Minneapolis Star Tribune*, March 31, 1989.
9. Bognanno, "Korea's Industrial Relations," p. 45.

10. Park Young-Ki, "Economic Democratization and Industrial Relations in Korea with Special Reference to the Role of Unions" (paper presented at the International Symposium on Economic Democracy and Industrial Relations, Soongsil University, Seoul, Korea, June 16–17, 1988), p. 9.
11. U.S. Department of Commerce, International Trade Administration, *Foreign Economic Trends, Korea*, FET 90-43, p. 3.
12. Bognanno, "Korea's Industrial Relations," p. 46.
13. Bank of Korea figures, cited in *Foreign Economic Trends, Korea*, FET 90-43, p. 4.
14. "Police Break Strike," *Minneapolis Star Tribune*, March 31, 1989.

CHAPTER 8 (Pages 139–152)

1. Jang Song-Hyon, "A Primer on What Makes Koreans Tick," *Business Korea*, February 1985, p. 36.
2. "Hanjin: Civilian Diplomats with Wings," *Business Korea*, January 1986, p. 51.
3. From company hand-outs: "An Introduction to the Daewoo Group," July 1988, Public Relations Department, Daewoo Group; "Hyundai Corporation in Profile," undated; Samsung Group hand-out, undated.
4. T. W. Kang, *Is Korea the Next Japan?* (New York: Free Press, 1989), p. 66.
5. Ira C. Magaziner and Mark Patinkin, "Fast Heat: How Korea Won the Microwave War," *Harvard Business Review*, January–February 1989, p. 86.
6. Bae Kyuhan, *Automobile Workers in Korea* (Seoul: Seoul National University Press, 1987), p. 73.
7. Robert F. Spencer, *Yogong: Factory Girl* (Seoul: Royal Asiatic Society, Korea Branch, 1988), pp. 70–71.
8. Ibid., p. 79.
9. Rose A. Horowitz, "Management Korea-Style: It's All in the Family," *Journal of Commerce*, April 8, 1987.
10. For an excellent discussion of this process, see Spencer, *Yogong*.
11. Karl Schoenberger, "Korea Shaken by Job Accident Rate," *Los Angeles Times*, July 25, 1988; "South Korea Survey: Division of the Spoils," *The Economist*, May 21, 1988, p. 20.
12. "Occupational Diseases Plague Industrial Workers in Onsan," *Korea Herald*, November 17, 1988.
13. Mark Clifford, "The Price of Democracy," *Far Eastern Economic Review*, January 26, 1988, p. 60.

CHAPTER 9 (Pages 153–165)

1. "Hyosung: Outside Weaknesses, Inside Strengths," *Business Korea*, January 1986, p. 52.
2. Kim Kyong-Dong, *Man and Society in Korea's Economic Growth: Sociological Studies* (Seoul: Seoul National University Press, 1979), p. 55.
3. S. M. Lee and S. Yoo, "The K-Type Management: A Driving Force of Korean Prosperity," in *Management International Review*, 27 (October 1987), p. 71.
4. Jang Song-Hyon, "Playing by the Rules—Korean Style: Hiring and Firing in Korea," *Korea Business World*, January 1986, p. 60.
5. Bae Kyuhan, *Automobile Workers in Korea* (Seoul: Seoul National University Press, 1987), pp. 44–49.
6. Kim Sookon, "Is the Japanese System of Lifetime Employment Applicable to a Developing Country such as Korea?" (paper presented at the International Industrial Relations Association Sixth World Congress, Kyoto, Japan, March 28–31, 1983), p. 47.
7. "216 Education Officials Altered Their Ages to Delay Retirement: Report," *Korea Herald*, October 26, 1988.
8. Kim Kyong-Dong, *Man and Society*, p. 57.
9. Kim Sookon, "Japanese System," pp. 54–56.
10. Jang Song-Hyon, "Playing by the Rules—Korean Style: How to Best Compensate Your Employees," *Korea Business World*, February 1986, p. 50.
11. Keong Deok-Soo, "The Labor Standards Act and the Rules of Employment" (paper presented at the American Chamber of Commerce in Korea's 1987 Labor Seminar), Seoul, February 26, 1987, p. 9.

CHAPTER 10 (Pages 166–186)

1. Bae Kyuhan, *Automobile Workers in Korea* (Seoul: Seoul National University Press, 1987), p. 22.
2. Ira C. Magaziner and Mark Patinkin, "Fast Heat: How Korea Won the Microwave War," *Harvard Business Review*, January–February 1989, p. 89.
3. Ibid., p. 85.
4. Leroy P. Jones and Il Sakong, *Government, Business, and Entrepreneurship in Economic Development: The Korean Case* (Cambridge: Council on East Asian Studies, Harvard University, 1980), p. 61.
5. Magaziner and Patinkin, "Fast Heat," p. 89.
6. Louis Kraar, "Korea, Tomorrow's Powerhouse," *Fortune*, August 15, 1988, p. 76.

7. "Samsung: Handpicked for Perfection," *Business Korea*, January 1986, p. 56.
8. Rhee Yang-Soo, "A Cross Cultural Comparison of Korean and American Managerial Styles: An Inventory of Propositions," in *Administrative Dynamics and Development, The Korean Experience*, ed. Kim Bun Wong et al. (Seoul: Kyobo Publishing, 1985), p. 84.
9. T. W. Kang, *Is Korea the Next Japan?* (New York: Free Press, 1989), p. 75.
10. Barun Roy, "Daewoo's Kim Woo Chong: The Sky Is the Limit in Perfection," *Asian Finance*, November 15, 1985, p. 65.
11. "Daewoo: Gambling Against High Odds," *Business Korea*, January 1986, p. 50.
12. Study conducted in 1983 by the American Chamber of Commerce.
13. Testimony by Pharis J. Harvey, executive director, North American Coalition for Human Rights in Korea, before the Overseas Private Investment Corporation, Washington, D.C., November 13, 1986.
14. Myoung Ho Lee, "An Assessment of the Korean Management System," *Quality* (Korean Standards Association), 3, no. 7 (April 1988), pp. 12–19.
15. Bae, *Automobile Workers*, pp. 56–69, 81.
16. Kang, *Is Korea the Next Japan?* p. 14.
17. Robert F. Spencer, *Yogong: Factory Girl* (Seoul: Royal Asiatic Society, Korea Branch, 1988), p. 59.
18. Kang, *Is Korea the Next Japan?* p. 12.
19. Ibid., p. 90.
20. For a discussion of attempts to expand quality circles, see "Campaign Expands to Guarantee Highest Standards," *Korea Herald*, November 12, 1988.

CHAPTER 11 (Pages 187–212)

1. Leroy P. Jones and Il Sakong, *Government, Business, and Entrepreneurship in Economic Development: The Korean Case* (Cambridge: Council on East Asian Studies, Harvard University, 1980), p. 352.
2. Ibid.
3. Unless otherwise noted, direct quotations from Lee come from his autobiography, excerpted in *World Executive Digest*, May 1988, pp. 38–56.
4. Jones and Sakong, *Government, Business, and Entrepreneurship*, p. 349.
5. Ira C. Magaziner and Mark Patinkin, "Fast Heat: How Korea Won the Microwave War," *Harvard Business Review*, January–February 1989, p. 84.
6. "Giving Big Business a New Role," *Business Korea*, December 1988, p. 15.

7. Jones and Sakong, *Government, Business, and Entrepreneurship*, p. 357.
8. Alan Freeman, "Koreans Press Ahead with Canadian Plant," *Wall Street Journal*, July 29, 1988.
9. Jang Jung-Soo, "Still Driving Hard at 70," *Business Korea*, January 1986, p. 19.
10. Laxmi Nakarmi, "Daewoo vs. Hyundai," *International Business Week*, December 15, 1986, p. 49.
11. Yi Sang-Won, "Excelling in PC Markets," *Business Korea*, November 1988, p. 50.
12. Nakarmi, "Daewoo vs. Hyundai," *International Business Week*, December 15, 1986, p. 47.
13. Ibid., p. 46.
14. Simon Caulkin, "Why Daewoo Works Harder," *Management Today*, July 1986, pp. 64–65.
15. Barun Roy, "The Sky Is the Limit in Perfection," *Asian Finance*, November 15, 1985, p. 63.
16. Jones and Sakong, *Government, Business, and Entrepreneurship*, p. 364.
17. Roy, "Sky Is the Limit," *Asian Finance*, p. 65.
18. Ann Charters, "Turning Point for a South Korean Giant," *Financial Times*, October 31, 1984.
19. Boyd Gibbons, "The South Koreans," *National Geographic*, August 1988, p. 239.
20. Ronald E. Yates, "How Daewoo Became a Global Giant in Just 17 Years," *Chicago Tribune*, October 20, 1985.
21. Louis Kraar, "The Hardest Worker in South Korea," *Fortune International*, August 20, 1984; "Daewoo: Gambling Against High Odds," *Business Korea*, January 1986, p. 50.
22. Kraar, "Hardest Worker," *Fortune International*, August 20, 1984.
23. "Czechs Buy Le Mans," *Korea Herald*, April 30, 1989.
24. Charters, "Turning Point," *Financial Times*, October 31, 1984.

CHAPTER 12 (Pages 215–225)

1. "14 Members Injured in Fight Between Rival Hoodlum Groups," *Korea Herald*, October 25, 1988.
2. Gregory Henderson, *Korea, the Politics of the Vortex* (Cambridge: Harvard University Press, 1968), p. 30.
3. *Korea Year 2000: Prospects and Issues for Long-Term Development, Summary Report* (Seoul: Korea Development Institute Press, 1986), p. 99.
4. Ibid., pp. 41–42.
5. Baek Sung-Won, "Care for the Elderly: Responsibility or Nuisance?" *Korea Herald*, October 29, 1988.
6. *Korea Year 2000*, pp. 86–90.

7. "Overly Generous Welfare System May Trigger Many Side Effects: KDI Fellow," *Korea Herald*, October 27, 1988.

8. *Korea Year 2000*, p. 78.

9. Korea Development Bank, *Industry in Korea, 1988* (Seoul, 1988), p. 11.

10. "South Korea Survey: A Man-Made Miracle," *The Economist*, May 21, 1988, p. 18.

11. *Industry in Korea, 1988*, p. 10.

12. "Goldstar: World-Class Electronics Producer," *Korea Herald*, October 22, 1988.

13. *Industry in Korea, 1988*, p. 10.

14. Bill Powell, "The Pacific Century," *Newsweek*, February 22, 1988, p. 48.

15. *Industry in Korea, 1988*, p. 194.

16. *Korea Year 2000*, p. 28.

17. "303 People Donated Average W4 Million to Land Teaching Jobs: Report," *Korea Herald*, October 29, 1988.

18. Chong Bong-uk, "Business Leaders Determined Not to Make 'Forced Donations'," *Korea Herald*, October 30, 1988.

19. Lho Joo Hyoung, "Korea Seeks Quantum Leap," *Korea Business World*, November 1988, p. 41.

20. "Economy Should Be Private-Led: Chung," *Korea Herald*, October 29, 1988.

CHAPTER 13 (Pages 226–239)

1. *Korea Year 2000, Prospects and Issues for Long-Term Development, Summary Report* (Seoul: Korea Development Institute Press, 1986), p. 50.

2. U.S. Department of Labor, Bureau of Labor Statistics, *International Comparisons of Hourly Compensation Costs for Production Workers in Manufacturing, 1975–1987*, August 1988, p. 5.

3. Korea Development Bank, *Industry in Korea, 1988* (Seoul, 1988), p. 113; *Korea Herald*, "Goldstar to Build Plant in Philippines," October 28, 1988.

4. U.S. Department of Commerce, International Trade Administration, *Foreign Economic Trends and Their Implications for the United States: Thailand*, FET 89-48 (May 1989), p. 4.

5. Ron Moreau, "Asia's New Economic Tiger," *Newsweek*, July 11, 1988, p. 52.

6. Louis Kraar, "The New Powers of Asia," *Fortune*, March 28, 1988, p. 129.

7. See *Industry in Korea, 1988*, p. 5.

8. "Happy Graduation, Tigers!" *Christian Science Monitor*, February 4, 1988.

9. The program was especially important for Korea; in 1984, the country

was the second largest beneficiary of the GSP program, exporting $1.5 billion to the United States, or 13.5 percent of the world total—everything from office machines and microwave ovens to fur coats.

10. Stephen L. Lande, "A Warning Before the Storm," *Business Korea*, December 1988, p. 19.

11. David R. Francis, "Asian Economic Tigers Grow Up," *Christian Science Monitor*, May 19, 1989; U.S. Department of Commerce, International Trade Administration, *Foreign Economic Trends and Their Implications for the United States: Korea*, FET 88-111 (October 1988), p. 3.

12. Thomas G. Donlan, "Son of Gephardt," *Barron's*, May 8, 1989, p. 17.

13. Art Pine, "U.S. Has New Weapon in Its Trade Arsenal," *Los Angeles Times*, May 21, 1989; "Administration Uses Super 301 and Special 301 Trade Tools," *Business America*, June 5, 1989, pp. 23–25.

14. Lande, "A Warning," *Business Korea*, p. 22.

15. Quoted in "Japan-Korea Trade," *Korea Herald*, October 27, 1988.

16. "Anti-American Feelings Appear to Be Higher Than Expected: Poll," *Korea Herald*, November 18, 1988.

CHAPTER 14 (Pages 240–248)

1. See Kim Kyong-Dong, "The Distinctive Features of South Korea's Development," in *In Search of an East Asian Development Model*, ed. Peter L. Berger and Hsin-Huang Michael Hsiao (New Brunswick: Transaction Books, 1988), p. 216.

2. Mark Clifford, "Seoul's Chinese Puzzle," *Far Eastern Economic Review*, March 3, 1988, pp. 50–51.

3. Ibid.

4. Lho Joo-Hyoung, "Korea Looks West—to China," *Korea Business World*, July 1988, p. 16.

5. Clifford, "Seoul's Chinese Puzzle," pp. 50–51.

6. Lho, "Korea Looks West," pp. 17–18.

7. "Goldstar to Import Black and White TVs from China," *Korea Times*, December 9, 1988.

8. Bill Powell, "The Pacific Century," *Newsweek*, February 22, 1988, p. 45.

9. U.S. Department of Labor, Bureau of International Labor Affairs, *Foreign Labor Trends, China*, FLT 89-15 (1989), p. 3.

10. "Contractors Employ More Foreign Workers at Overseas Construction," *Korea Herald*, October 25, 1988.

11. "South Korea Survey: A Man-Made Miracle," *The Economist*, May 21, 1988, p. 19.

12. Dave Hage, "Busier Than Ever: Pace of Work is Changing the Way Americans Live," *Minneapolis Star Tribune*, September 5, 1988.

Index

267

Wages (*cont'd*)
control of, 115–16
increases in, 219, 245
minimum, 129–30, 151
productivity and, 24
at Samsung, 192
in Thailand, 232
of women, 21, 28
Wall Street Journal, 198
Warring States, era of, 66
Waseda University, 189
Welfare system, 218
Westinghouse, 200
Women, 21
discrimination against, 130
as labor activists, 120–22
labor force participation of, 20, 27–29
paternalism toward, 147, 148–50
wages of, 21, 28
Work force, 17–35
accident rate of, 34
activism of, 25–26
education of, 31–34
length of workweek for, 21–22

productivity of, 23–25
shortages in, 220–23
size of, 19–20
standard of living of, 29–31
wages of, 21–23
women in, 20, 27–29
Workweek, length of, 7, 21–22, 28, 131, 166–69, 206
World Bank, 9, 19, 31, 115
World War I, 87
World War II, 82, 92, 94, 95, 99, 101, 107, 242

Yamagata, Prince, 82
Yang Chang-Mo, 42
Yangban (landed aristocrats), 65, 66, 71, 181
Yemen, 47, 201
Yi dynasty, 65–72, 76, 84, 86, 89
Yi Song-gye, 65
Yi Sun-sin, Admiral, 63, 66, 72–73, 76
Yomiuri Shimbun (newspaper), 237
Yonsei University, 31, 74, 159, 204

Zaibatsu (Japanese conglomerates), 82